Sunburst Farm
Family Cookbook

Sunburst Farm
Family Cookbook

Good Home Cookin' the Natural Way

By Susan Duquette

Illustrations by Donna Wright
Photography by Mehosh Dziadzio

From the Brotherhood of the Sun

Published by
Woodbridge Press Publishing Company
Santa Barbara, California 93111

Published and Distributed by

Woodbridge Press Publishing Company
Post Office Box 6189
Santa Barbara, California 93111

Library of Congress Catalog Card Number: 76-427.

International Standard Book Number: 0-912800-28-3.

Published simultaneously in the United States and Canada

Printed in the United States of America

Brotherhood of the Sun

The Brotherhood of the Sun is a family of more than 250 men, women, and children who have dedicated themselves to living in harmony with all people and all things.

Our desire is to follow the simple laws of God and Nature. In order to create an environment in which this is possible, we have established, in the mountains above Santa Barbara, California, three farms where most of our members live. We try to care for our basic needs by relying on the land. We have our own gardens and field crops, we rear livestock (including goats, cows, horses, donkeys, and chickens), build our homes, make some of our own clothing and are learning other necessary skills. We also own a large, old wooden schooner called, "The Galilee." We use it for fishing; and, of course, sailing and experiencing the ocean.

In order to help support ourselves and to share with other people our way of life, we have established a large organic foods complex in Santa Barbara called Sunburst Organic Foods.

This organization includes a large wholesale warehouse that ships food to stores across the country, three large retail markets, a community store, a restaurant called "The Farmer and the Fisherman," a whole-grain bakery and a fresh juice-bottling plant that distributes along the west coast.

Our dream is to provide a home in natural surroundings for people who long to live a simple, virtuous life full of love and service to each other and to all mankind. We hope that through our efforts and example we may help to bring the Garden of Eden back to this, our Mother Earth, and to see all men live in brotherhood under the Fatherhood of God.

Everyone Helped

As members of a family, we accept varied individual responsiblities all of which combine to benefit and sustain the family as a whole. Each job is of equal importance. One of my responsibilities happened to be the writing of this book.

I was lucky to have some help from those who had time and experience. So, thanks to the cooks, Susan, Dyan, Alicia, Deborah, Sandy, Katie, and our famous baker, Dana.

To Jill and Dorothy, our experienced canners.

To Welmoet who lends a sympathetic ear and an editorial hand.

To David, Barbara, Mary, and Grandfather, my loyal and faithful testers.

To Andrew for that extra inspiration.

And to my buddies, Mehosh and Donna. Who, with me, now truly know what it takes to make a book!

Last, and most important, I give my thanks to all my brothers and sisters who by doing their jobs gave me the time and inspiration to write this book. I am blessed to share this life with them.

As we continue to grow,

Susan

6

A Guide
To This Book

(List of Recipes, Page 298)

The Honor of Cooking

As we search our Mother Earth we find an unlimited wealth of imagination creating the many different cultures existing today. Still we find that people all over the world have certain common necessities, one of them surely being food. Man works daily to provide the nutrition needed to sustain his life.

As a family of 250 persons we are influenced by many varied backgrounds and nationalities. The past five years of change have brought us through many ideas, tastes, and opinions concerning food. We've found that as we strive daily to live our lives as natural men and women, choosing a diet to suit everyone's taste is becoming second nature to us. Our bodies know and if we listen they will tell us what we need. In addition to the food that we eat, we also regard fresh air, sunshine, exercise, and rest as "nourishment" imperative for our well-being.

We've learned much by growing our own foods. Gardens flourish and become as schools providing many lessons from the

Susan

book of life. Nutritionally, home-grown organic foods are best, especially when brought to your table right after picking. The vibrant colors tell you that they are filled with life.

A garden can be grown in even the smallest of areas. If this is not possible, then purchasing locally grown or organic foods is the next best thing.

In the quiet of your kitchen you accept the honor of cooking. You are the exchange between the food and your family. What you give of yourself, to the food, is what others will receive. It is so important to prepare this food with care in order to sustain the life-force which is the nutrition in all foods.

Cooking as an art offers a limitless range for creativity. It opens the door to discovering ways of efficiency and ecology, which means using foods to their fullest capacity, utilizing leftovers and giving back to our Mother Earth what we are unable to use.

This book contains recipes that have been tried and tested in our homes, our bakery, and our restaurant and have proven to be our favorites.

Enjoy!

Soups and Snacks

At our ranch nestled in the wilderness we have no electricity or gas so we cook on our ever-faithful wood stove.

Whatever the means of cooking, we have found that preparation of meals on a wood stove truly enhances the flavor of food. It takes a little longer because there's wood to be gathered and chopped and a fire to be built. But with a little practice at cooking on this kind of stove you'll be surprised how simple it is to prepare a meal with satisfying results.

A cook can be successful in creating a good meal in just one large pot. With imagination, you are able to use the bounty of foods around you—including many leftovers. The full and steaming pot of soup seems always to bring a warm and hearty feeling whether it is only an introduction or the main course itself.

Some special little touches to give the perfect "finish" to your soups can be seeds or nuts, croutons, grated cheese or vegetables, scallions, or a pinch of dried herbs.

These recipes will yield 4-6 servings unless otherwise indicated.

Vegetable Stock Pot

I use my vegetable tops and peelings—and vegetables that have "gone limp" to start a stock pot. I put all those "vegies" into water and cook them for a couple of hours, then strain the broth. There you have a beginning or base for a vegetable soup. I also save water from cereals, grains, and steamed vegetables for use as soup bases.

Vegetable Soup

4 c. water with
    4 bouillon cubes or
    equivalent powder (or use
    4 c. Stock Pot broth—above)
½ med. onion, sliced
1 med. carrot, sliced
½ c. celery
½ c. zucchini, chopped or
    sliced

½ c. potatoes, chopped
2 tomatoes, chopped
1 t. garlic powder (or fresh)
1 t. sea salt
3 T. tamari (soy sauce)
½ t. thyme
½ t. oregano
½ t. basil
sea salt to taste

In a large pot bring water (or broth) to boil. Add all ingredients and simmer 45 minutes over medium-low heat.

Variations:

Add tomato juice to broth.
Use fresh herbs whenever possible.
Add homemade noodles.
Add rice, barley, lentils, beans.
Puree soup in blender.

String Bean Soup

4 lbs. potatoes, boiled
½ lb. butter or margarine
5 T flour

4 T. garlic cloves, chopped
2 lbs. cooked green beans
2 pts. sour cream

Boil potatoes in enough water to cover and slice. Save water. Heat margarine, add flour and mix in with a whisk until smooth. Add chopped garlic cloves. Pour in potato water. Add potatoes, cooked beans, and boil slowly for 15 minutes. Add 2 pts. sour cream and serve.

Minestrone

½ c. pinto beans
2 c. water
2 lg. onions
2 tomatoes, chopped
3 garlic cloves, minced
3 carrots, cut lengthwise in
    slices

¾ c. celery ribs and leaves
1 c. fresh spinach, chopped
1 c. tomato or V-8 juice
1 T. oregano
1 T. parsley
5 c. water
sea salt to taste

Soak pinto beans overnight (or pressure cook), or use up leftover pintos from a Mexican meal.

Put uncooked pintos in a pot with the 2 c. water, onion, and tomatoes. Simmer for 2 hours.

Meanwhile, sauté in oil until tender the garlic cloves, onion, carrots and celery. (Use olive oil if you wish.) Add chopped fresh spinach. Cook 1 minute.

Place vegetables and bean mixture in a pot with water. Add tomato or V-8 juice, oregano, parsley, the 5 c. water and salt to taste. Simmer for ½ hour and serve.

Variation:

Add Parmesan cheese.

French Onion Soup

4 garlic cloves, minced
4-5 med. onions, sliced
3 T. paprika
3 T. butter
2 T. oil

5 c. water
3 T. tamari or 2 T. sea salt
croutons
Parmesan cheese
Muenster cheese

Sauté garlic and onions in butter and oil. Add paprika. Cook until onions are transparent. Add water and tamari (soy sauce), and bring to a boil.

Serve with croutons on top, sprinkled with Parmesan. Or, put in a casserole or individual oven-proof dishes, top with croutons, then a slice of Muenster, then Parmesan. Put back in a very hot oven or put under broiler until cheese browns.

Dill-Cabbage Soup

4 c. green cabbage, chopped
1 lg. onion, chopped
5 c. hot water
3 T. tamari
4 T. dill

1 T. garlic powder
3 or 4 tomatoes, chopped
1 pt. sour cream
sea salt to taste

Sauté cabbage and onion. Add hot water, garlic powder, tamari, dill. Simmer for ½ hour. Add chopped tomatoes, salt if needed.

Serve plain or top each serving with 1 T. sour cream.

Czechoslovakian Sauerkraut Soup

6 c. mushrooms, sliced and
   sautéed in butter or
   margarine
1 16-oz. can of sauerkraut

6 c. bouillon water (2 cubes
   per cup)
2 qts. tomato juice
salt and pepper to taste

Very simple but very different. Just put all ingredients together and simmer for 2 hours. Do not let it boil. Serve very hot. *Yield: 8-10 servings.*

Japanese and Chinese Soups

The broth is the main ingredient; simple to prepare. You can use: dulse, kombu; bouillon and tamari; miso; fish broth with tamari. (See "sea vegetables" in Vegetable section.)

Tofu-Vegie Soup

When the broth is heated thoroughly have your serving bowls ready. Put in a small square or two of tofu, a few mung bean sprouts, and a little chopped green onion. Pour hot broth in and serve immediately.

Spinach and Hard-Boiled Egg Soup

Chop spinach leaves small. Slice hard-boiled eggs. Have your broth heated thoroughly, put spinach and eggs in bowls, pour broth over and serve.

Egg-Drop Soup

When the broth is ready, add a raw egg and stir until egg becomes stringy. Serve immediately. You may also add chopped green onions, tofu, sliced cucumbers.

Miso-Onion Soup

4 c. water	⅛ t. ginger
2 c. onion, chopped	⅛ t. thyme
3 T. miso	1 T. nutritional yeast

Sauté onions in a little oil. Add onions and other ingredients (except yeast) to the water and simmer about 10 minutes to blend flavors. Add yeast just before serving.

Chowder

1 lg. onion, chopped	4 T. parsley
2 carrots, chopped	2 T. sea salt
1 c. celery, chopped	4 T. butter
6 med. potatoes, boiled	2 t. paprika
8 c. milk	

Sauté onion, carrots, and celery in a skillet. Slice potatoes and put them in a pot with "vegies." Add milk and seasonings and heat until almost boiling. Taste to correct seasonings. Serve with a dot of butter and sprinkle with parsley.

Potato-Buttermilk Soup

1 lb. (3) potatoes, diced	1 t. sea salt
4 c. buttermilk	½ t. celery salt
1 T. flour	½ t. dill
1 onion, chopped	1 t. curry powder (optional)
½ c. baco-bits	½ t. pepper (optional)

Dice potatoes and cook in a small amount of boiling, salted water until tender. Set aside; don't drain.

Meanwhile, pour ¼ c. buttermilk into a jar, adding flour; shake until smooth.

Put this mixture and rest of buttermilk into a pot and slowly bring to boiling point, but do not boil.

Sauté onion in a little oil and cook until golden. Add onion, baco-bits and seasonings to buttermilk. Add potatoes and their liquid and heat almost to boiling. Serve garnished with chives.

Variations:

Grate ½ c. carrots and add or substitute them for potatoes.
Slice leeks and substitute for onions.

Lentil-Barley Soup (Stew)

¼ c. butter or margarine	⅓ c. med.-sized barley
⅓ c. chopped onion	½ t. sea salt
½ c. chopped celery	dash pepper
1 1-lb. can stewed tomatoes	⅛ t. crushed, dried rosemary
2 c. water	leaves
½ c. lentils, well-rinsed	⅓ c. shredded carrots

Melt butter in a large, heavy saucepan over moderate heat. Add onion and celery and cook until onion is lightly browned. Stir in tomatoes, water, lentils, barley, salt, pepper, and rosemary. Bring to a boil.

Cover tightly and boil gently 25 minutes, stirring occasionally, Add carrots and cook 5 minutes longer. If a thinner soup is desired, add more water or tomato juice.

Sun Seed Soup

1 c. sunflower seeds   4 c. vegetable broth
2 c. onions, halved and sliced

Sauté seeds and onions until browned, add broth and cook over medium-low heat ½ hour. Serve with a garnish.

Split Pea Soup I

1 lb. split peas   1 sprig parsley
2 T.butter   ⅛ t. pepper
2 qts. water, hot   2 T. sea salt
1 med. onion, sliced   dash paprika
1 carrot, grated   tamari
1 branch celery   garlic powder

Heat butter in kettle. Add onion and sauté until lightly browned. Add boiling water to peas and all the remaining ingredients.

Cover and simmer 1½ hours, or until peas are mushy. Stir occasionally. Serve topped with baco-bits.

Split Pea Soup II

1 qt. split peas   1 T. flour
1 pt. hot water   1 c. milk
1 onion, sliced   1 c. cream
2 T. margarine

Cover the peas with hot water. Add onion and cook until peas can be mashed. Mash the peas and add the hot water. Blend the margarine and flour, and cook a minute or so with constant stirring, but don't brown. Add peas, then the milk and cream.

Season to taste with salt and white pepper and allow to boil up once. Strain and serve.

For variation add baco-bits.

Cream Soups

Cream soup can easily be made without a specific recipe once you know the base, which is simply a thin cream sauce. It is best to make it in a double boiler, making sure the water in the lower pan is not touching the top pan.

To get the most flavor out of the vegetable you plan to use, either sauté the vegetable in the butter to be used in the cream base, or if you are steaming the vegetable, use the water left over from steaming as part of the water in the broth. You can substitute egg yolk (but watch the heat) for flour or part of the flour. It makes an even richer and more nutritious soup.

The fat will rise to the top the longer it sets. Stir vigorously before serving. If a cream soup does curdle on you, it is not lost. Try putting it in a blender, vegetables and all. If necessary, add a few more "vegies" for "something to chew."

A few good combinations: green bean-almond; cucumber-watercress; brussel sprout-cheese; asparagus-squash blossoms; nettles.

Rich Cream of Mushroom Soup
(From our restaurant.)

½ c. butter or margarine
⅓ c. unbleached white or
   pastry flour
2 c. whole milk
5 cubes bouillon, dissolved in
2 c. water
½ pt. whipping or heavy
   cream

½ lb. mushrooms, sliced
1 T. parsley, chopped
1 T. rosemary leaves (bruise in
   palm of hand)
½ c. green onions, chopped
sea salt
pepper
nutmeg

Sauté mushrooms and green onions in butter. Add flour and bouillon water as needed. Transfer into larger pot. Add rosemary and the rest of the water. You can add 4 egg yolks to the mixture for a richer soup.

Keep the temperature low. Add milk and when soup is thickened, add cream. Turn off heat. Add salt, pepper, and nutmeg to taste.

Cheese-Brussel Sprout Soup

2 T. butter
2 T. unbleached white flour
1 c. sharp cheddar, thinly
   sliced

4 c. milk
1 lb. brussel sprouts,
   quartered
1 t. sea salt

In a skillet, melt butter, add flour, and brown. Slowly add milk and stir with a whisk until smooth and creamy over low heat. Meanwhile, steam brussel sprouts. To the soup base, add salt and ½ c. of the water from the steamed brussel sprouts.

Add cheddar cheese slices and brussel sprouts and serve plain or garnished. Try adding 2 t. curry powder.

Pumpkin Soup

½ c. butter
½ c. unbleached white or
   brown rice flour
3 c. evaporated milk
5 c. pumpkin, pureed
2 c. whole milk

1½ bouillon cubes
2 c. onions, chopped fine
1¼ t. sea salt
1 t. ginger
1¼ t. nutmeg

If you are using whole, fresh pumpkins you must prepare them first (see vegetable section). When cooked, run through a sieve or a food mill or blender to puree.

In a soup pot, melt butter, add flour and whisk to a smooth paste. Begin browning paste. Add evaporated milk, blending well, then add pumpkin and whole milk.

Sauté onions in a little oil until tender. You can add them to soup as is or run them through a sieve first if you prefer them smooth. Add bouillon and spices, mix well, heat. Serve hot or cold. You can sprinkle some roasted seeds on top if you wish.

Yield: 6-8 servings.

Variation:

Use same ingredients. Prepare pumpkin by steaming or baking. Do not cook until soft. Remove about 10 minutes before well done. Cut into chunks (½") and sauté for 5 minutes with onions and the cleaned seeds from pumpkins. Add to creamed broth, season, and cook about ½ hour.

Gazpachio

2 lbs. ripe tomatoes
1 c. bouillon water
2 c. tomato or V-8 juice
4 green onions
1 stick celery
2 T. horseradish
½ c. cucumber, chopped

1 clove garlic
½ c. green pepper
1 T. vinegar
1 T. olive oil
½ c. bread crumbs
sea salt and cayenne to taste

Blenderize the vegetables and tomatoes, using broth to liquefy. Save a little of green pepper and green onion (finely chopped). Add rest of the ingredients and chill until very cold. Serve with finely chopped parsely to garnish. Very nutritious.

Casserole Soup (Yesterday's Soup)

You can take many casseroles or leftovers and recreate them into other very appetizing dishes—like soup. I have added scalloped potatoes, quiche, etc. to cream sauce for a quick, delicious soup.

Also, if you have leftover steamed vegetables, add them to a clear broth or tomato or cream broth.

It is a good feeling to make good use of leftovers from the ice box. Soups are a great way to keep and use those nutrients.

Leftover Gravy Soup

1 c. gravy
2 c. milk

1 c. mashed potatoes
1 c. onions

Sauté onions until browned. Meanwhile, begin beating gravy and milk. Stir in mashed potatoes and onions. If soup needs seasoning, add salt or kelp and ground celery seed.

Cumin-Carrot Soup

1 c. cream sauce
1 c. milk
1-2 c. "vegie" bouillon or
    broth

2 c. carrots, grated
2 c. onions, chopped
2 T. tamari
1 t. cumin

Mix cream sauce, milk, broth, and begin beating. Meanwhile sauté carrots and onions until browned. Add to broth. Then add tamari and cumin. If soup is too thick, thin with 1 c. broth—or, if you want it really creamy, use 1 c. milk. Serve hot or cold.

Fish Chowder
(From our restaurant.)

Follow the recipe for chowder. You may use an inexpensive fish like sheepshead, Johnny bass, or cod.

Cut fish into 1-inch cubes. Put in a large skillet and add a little water. Cover, and poach about 2 minutes. Put fish in bowls and pour over chowder to serve.

For an even fishier-tasting chowder, ask at the fish market for fish heads and remnants. Boil in a little water for about 30 minutes and strain. Use the broth in chowder.

Manhattan Fish-Noodle Chowder

6 c. broth (if you have any broth left over from fish, use it)	2 c. fish
	1 c. corn
	2 c. noodles
2 c. tomato juice	1 t. garlic powder
1 c. carrots, sliced in rounds	1 t. sea salt
2 c. onions	1 T. tamari
1½ c. tomatoes, chopped	2 T. butter

Put broth and juice in soup pot. Add vegetables and bring to a boil. Add noodles and spices. Cook until noodles are tender. Meanwhile, in a skillet, put some water (¼ inch) and fish; cover and poach about 3 minutes. Pour any remaining juice in chowder. When noodles are done, add butter and fish. Serve immediately so fish doesn't get to mushy. This one is sure to be a winner.

Yield: 6-8 servings.

Abalone Chowder

2 c. abalone, cut into small strips	1 c. evaporated milk or cream
	1 c. milk
1 c. carrot grated	2 t. curry
1 c. onion, chopped	1 t. paprika
6 T. butter	2 t. basil

Melt butter in a large, heavy skillet. Add abalone, carrots, and onions. Sauté over low heat until soft. Add evaporated milk. Transfer to a soup kettle and add remaining milk and spices. Continue cooking over low heat until well heated.

Serve with a little parsley garnish. If desired, add a grain and turn this chowder into a main dish! *Yield: 2-4 servings.*

Mock Meatball Soup

Prepare Mock Meatball recipe. Prepare Manhattan Fish-Noodle Chowder, eliminating the fish. When noodles are done add butter and Mock Meatballs and serve.

Cold Papaya-Pear Fruit Soup

1 c. half and half or buttermilk
½ c. honey
4 eggs
1 papaya, skinned and seeded

1 pear, cored
1 T. cinnamon
1 t. nutmeg
1 c. strawberries, slivered

Blenderize all ingredients except the strawberries. Serve in chilled bowls with a sprig of mint and slivered strawberries. *Yield: 2-4 servings.*

Snacks

Roasted Seeds

To roast seeds, put them in a skillet and cook over medium to medium-high heat, stirring often until browned. Or, put on a cookie sheet in a 400° oven and roast until golden, stirring occasionally.

Roasted Seed Mix

1 c. cashews
1 c. sunflower seeds
½ c. sesame seeds
¾ c. baco-bits
4 T. tamari
½ t. onion

1 t. garlic, granulated or
   powder
½ t. thyme
½ t. basil
oregano
¼ c. Parmesan (optional)

In a large skillet, roast seeds, cashews and baco-bits. Stir in tamari and coat well. Add seasonings. Continue roasting until golden brown. Add Parmesan, mixing in well. Roast for 1 minute or more. Serve as a snack or in soup and salads. *Yield: 3 cups.*

Gamasio

Roast sesame seeds in an unoiled skillet. Remove and crush, with salt, using a mortar and pestle or a blender. Serve on rice, vegetables, soups.

Seven-Grain Crackers

½ c. rice grits*
1 c. wheat germ
1 c. oats
½ c. millet meal
½ c. whole wheat flour
½ c. sesame seeds

3 c. milk
½ c. oil
3 cloves garlic, minced or
   pressed
cayenne, sea salt

Soak rice grits and pressed garlic in milk for 10 minutes. Add oats, wheat germ, sesame seed or meal, whole wheat flour, millet meal. Add oil to grain mixture and mix well. Add salt and cayenne to taste.

Mix in milk, rice mixture, adding enough liquid to form dough. Spread out ¼ inch thick on a cookie sheet, and score. Bake at 375° for 15-20 minutes. *Yield: 48 crackers.*

* (Grits are just rice that is coarsely ground.)

Crackers from Leftover Cereal

To make that extra cereal into crackers, all you need to do is add enough flour to make a stiff, pliable dough that you can roll out. Season with salt or whatever your taste buds suggest—sesame, sunflower, or caraway seeds. Roll out and score, then bake at 375° for 15-20 minutes. Remove. Cool a little, then cut.

Sesame Crackers

½ c. water
4 T. oil
2 T. milk
½. t. sea salt

1½ c. whole wheat flour
½ c. soy flour
½ c. sesame seeds

Mix all ingredients and make a stiff, pliable dough. Roll out—the thinner the better. Lay on an oiled and floured cookie sheet, sprinkle with salt and sesame seeds. With a fork, prick the crackers and mark into squares. Bake at 350° for 20 minutes.
Yield: 36 crackers.

Tortilla Chips

Cut tortillas into sixteenth's and drop in a skillet or wok or pot containing very hot oil. Cook until crisp and browned. Remove and drain on paper towels. Salt.

Wheat Sticks

1 c. flour	2-3 T. soy flour
3 c. whole wheat flour	¾ c. oil
1 c. graham flour	1 t. sea salt
1 c. wheat germ	½ c. honey (optional)
1¼ c. water	1 c. coconut, grated (optional)

Mix dry ingredients and work in oil. Add enough water for a stiff dough. Knead until smooth. Roll out to ¼ inch thickness. Cut into sticks. Bake at 350° until browned. *Yield: 60 sticks.*

Sandwich Suggestions

Caraway Melt

Toast rye bread and top with a mixture of half Swiss cheese and half jack cheese. Sprinkle with caraway seed and melt in oven or broiler. Serve with tomatoes and sprouts.

Sauerkraut-Caraway Melt

After toasting rye bread, put drained sauerkraut on top, then cheese. Melt in oven or broiler. Sprinkle with caraway seed and serve with Thousand Island dressing, tomatoes, and sprouts.

Cream Cheese

Cream cheese goes with so many things. Here are a few that we really like: chives, baco-bits; Worcestershire sauce, basil, salt; pineapple, curry and raisins (optional); olives; cucumber and paprika; banana, honey, dates and/or walnuts.

Avocado I

Avocado slices, jack cheese, tomato, sprouts, and mayonnaise.

Avocado II

Avacado, hard-boiled eggs, lemon juice, mayonnaise, salt or tamari.

Open Face

Slice of bread with fresh, sliced mushrooms, onion, and sliced tomato—topped with cheese, oregano sprinkled on top. Put under broiler until cheese is melted.

Baco

Baco-bits, mayonnaise, lettuce, tomato, and sprouts.

Cucumber

Cucumber slices, lettuce, tomato, mayonnaise, and sprouts.

Stuffin'

Leftover stuffing on toast with cheese melted on top, lettuce, tomato, and sprouts.

Bible Bread

Bible bread or chapatis stuffed with cheese, sautéed mush-mushrooms, onions, avocado, tomato—cook in a fry pan with a little butter until the cheese melts. Add sprouts, lettuce, mayonnaise, or Tahini Dressing (see recipe in next section).

Salads and Dressings

An afternoon or evening meal doesn't seem complete without a salad. The requirements for a good-tasting salad include color, variety, texture, ingredients that are crisp and crunchy, and a complementary dressing.

The main base for salad is lettuce, in many varieties that offer different tastes and textures.

The best way to maintain freshness and nutrients is to pick the greens from your own garden and serve them as soon as possible. A very small patch of land can provide you with many salad "fixings."

Don't limit your salad ideas to domestic greens. There are many wild edibles which grow right in your own yard.

Here are some of the many varieties of greens and vegetables you can use in salads:

Lettuce

Head, red leaf, boston, bibb, butter, salad bowl, romaine, and others.

Other Leafy Greens

Chinese cabbage, escarole, spinach, watercress, chicory, mustard greens, beet greens, kale, dandelion greens, nasturtium leaves, burnet, nettles, miner's lettuce.

Vegetable Additions

Fresh corn, peas, broccoli, cauliflower, asparagus tips, sliced mushrooms, radishes (try white ones, also known as daikon), grated beets, carrot curls, green onions, cucumber, tomatoes, grated summer squash, nasturtium flowers, marigolds, geranium leaves and flowers.

Extra Delights

Olives, artichoke hearts, cheeses, eggs, croutons, sprouts of all kinds, and fresh or dried herbs.

Croutons

Dry bread at room temperature (uncovered) for a few days, or put in the oven at 250° until dried. When dry, cut into 1-inch cubes. Toss with oil, garlic powder, and herbs of your choice. Parmesan cheese is good, too. Bake at 400° until golden and crisp: 10 minutes. Cool and store. You may sprinkle seeds on top, raw or toasted.

Shepherd's Salad
(From our restaurant.)

1 bunch fresh spinach
2 oz. feta, crumbled
2 hard-boiled eggs

6 green olives
2 oz. sunflower seeds (roasted)

Fill bowl with spinach and top with remaining ingredients. Serve with herb dressing. You may also top with two artichoke hearts. *Yield: 2 large salads.*

Creamy Cucumber Salad

2 c. cucumbers	½ c. sour cream
½ small onion	4 T. milk
3 T. fresh parsley, chopped	¼ c. chives

Slice cucumbers thin. Soak in salt water 1 hour. Drain, mix in other ingredients, chill. *Yield: 4 4-oz. servings.*

Variations:

Try 1 c. yoghurt, 1½ t. mint and ¼ c. lemon juice instead of sour cream and chives.

Serve with watercress.

Potato Salad

4 large potatoes	6 hard-boiled eggs (if you don't
1 med. onion, finely chopped	want so much egg flavor,
½ c. chopped celery	use 4)

Cube potatoes, chop eggs, combine with onion, celery, and dressing. *Yield: 6 cups.*

Dressing:

½ c. mayonnaise	¼ t. sea salt
1 T. mustard	1 T. parsley
1 T. milk	½ t. honey

Variations:

Add curry or cayenne.
Add sunflower seeds and chopped broccoli.
Add baco-bits.

Sunchoke Salad
(Jerusalem artichokes.)

2 c. grated sunchokes	¼ c. olive oil
1 c. grated carrots	1 c. fresh lemon juice
¼ c. chopped, fresh celantro	¼ c. nasturtium flowers,
½ t. ground rosemary	chopped (if available)
1 t. ground ginger	

Mix together and chill. Serve on a bed of romaine. You may add ¼ c. roasted and salted peanuts. *Yield: 6 4-oz. servings.*

Marinated Vegie Salad

1 c. chopped broccoli
1 c. green beans
1 c. cauliflower, cut small
¼ c. mung bean sprouts
½ c. shirred carrots
1 c. green onions, chopped

½ c. green olives, sliced
1 c. mushrooms, sliced
1 c. canned water chestnuts,
   sliced or 1 c. sun-
   chokes, sliced thin

Combine all ingredients. Follow recipe for Marinade in this section. Pour over vegetables, mix well, and put in the refrigerator overnight. Mix again. Serve on a bed of lettuce. For an oriental touch try any of these: grated white horseradish, lotus roots, bamboo shoots, laver, mung bean sprouts, freshly grated ginger. This salad will last a few days in the refrigerator.

Yield: 16 4-oz. servings.

Bean Salad

½ c. cooked kidney beans
½ c. cooked garbanzos
½ c. green beans

½ c. soy beans or pintos
½ c. chopped onions
½ c. chopped celery

Cook beans according to bean recipes. Chill and add onions and celery.

Mix together:

⅓ c. apple cider vinegar
1 T. oregano
1 t. garlic powder

1 t. sea salt
⅓ c. oil

Pour over beans and chill. *Yield: 6 4-oz. servings.*

Macaroni Salad

4 c. cooked elbow macaroni
2 c. chopped celery
2 c. cucumbers, quartered and
  sliced

3 c. chopped tomatoes
1 c. scallions
¼ c. fresh parsley, chopped

Dressing:

2 c. mayonnaise
½ c. milk
½ t. sea salt

¼ t. black pepper
½ t. curry

Chill and serve. *Yield: 20 4-oz. servings.*

Cole Slaw

2 c. grated cabbage
½ c. grated carrot
⅛ c. finely chopped or grated
  onion

⅓ c. mayonnaise
1½ t. garlic powder
sea salt

Mix all ingredients. As an alternative you can just grate cabbage and carrot and use yoghurt as a dressing—or use French dressing. *Yield 6 4-oz. servings.*

Daikon Salad
(White radish)

2 c. grated radish   ¼ c. grated carrot

Mix together:

4 oz. vinegar   1 t. sugar
2 oz. lemon juice   1 T. tamari
1 t. kelp

Pour mixture over daikon and carrot. Set aside and chill at least 1 hour. Serve with grated, fresh ginger on top. You can add 1 c. chopped cucumber. *Yield: 9 2-oz. servings.*

Bulghur Salad

1 c. bulghur wheat   1 c. minced parsley
2½ c. water   ¼ c. sesame or olive oil
1½ t. sea salt   2 T. lemon juice
2 scallions   ¼ t. mint or thyme

Add bulghur to boiling, salted water. Reduce heat and simmer, covered, for 30 minutes. Remove cover and cool to lukewarm. Mix with scallions, celery, and parsley, and place in refrigerator to chill.

Mix oil, lemon juice, and herbs. Pour over bulghur and serve. *Yield: 4 2-oz. servings.*

Variations:

Top with grated sesame seeds.
Top with a sprig of mint, parsley, or watercress.

Angel Egg Salad

8 hard-boiled eggs (remove yolks)

Add to yolks:

1 t. finely chopped onion   ⅛ t. cumin
⅛ t. curry   1 t. sage
½ t. garlic powder   ½ c. mayonnaise

Mix and stuff whites, then chill. (If you wish, you can add 2 T. Parmesan cheese.) *Yield: 16 stuffed egg halves.*

Farmer & Fisherman Salad
(From our restaurant.)

2 c. red snapper	1 green pepper
8 large prawns	2 tomatoes
¼ c. mushrooms	8 romaine lettuce leaves
¼ c. green onions	3-4 c. tossed green salad
1 avocado	1 cucumber
2 lemon wedges	2 watercress sprigs

Prepare the snapper two to three hours ahead of time. Cut into 1-inch cubes, place in a skillet with a little boiling water, and cover. Cook over medium heat until pink is gone; about 3 minutes. Remove from heat and drain, saving the liquid for your next batch of chowder.

Boil water and cook prawns (see Cooked Shrimp, in Fish section). Chill fish and shrimp. After one hour, pour Marinade (see this section) over the fish and shrimp, and return to refrigerator.

When the fish has chilled, add mushrooms and green onions to mixture.

Now you can begin to assemble your salad. Line a large salad bowl (chef's salad size) with romaine lettuce leaves. Fill bowl three-fourths full of tossed green salad. Slice an avocado in half, then in lengthwise strips. Cut green peppers and cucumbers in rounds, and tomatoes and lemons in wedges.

In the middle of the tossed salad, place some of the fish/vegie mixture and put large shrimp around it. Line the outer edges, alternating as you go, with avocado, green pepper, tomato wedges. Stick cucumber strips upright along the sides. Put a long toothpick into a cucumber round, then into a lemon wedge, and set on top with a sprig of watercress. Sprinkle on a few croutons and you have created a meal in itself!

Serve with your favorite dressing and with some bread or rolls. *Yield: 2 large salads.*

Tuna-Stuffed Avocado Salad

1¼ c. fresh tuna, poached
¼ c. green onions
¼ c. cucumbers, cut small
2 large avocados
¼-½ c. sour cream
juice of 1 lemon

1 t. Worcestershire sauce
½ t. dry mustard
2 dashes cayenne
½ t. kelp
paprika
sea salt to taste

Combine tuna and vegetables. Mix sour cream and spices and combine with tuna. Cut avocados in half and remove pit. Top with lots of filling; sprinkle paprika on top. Serve with crackers or tortilla chips and a lemon wedge.

You can also use other kinds of fish or shrimp.

Yield: 4 stuffed avocado halves.

Cabbage Salad

2 c. red cabbage, grated
1 c. beets, grated
1 c. carrots, grated
1 c. parsnips or turnips (young and tender)

1 c. zucchini, grated
1 c. yellow squash, grated
¼ c. green onions, chopped
¼ c. parsley, chopped fine

Mix vegetables together in a bowl and serve on a bed of greens or spinach, with sprouts and your favorite dressing. Top with ground seeds or dried herbs. *Yield: 15 4-oz. servings.*

Sprouts

Almost all seeds will sprout. Many you can eat raw; some require some steaming. Sprouting not only maintains, but also increases the nutritional value of foods—and makes them easier to digest.

We sprout our seeds by putting them in a jar, filling it with water and soaking the seeds overnight. Drain and rinse the next morning and place mosquito netting, cheesecloth, or nylon net on the end of the jar, and secure with a rubber band. If a canning jar is used, use the metal rim over the cheesecloth.

Put jar in a dark place, tilted on an angle so all the water can drain out. (It's a good idea to build a sprout rack—see illustration.)

Continue rinsing twice a day until sprouts have developed. If you are in a hot climate, rinse three times a day.

When sprouts are almost ready, put them directly in sunlight so they can develop a nice green color and chlorophyl.

Amount of Seeds and Sprouting Time

Seed or bean	Amount of seeds per quart of water	Time for sprouting
Alfalfa seeds	3 T.	3-4 days
Mung beans	¾ c.	2-3 days
Lentils	¾ c.	3 days
Sunflower seeds*	1 c.	2 days
Garbanzos	1 c.	3 days
Wheat*	1 c.	3 days
Barley*	1 c.	3 days
Soybeans	1 c.	3 days
Peas	¾ c.	3-4 days
Oats*	1 c.	2-3 days

* These seeds are great in sprouted bread (see Bread section).

To cook sprouts, steam for 20-30 minutes; or use them in breads, casseroles, or burgers.

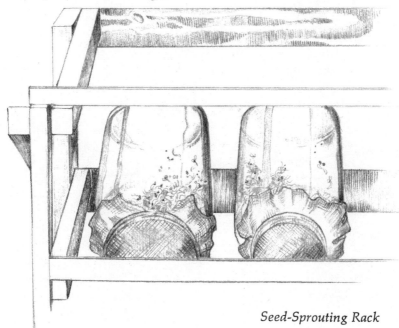

Seed-Sprouting Rack

Dressings

Oil and Vinegar — or Lemon Dressing

¾ c. oil   ¼ c. vinegar or lemon juice
1 t. sea salt

Mix and serve.

Herb Dressing
(From our restaurant.)

1 c. oil	½ t. tarragon
½ c. apple cider vinegar	½ t. rosemary
¼ c. lemon juice	½ t. sea salt
2 T. tamari	1 t. kelp
1 t. garlic powder	½ t. dry mustard (optional)
1 t. whole thyme	2 T. Parmesan (optional)
1 t. oregano	¼ c. sesame seeds, roasted
½ t. marjoram	

Put everything in a blender, except sesame seeds. Blend, then add seeds—or just put in a jar and shake. *Yield: 1 pt. (16 oz.).*

French Dressing

⅔ c. oil	1 t. sea salt
⅓ c. apple cider vinegar or lemon juice	1 t. oregano
	1 t. rosemary
½ t. garlic, grated or powdered	1 t. thyme

Mix in a blender or put in a jar and shake. *Yield: 1 c. (8 oz.).*

Honey French Dressing

Follow recipe for French dressing, using lemon juice and ½-⅔ c. honey.

Clipper Belle Dressing

¾ c. olive oil
¼ c. vinegar or lemon juice
¼ c. ketchup
2-3 t. honey

1 t. sea salt
½ t. garlic powder
½ t. paprika

Mix ingredients in a blender or put in a jar and shake.
Yield: 12 oz.

Herbed Marinade
(For fish or vegetables.)

1 c. olive oil
½ c. lemon juice
1 t. oregano
½ t. garlic powder
1 t. thyme

1 t. basil
1½ t. Worcestershire sauce
½ t. dry mustard
few leaves celantro

Put in a jar and shake. (The blender makes this marinade too
creamy.) *Yield: 12 oz.*

Spiral Dressing

2 c. sesame oil
¼ c. vinegar
¼ c. tamari

⅛-¼ c. honey
½ medium onion
½-⅓ c. miso

Put mixture in blender. If it looks too thick, add water.
Yield: 3¼ c. (26 oz.).

Creamy Dressings

(If they become too thick it is best to thin them with buttermilk.)

Bleu Cheese Dressing

1 c. bleu cheese, crumbled	½ t. garlic
1 c. sour cream (thin with buttermilk)	½ t. Worcestershire sauce

Break up cheese with a fork. Mix in sour cream and season, or put in a blender until smooth. Salt if needed. *Yield: 16 oz.*

Thousand Island Dressing I

1 c. mayonnaise	2 T. pickle relish
¼ c. ketchup	sea salt

Mix everything together until smooth. *Yield: 12 oz.*

Thousand Island Dressing II

1 c. mayonnaise	1 t. sea salt or tamari
¼ c. ketchup	1 t. kelp
3-4 hard-boiled eggs	1 t. honey/brown sugar
½ t. sweet basil	1 t. garlic powder
½ t. oregano	

Mix everything together until smooth. In place of ketchup you can use chile sauce, green pepper, or ½ t. dry mustard.
Yield: 12 oz.

Top o' the Vegies Dressing

½ bunch carrot tops	1 bunch (¼ c.) beet tops

Grind tops through a food mill. When choosing your vegetable tops be sure they are not too bitter. Press out juice and mix with:

½ c. oil	1 t. tamari
¼ c. lemon	¼ t. cayenne
¾ t. garlic	½ t. thyme
½ t. cumin	

For variety you can add ¼ c. fresh spinach, or 1 c. cottage cheese or sour cream, or other types of greens like kale.
Yield: 8-12 oz.

Vegies Dressing
(Or: Poor Man's Dressing)

2 green peppers
2 tomatoes
3 green onions
1 t. garlic powder
¼ t. sea salt

⅛-¼ c. lemon juice or
  1-2 lemons
½ t. marjoram
1 t. basil

Grind vegetables and garlic. Add lemon juice and spices. *Yield: 8-12 oz.*

Guacamole I

3 ripe avocados
1 t. sea salt
1 T. lemon juice

1 t. garlic powder or
2 t. fresh, chopped garlic
  cloves

Mash avocados and add seasoning. (I also like to add the pulp of one or two tomatoes.)

When making guacamole, save the pits from your avocados. If you stick them in the guacamole, they will keep it from turning brown. *Yield: 16-24 oz.*

Guacamole II

3 large ripe avocados
1 t. sea salt
juice of 3 lemons
¼ c. onions, chopped
  (optional)

1 c. sour cream
1 t. garlic powder
1 t. kelp
2 t. tamari
2 t. bouillon powder

Mix in blender. *Yield: 3 c.*

Guacamole III

3 avocados
½ c. oil
¼ c. lemon juice

2 t. kelp
⅛ c. onion, minced
1 t. tabasco

Mix in blender. *Yield: 3 c.*

Yoghurt Dressing I

1 c. yoghurt
1 c. tomato juice
1 t. tamari
¼ c. lemon juice

1 t. garlic powder
½ t. basil
½ t. rosemary
¼-½ t. sea salt

Put in blender or shake in a jar. *Yield: 16 oz.*

Yoghurt Dressing II
(Rich and a touch of tang.)

1 c. yoghurt
4-6 oz. bleu cheese or
   Gorgonzola
½ c. oil
⅛ c. vinegar
1 t. Worcestershire sauce

1 t. basil
1 t. garlic powder
1 t. thyme
1 t. oregano
½ t. sea salt

Put in blender or shake in a jar. *Yield: 2½ c. (22 oz.).*

Yoghurt Dressing III

1 c. yoghurt
1 T. lemon juice
¼ t. garlic powder
½ t. basil
1 t. dill

½ t. thyme
½ t. sea salt
½ t. tamari
1 T. milk (optional, if you
   desire thinner dressing)

Put in blender or shake in a jar. *Yield: 8-12 oz.*

Cuke 'n Yoghurt Dressing

1 cucumber
½ t. garlic
juice of 1 lemon
1 c. yoghurt

¼ t. basil
¼ t. dill
¼ t. kelp

Put in a blender or shake in a jar. *Yield: 12-16 oz.*

Ground Seed I

1 c. ground sunflower seeds	1 t. ground basil
1 c. ground sesame seeds	½ t. tarragon
1¼ c. oil	1 t. thyme
½ c. lemon juice	¼ t. celery seed
1 t. oregano	2 T. tamari

Put in a blender or shake in a jar. *Yield: 1 qt.*

Ground Seed II

(This makes almost 1 qt. of dressing.)

1 c. ground sunflower seeds	½ t. garlic powder
1 c. buttermilk	½ t. celery salt
¾ c. ketchup	½ t. kelp

Mix in a blender or shake in a jar. *Yield: 3 c.*

Ground Seed Dressing III

(Or special sandwich sauce.)

1 c. ground sesame seed	½ t. Worcestershire sauce
1½ c. mayonnaise	¼ t. ground oregano
½ c. ketchup	½ t. sea salt
¼ t. garlic powder	buttermilk to thin

Leave thick as a dressing for sandwiches (great with soyburgers). Thin with buttermilk for a salad dressing. *Yield: 3 c.*

Mayonnaise

1 c. oil	2 T. lemon juice
1 egg	¼ t. sea salt

Begin by breaking egg into a blender with ¼ c. of oil and 1 T. lemon juice. Turn blender on (have the rest of your oil there and ready). After 8 seconds begin *very, very* slowly to pour in the rest of oil. Keep pouring until it has all been added.

Turn off blender and add salt and rest of lemon juice. Turn blender on until all is mixed in. *Yield: 1 c.*

There are some important tricks to remember in making a successful batch of mayonnaise:

Your selection of oil is important because it will provide the dominant taste.

Don't make more than one batch at a time.

Be sure to pour in the oil very slowly.

It is best to make mayonnaise in cool, dry weather.

If a batch doesn't work out, set it aside and make a new batch. With the new batch in the blender, turn the blender on and pour in the old, unemulsified batch, very slowly. It should thicken up this time.

Eggless Mayonnaise

1 c. lemon juice	¼ c. oil
1 t. honey	½ c. Tahini or nut butter

Mix well, in a blender, if possible. *Yield: 12 oz.*

Vegetable Mayonnaise

2 tomatoes
2 stalks celery
1 small onion, grated
¼ c. oil

1 c. eggless mayonnaise, or
   ground seed or nut butter
cayenne
sea salt

Mash the tomatoes, first removing the peeling. Add celery, mayonnaise or nut butter, and oil. Add salt and cayenne to taste. Whip together well. *Yield: 16-22 oz.*

Ketchup

4 lbs. ripe tomatoes, chopped
3 medium onions, chopped
4 cloves garlic, minced
3 T. honey
1 t. allspice
½ t. cumin

1 t. ground cloves
1 t. pepper
½ t. cinnamon
1 t. mustard
½ t. cayenne
1 t. sea salt

Put tomatoes, onions, and garlic in a pot to simmer. When mixture has begun to cook down, add honey and spices. Continue simmering until ketchup reaches desired thickness. Remove from heat and run through a food mill. Add ½ c. apple cider vinegar, then cool and use, or can and store. *Yield: 1½ qts.*

(Also see ketchup in Canning and Drying section.)

Herbs for Seasoning

One-fourth t. dry herbs equals 1 t. fresh herbs. When using whole herbs instead of powdered, use a little more. If you want them slightly smaller, or powdered, roll between your hands.

Anise

Seed or ground. Sweet licorice aroma and taste. Cakes and cookies, fruit sauces, good to chew for stomachaches.

Basil

Broken leaves or ground. Pleasant, mild, sweet. Tomato sauce, cream sauce, fish, soups, eggs, omelettes, soufflés.

Bay

Leaves or ground. Helps digestion of beans. Tomatoes, stews.

Borage

Cucumber-like flavor. Salads, tea.

Caraway

Seeds. Rye bread, sauerkraut, cheese, cottage cheese. Gives rye bread its flavor.

Cardamom

Whole pods with seeds, or ground. Tea and hot milk, bitter-sweet, pastries and coffee cakes, fruit salad dressings.

Cayenne

Many different kinds. Vary in hotness. Beans, salad dressings, sauce, guacamole.

Celery Seed

Seeds or ground and combined with salt. Salad dressing, soups, stews, stuffing.

Chervil

Leaves. Delicate, licorice flavor, similar to parsley. Salad, butter and sauces, fish, eggs, cheese spreads.

Chives

Garnish for soups, baked potatoes, with sour cream. Great in cheese spreads, garlic butter for bread, cold stuffings for tomatoes, fish.

Cinnamon

Sweet 'n spicy. Good in hot drinks, cakes, cookies, desserts, pies, yoghurts, sour cream, jams, sauces, pancakes, breads, pudding, cereal, chocolate. Chutney, for taste.

Cloves

Whole or ground. Sharp and spicy. Good in hot drinks, preserves, pies, cakes, sweet stuffing, chutney, French toast.

Coriander

Whole or ground. Apple and pumpkin pie, cookies, cakes, and pudding.

Cumin

Whole or ground. Strong flavor. Enchilada sauce, beans, chili, stews.

Dill

Leaves, stems and seeds. Pickling, potato salad, salad dressing, potatoes, fish sauces, bread, soup.

Fennel

Whole or ground. Cookies, cakes, breads, soups and stews, rice and grains. Sweet licorice anise.

Garlic

Vegetable dishes, soups, sauces, gravies, beans, bread, crackers, fish, salads.

Geranium

Fruits and salads.

Ginger

Fresh root or ground. Sauces, sautéed with vegetables, rice, hot drinks, candies, cookies, cakes, puddings, pies, chutney preserves, fish, salads, and dressings.

Juniper Berries

Fish, stews, especially when roasted outdoors.

Kelp

Strong, high in iodine. Use in vegetable dishes, salads, dressings.

Lemon Verbena

Strong lemon flavor. Fish, stuffing, desserts, preserves, sauces, teas.

Marigold

Petals. Soups, stews. Color substitute for saffron.

Marjoram

Leaves or ground. Salads, dressings, fish, stuffing, vegetable loaves, sauces, soups, stews, eggs, cheese, vegetables.

Mint

Fresh or dried leaves, flakes, extract. Salads, dressings, drinks, garnishes, frosting.

Mustard

Whole or powdered. Salad dressings, sauces.

Nasturtiums

Salads.

Nutmeg and Mace

Whole or ground. Cakes, cookies, sauces, eggnog, hot drinks.

Oregano

Leaves or ground. Similar to marjoram and thyme. Sauces, salads, dressings, spaghetti, pizzas, fish, soups.

Paprika

Powder. Potatoes, vegetables, fish, garnish.

Parsley

Leaves, stems, flakes, fresh or dried. Fish, soups, sauces, spreads, cheese, vegetables, eggs. Fresh as garnish in salads.

Pepper

Whole corns, and cracked, coarsely ground.

Poppy Seeds

Whole. Sweet, nut-like. Use in baking, vegetable dishes.

Rosemary

Needle-like leaves. Soups, stuffing, fish, garnish.

Saffron

Strands or ground. Cakes, breads, rice, as a coloring for cheese, butter.

Sage

Rubbed or ground. Stuffing, dressings, vegetable loaves, soups, stews, beans.

Savory

Leaves or ground. Sauces, dressings, soups, soufflés, eggs, fish.

Sesame

Whole. Nut-like flavor.

Tarragon

Leaves, chopped. Salads, tomato sauce, dressings, fish, marinades.

Thyme

Leaves or ground. Grains, rice, sauces, dressings, eggs, soufflés, potatoes, soups, stews, vegetables, fish, stuffing.

Turmeric

Ground, bright yellow, slightly bitter. Sauces, gravies, beans, spreads, pickles, dressings, curries; also for coloring.

Sauces

Let your imagination transform a plain entrée into a work of art, pleasing to the palate—with creative sauces!

Sauces can complement fine foods or turn dull foods into interesting and tasty dishes. Some can be prepared with basic ingredients you usually have on hand. You can prepare many of them ahead of time to make your meal preparation easier.

Cream Sauce
(With many variations.)

Melt ½ lb. butter or margarine over medium heat; slowly add 1 c. flour* stirring constantly with a whisk to remove all lumps. Add 1 qt. milk** and stir until well blended. Add sea salt to taste and remove from heat.

As sauce cools, it will thicken more; so, if storing, you may have to thin with milk when you reheat it.

* Brown rice flour is great, but expensive. You can use wheat or white.

** I use half and half, cream, or evaporated milk, depending on the richness I desire. *Yield: 4-6 c.*

Variations:

Add basil and Worchestershire sauce.
Add curry and tamari.
Instead of flour, use ground sesame seeds.
Use vegetable bouillon and tamari to thin for gravy.
Use as a base for cream soup.
Add dry mustard.

53

Cheese Sauce

Follow recipe for cream sauce; add 2 c. grated cheese.

Curry Powder

½ c. ground cumin seed
¾ t. ground mustard seed
3 T. dried, ground ginger root
½ c. turmeric

½-1 T. coriander
1 T. cayenne
2 peppercorns
1 T. cardamom

Grind all the spices. Store in an airtight jar. *Yield: 4 c.*

Curry Sauce
(From our restaurant.)

5 pippins (or other cooking
apple), sliced thin
3 onions (equal in amount to
apples), sliced in half-moons
1 lb. butter
½ T. sea salt

2½ T. whole wheat pastry
flour
3½ T. curry powder
1 T. ginger
¾ t. nutmeg

Sauté apples and onions slowly in butter until onions are transparent. Blenderize three-fourths of the mixture and return to pan. Mix flour and spices with remaining one-fourth of mixture, to make a smooth paste. Stir in with rest of mixture and cook to desired thickness. Serve with noodles or rice. *Yield: 3 c.*

Chinese Sauce

¼ c. butter or margarine
1 c. onion, chopped
2 cloves garlic, chopped
1 t. sea salt
⅛ t. pepper
1 c. celery, finely chopped

¾ c. water
⅓ c. cold water
2 t. tamari
2 T. arrowroot
1 t. honey

Melt butter in a large skillet. Add onions, garlic, celery, salt, and pepper. Sauté for a minute, then add ¾ c. water. Cover and cook 5 minutes. Mix cold water, tamari, arrowroot, and honey. Make sure there are no lumps. Add to above mixture and cook just to boiling point. Serve over rice or see Chop Suey recipe in Vegetarian Main Dishes section. *Yield: 3 c.*

Black Bean Sauce

2 c. cooked black beans
¼ c. vinegar
¼ c. tamari
¼ c. water

2 T. fresh, ground ginger
7 lg. cloves garlic, grated or
finely chopped

Mix beans with vinegar, tamari, and water. Meanwhile, sauté ginger and garlic in a little oil until browned. Add to beans. Run mixture through a blender or food mill. Serve with grains or pasta. (See Fish section: Shrimp in Black Bean Sauce.)
Yield: 2¾-3 c.

Tomato Sauce for Spaghetti

¼ c. oil (preferably olive)
2 cloves garlic, sliced
1 onion, sliced
2 c. vegetable broth (see Soup
    section)
1 10-oz. can tomato
1 10½-oz. can tomato puree
1 12-oz. can tomato paste
3 t. honey

1 t. sea salt
1 t. kelp
½ t. garlic (granulated)
3 T. tamari
2 t. oregano
1 t. basil
1 t. thyme
½ t. marjoram
1 c. Parmesan cheese

Put ¼ c. oil in a deep pan. Add garlic and onions; brown garlic. Add vegetable broth and tomatoes. Cook, adding 3 c. water or tomato juice as needed. After cooking an hour, add seasonings—except Parmesan. Cook 2-3 hours, stirring often. Add Parmesan and serve. *Yield: 6 c.*

(Some suggestions: cook sauce the night before—it improves with aging; you may like fresh tomatoes added to this sauce.)

Tomato Sauce "from Scratch'"

Some soft tomatoes are all you really need. Scald 1 minute, then dip in cold water to remove skins. (If you don't mind the skins, cook tomatoes with skins on.)

Cut tomatoes in halves or quarters. Cook until thick. If necessary, add water. If a smoother sauce is desired, run through a sieve or blender. Season as above or use whatever you think is good. If you use onions and garlic be sure you add them during the early part of the cooking.

Easy Tomato Sauce

8 c. whole tomatoes (canned or
  fresh)
1 onion, sliced
3 garlic cloves, chopped
1 c. celery, finely chopped

¾ c. green peppers, chopped
1 t. sea salt
1 t. kelp
2 t. oregano
1 c. broccoli, chopped

Sauté onions and garlic in a large skillet until browned. Add tomatoes and seasonings. Cook about 45 minutes. Add broccoli the last 5 minutes. Serve with shrimp, vegetables, rice, or pasta. *Yield: 6 c.*

Another Easy Tomato Sauce

½ c. oil
3 garlic cloves
1 onion, sliced
2 c. vegetable broth

2 cans tomato paste
4 c. tomatoes, chopped
2 c. tomato juice or water

Prepare sauce and season as in Easy Tomato Sauce, leaving tomato juice until later. If sauce is too thick after cooking a few hours, add more tomato juice or water. *Yield: 8 c.*

Sweet 'n Sour Sauce

2 c. unsweetened pineapple
juice
1 c. apple cider vinegar
¼ c. honey
¼ c. tamari
1 T. arrowroot

2 t. ginger, ground
1 lg. tomato, cut in
half-moons
1 pineapple, cut in chunks
(3 c.)
1 lg. green bell pepper, sliced

Put juice and vinegar in a large saucepan and heat. Add honey, tamari, and ginger. Remove some of the juice, add arrowroot to it. Mix to a smooth paste, then add it to sauce. When sauce thickens, add tomato, pineapple, and bell peppers. Cook 1 minute; remove from heat.* Serve with refried rice, udons, egg rolls, or vegetables.

* At this time check your sauce. If it is too sour, add a little more pineapple juice and honey. *Yield: 4 c.*

Mustard Sauce

2 t. prepared spicy mustard
½ c. heavy cream
¼ t. curry powder

sea salt
pepper
pinch of paprika

Blend ingredients. Salt and pepper to taste. Refrigerate 1 hour before serving. *Yield: ½ c.*

Butter Sauces

Lemon Butter Sauce

Combine 2 T. butter and ¼ c. lemon. You may wish to add garlic powder; and, for green beans or garlic bread, Parmesan cheese. *Yield: ⅓ c.*

Cocktail Sauce I

Good for omelettes, raw vegetables, tempura dishes. Combine 1½ oz. ketchup and 1 T. horseradish; and, perhaps, ½ T. Worcestershire sauce. *Yield: ¼ c.*

Cocktail Sauce II

2 oz. ketchup
1 t. horseradish
1 T. lemon juice

½ T. spicy mustard
¼ t. Worcestershire sauce

Combine all ingredients. *Yield: 3 oz.*

Herb Butter Sauce

½ c. butter
3 T. tamari
1 t. garlic   ⋅
½ t. basil

1 t. oregano
¼ t. thyme
½ t. rosemary
¼ t. tarragon

Melt butter and add tamari; spices. Very rich; great for fish.
Yield: ½-¾ c.

Quick Sauce for Pizza or Vegetable Dishes

1 T. olive oil
1 med. onion, chopped
1 clove garlic, chopped fine
1⅓ c. peeled tomatoes,
   chopped (reserve juice)
2 T. tomato paste

1 t. dried oregano
½-¾ t. basil
½ bay leaf
½ t. honey
½ t. sea salt

Heat oil in skillet. Sauté onion in oil until transparent. Add
garlic and sauté 1 minute; don't brown. Stir in remaining
ingredients and simmer sauce at very low heat (uncovered) for 1
hour or until thick. Stir from time to time to prevent burning.
Yield: 1½ c.

Barbecue Sauce

¼ c. ketchup
¼ c. molasses
1 t. mustard

½ t. garlic powder (optional)
1 t. tamari (optional)

Mix ingredients together and pour over food, or steep food in
sauce. *Yield: ½ c.*

Tartar Sauce

1 c. mayonnaise
¼ c. sweet pickle relish

½ T. lemon juice

Combine ingredients. Serve with fish. *Yield: 1¼ c.*

Hot Sauce I

4 med. peeled tomatoes, finely
  chopped
½ c. onion, finely chopped
½ c. celery, finely chopped
¼ c. green pepper, finely
  chopped

2 c. chopped chilies
¼ c. oil (preferably olive)
1 t. mustard seed
1 t. coriander seed
1 t. sea salt
dash pepper

Combine ingredients. Cook over medium heat, stirring occasionally; or just chill, stirring occasionally. *Yield: 4 c.*

Hot Sauce II

2 med. onions, chopped
15 med. tomatoes, diced
10 tomatillos, diced
4 Anaheim chilies, chopped
2 to 4 jalapenos, chopped*
1-2 t. cayenne
1 T. cumin

4 t. garlic powder
1 T. sea salt
2 t. oregano
1 t. thyme
1 t. marjoram
1 t. kelp (optional)

Put onions, tomatoes, tomatillos, chilies in a pot and begin cooking down.

If you have a blender, shorten the cooking time in this way: after 30 minutes or so, remove mixture from heat, add spices, put in your blender, puree—and you're done. If the mixture is still watery, return it to the stove and cook uncovered a little more until it reaches desired consistency.

If you don't have a blender, add spices after 30 minutes and continue cooking until sauce is of desired consistency. *Yield: 2 c.*

* (Actually, the number of jalapenos you put in is up to you. I used 4 in this batch and found it about medium hot.)

Enchilada Sauce I

Follow above recipe for Hot Sauce II, with these additional steps. Melt 2 T. butter and stir in 3 T. flour to a smooth paste. Cook about 1 minute, stirring constantly. Remove from heat. If blenderizing, puree Hot Sauce mixture, return to cooking pot and add butter and flour mixture. Cook over low heat until thickened; about 30 minutes.

If you don't use a blender, add butter and flour mixture after sauce has cooked about 2 hours and continue cooking until sauce is of desired consistency. You may want to add another tablespoon of cumin. *Yield: 8 c.*

Enchilada Sauce II

2 T. oil (preferably olive)
2 cloves garlic, finely chopped
1 onion
1 lg. can tomato puree (12 oz.)

½ c. vegetable broth
1 t. cumin
2 T. chili powder

Heat oil. Add garlic and onions and sauté a minute or two. Add puree and broth, cumin, and chili powder. *Yield: 2 c.*

Red Chili Sauce

12 chili pods   sea salt

Remove stems, seeds, and veins from pods. (Keep seeds if you want a hotter sauce.) To remove seeds, put pods in cold water and bring to a boil.

Simmer 1 hour, stirring gently. Cool, then press small end of pod. Seed and pulp will slip out the cut stem end. Rub through a sieve to remove any remaining seeds. Boil this pulp for 15 minutes in the same water the pods were boiled in, then salt to taste. This chili sauce is a very good flavoring for general use in cooking. (1 c. sauce = 6 T. chili powder.)

Lemon-Egg Sauce

1 c. cream sauce
½ c. milk
2 T. butter

2 T. lemon juice
2 beaten egg yolks
1 T. parsley

Combine all ingredients except parsley. Heat over low heat until thickened; don't boil. Add chopped parsley, serve warm. *Yield: 1½ c.*

Sea-of-Green Sauce

1 c. mayonnaise
2 dill pickles (small)
½ c. green onions

1 c. sour cream
2 c. spinach
½ c. parsley

Put all ingredients in a blender and blend until well mixed. Good for hard-boiled eggs, potatoes, tomatoes. *Yield: 2 c.*

Golden Sauce

4 yolks from hard-boiled eggs
¼ c. cream
2 T. butter
2 T. flour

1 c. milk
½ t. dry mustard
¼ t. sea salt

Mash yolks to a paste. Gradually add cream. Cream together butter and flour and mix with yolk paste. Add milk and seasonings. Put into a double boiler and cook until mixture becomes a golden sauce. *Yield: 1¾ c.*

Variations:

Try blenderizing with 1 c. spinach.
Great on vegetables, rice, or noodles.

Creamy Cucumber Sauce

1 med. cucumber, peeled and
chopped finely
1 c. chopped, grated green
onion
1 c. light cream

1 T. cornstarch
1 t. lemon juice
½ t. dill seed
2 T. butter or margarine

Mix all ingredients (except the cucumber) in a blender and cook until thick. Add the cucumber and cook a minute or two. Pour hot over cooked vegetables or hard-boiled eggs. *Yield: 1¾ c.*

Mint Sauce

2 c. brown sugar
4 c. water
4 T. arrowroot

¾ c. butter
2 t. sea salt
4 T. mint extract

In a double boiler, combine sugar, water, and arrowroot. Cook until thickened. Remove from heat and stir in butter until melted. Add salt and mint. Serve with desserts. *Yield: 4 c.*

Papaya-Orange Sauce

2 med. Hawaiian papayas
1 c. orange juice
1 c. honey
¼ c. butter or margarine

3 T. cornstarch or arrowroot
2 egg yolks
1½ c. light cream

Blenderize or mash papayas together with orange juice and cook for 15 minutes. (If the papaya is unripe it will need to cook longer, and you may need to add as much as a cup of water.) Meanwhile, blenderize, or mix thoroughly, all the other ingredients (except the egg yolk) and cook until thick. Mix all together, add yolk and cook 2 minutes longer.

You can serve sauce hot on ice cream or put it in the refrigerator to use as an icing for spice cake or on a steamed papaya. *Yield: 3¾-4c.*

Plum Sauce

1 c. plums
½ c. buttermilk

¼ t. mace
2 dashes sea salt

Mash or blenderize plums. Add buttermilk and seasonings. Pour over fruit salads, pies, or rice. *Yield: 1½ c.*

Pan Gravy

2 c. milk (or 1 c. milk and
   1 c. vegetable broth)
3 T flour

sea salt or tamari to taste
pepper to taste

The browning or sautéing of food like Mock Meat Balls, fried eggplant, or fish, leaves some nice "browning" in the pan which makes a great base for gravy! If there is much oil in the pan it is best to drain off most of it. Then return to heat. Put milk and flour in a jar, shake until well mixed and smooth, pour into frying pan—stirring with a whisk.

As the mixture is heating it is important to keep stirring to prevent flour from sticking. The gravy will be thick. To thin down, add more milk or vegetable bouillon. Add mushrooms if you like. You may also wish to substitute oat flour or another of your choice. *Yield: 2 c.*

Almond or Cashew Gravy

Grind 1½ c. nuts in mill. Heat 3 c. milk and stir in meal until smooth and thick. Salt to taste. As a variation, substitute roasted and ground sesame seed and tamari. *Yield: 4 c.*

Sun Seed Gravy

⅛-¼ c. oil
6 T. fine sunflower seed meal
1 T. arrowroot

2 c. water
pinch sea salt
2-3 T. finely chopped onion

Fry onions in oil until transparent. Add "sun meal," arrowroot, water and salt. Cook 1 minute, stirring slowly, adding water. Lower heat and cook until thick. Add more water if necessary. *Yield: 2½ c.*

Tamari-Onion Gravy

1 c. onions, chopped
¼ c. oil
3 c. milk or water

½ c. flour
tamari to taste

Sauté onions in oil for 2 minutes. Add 2½ c. milk. Mix flour in remaining milk until a smooth paste is formed. Mix with milk and add tamari. Cook until it thickens. You may add sliced mushrooms.
Yield: 4¾ c.

Vegetarian Main Dishes

The preparation of good food in our restaurant, The Farmer and the Fisherman, taught me that there are indeed many things to consider in cooking and arranging an attractive meal.

The beauty of a meal first reaches the eye. That is why much care must go into the arrangement of the plate. The main dish, the center of the meal, is enhanced and highlighted by side dishes and garnishes. Together, these can have a colorful and pleasing effect—the final "spice" to the meal!

In this chapter you can share with me some experiences in the creative preparation and arrangement of main dishes.

(Other main dishes can be found in the sections on Grains, Pastas, Corn, and Milk.)

The recipes in this section yield 4-6 servings unless otherwise indicated.

Vegetables

Vegetables are an important part of our diet. They not only give us the necessary vitamins and minerals, but they add vibrant color to our plates. We grow many of our own. If you are not able to do that, the next best thing is to buy them organically or locally grown.

When buying organic vegetables, don't let looks fool you. They may sometimes be slightly limp or spotted, but this is due to not being sprayed and not being treated with preservatives. Limpness may, of course, be caused by evaporation, in which case you will not want to serve the vegetable raw, but it still has good nutrients and is tasty when cooked.

I usually never *peel* my vegetables because that's where many of the vitamins are stored.

These are my basic cooking methods.

Steaming

Put a little water (as little as possible) in the bottom of a pot. Put in steam basket and add vegetables. (Make sure water doesn't touch vegetables.) Cover, bring water to a boil, reduce heat to medium-low so water continues to slow boil. Cook vegetables until tender.

Sautéing

In a skillet, I add enough oil to cover bottom of skillet and get it hot. Then I add vegetables and cook until tender, usually 5-10 minutes* (be watchful—you may have to add a little more oil).

Sautéing and Steaming

Follow above instructions for sautéing. After about two minutes, add some water or vegetable broth. Cover immediately and steam until tender, usually 5-10 minutes.*

* Save all liquids from cooking for soup stocks or sauces, or just to drink. Cooking vegetables too quickly causes discoloration. Also, since acids cause discoloration, you can leave the lid off for 1 or 2 minutes to let acids escape with the steam.

Boiling

I try not to use too much water when boiling vegetables. I can use the same water as a broth or sauce for the vegetables in order to maintain most of the nutritive value. Boiling time depends on the vegetable. 5-10 minutes for some, 30-40 minutes for others.

Baking

Put vegetables in an oiled pan in the oven with a little water. You can rub oil on the skin of most vegetables. Bake for 30-60 minutes.

Asparagus

4 c. asparagus	1 c. crackers, coarsely broken
1 T. butter	pepper to taste
1 c. milk	paprika or cayenne to taste

Steam asparagus in a little water until tender. Heat milk and butter. Break up crackers and add to asparagus, then pour hot milk and butter over it. Add dash of paprika or (if you are a little more daring) a dash of cayenne. Serve as a side accompaniment.

Eggplant

1 lg. eggplant, sliced	1 c. cornmeal or cracker
2 eggs, slightly beaten	crumbs (or try using half
1½ t. sea salt	cornmeal and half
¼ t. pepper	cracker crumbs)

Slice eggplant, sprinkle slices with sea salt and put on paper towel to drain the water.

Beat eggs, salt, and pepper in a bowl. Put cornmeal in another bowl. Dip drained eggplant slices in eggs, then in cornmeal. Put ¼-inch oil in a heavy skillet and heat until almost smoking. Drop in slices and cook until browned on each side. This takes about 10 minutes. (A note on frying eggplant: it is important to have your oil hot before putting in the eggplant because it is very porous and will absorb a lot of oil.) Serve plain or with a tomato sauce.

Eggplant Parmigiana

Follow above recipe. After browning, lay eggplant slices in a baking pan, cover with Tomato Sauce (see section on Sauces). Top with fresh mushroom slices and grated mozzarella. Sprinkle with crushed oregano leaves. Bake at 375° until cheese melts. Serve with noodles.

Eggplant Patties

1 med. eggplant, cubed
1¼ c. cracker crumbs
    (20 crackers)
1¼ c. cheese, grated
2 T. minced parsley

¼ c. sliced green onion
1 clove garlic, minced
½ t. sea salt
⅛ t. pepper
2 T. cooking oil

Steam eggplant until tender (7 minutes). Mash and mix in cracker crumbs, cheese, eggs, parsely, onion, garlic, salt, and pepper. Shape into 8 patties. Cook in hot oil 3 minutes on each side until golden brown. You can serve these open-faced with tomato sauce and/or onions.

Eggplant Casserole

1 lg. onion
1 lg. eggplant, sliced (½ inch
    thick)

1 egg, beaten
1 t. unbleached white flour

Sauce:

½ t. sea salt
1 t. garlic powder
1 t. rosemary

1 t. parsley
milk
¼ c. baco-bits (optional)

Sauté onion in oil until transparent. Prepare eggplant as in recipe for eggplant and fry until crisp. Lay slices in a baking pan with onions. Meanwhile, in a 2-cup measuring cup, put egg, flour, and seasonings. Add enough milk to reach the 2-cup mark. Pour over eggplant. Sprinkle with baco-bits. Bake at 375° for 25 minutes.

Durango Potatoes

3 med. potatoes, sliced thin
½ med. onion, sliced in half
    moons
3 cloves garlic, minced
½ green pepper, chopped

4 T. oil
¼ c. wheat germ
1 t. sea salt
¼ t. pepper

Begin heating oil in a large skillet. Add potatoes and begin sautéing over medium heat. Cook about 15-25 minutes until almost tender.

(Add the potatoes first if you are using raw ones because they take longer to cook. If you are using precooked potatoes add them along with the rest of the vegetables.

Now add the rest of the vegetables and continue sautéing for 10 more minutes. Add wheat germ, salt, and pepper, if needed. Add a little more oil or butter. Cook until wheat germ is browned along with the rest of the vegetables.)

Durango Potatoes with Extra Fixin's

⅔ c. tomatoes, cut in wedges   ½ c. cheese, grated

Follow the above recipe, but after adding wheat germ, add tomato wedges. Sprinkle cheese on top, cover, and cook 2 more minutes and serve. When you add wheat germ you may also try adding ¼ c. nutritional yeast.

Potato Dumplings

2 c. mashed potatoes   1 c. flour
1 egg   sea salt
½ small onion, grated or   pepper
    finely chopped   nutmeg
2 T. butter

Mix cold potatoes with onion. Beat in butter. Add egg and mix well. Season to taste with salt, pepper, and nutmeg. Work in flour to make a dough that can be handled, adding more flour if needed. Shape into balls and drop in boiling broth. Cover and cook 15 minutes. Test by breaking with a fork.

Scalloped Potatoes

4 med. potatoes   4 to 6 T. flour
3 med. onions, cut in rings   4 to 6 T. butter
3-4 c. white cheese   sea salt to taste
⅔ c. milk, half and half, or   pepper to taste
    cream

Oil a large Dutch oven or deep casserole and begin layering potatoes. Pour milk over each layer, sprinkle with flour, then put on a layer of onions dotted with butter. Then sprinkle on salt and pepper and a layer of cheese.

Repeat layers until all ingredients are used up. End with grated cheese on top. Bake at 375° for 1½ hours or until golden brown on top.

Shepherd's Pie

4 med. potatoes	2 c. vegetables (carrots, celery,
¾ c. milk	fresh corn, onions)
¼ c. butter	paprika
parsley	

Shepherd's pie is a good way to use up those extra potatoes, vegetables, cream sauce, or whatever. If using leftover potatoes, mash them with milk and butter. If using raw potatoes boil first, then mash. Set aside. Steam vegetables when tender. Add peas and moisten with cream sauce and salt. If you don't have cream sauce, moisten with leftover gravy, soup, or just milk.

Put vegetables in a casserole dish and spoon the mashed potatoes on top. Dot with butter and sprinkle with parsley and paprika. Bake at 400° until potatoes are golden brown, about 20 minutes.

Stuffed Mushrooms

1 lb. large mushrooms	½ c. grated cheddar cheese
2 T. butter	¼ c. sunflower or
1 T. minced onions	sesame seeds
¼ c. fine bread crumbs	½ t. garlic powder
¼ c. baco-bits	1 t. tamari
½ c. light cream	

Wash mushrooms and remove stems. Reserve caps. Chop stems, and sauté with onion in butter in a small skillet; 5 minutes or until tender. Add crumbs, cook 2 minutes. Stir in baco-bits, lemon juice, and seeds, plus the garlic, tamari, and spike. Fill caps.

Place in 8" x 10" baking dish. Pour cream around mushrooms. Bake at 400° for 15 minutes. Top with cheese and bake 8-10 minutes longer, or until cheese melts. Serve as an accompaniment with grains, fish and other vegetables.

Stuffed Cabbage

Cut heart from head of cabbage. Lift large leaves without breaking. Steam leaves. Use Rice Stuffing (see this section) and roll inside cabbage. Stick toothpicks in to hold leaves together. Place in baking pan, pour tomato juice over top. Bake at 350° for 45 minutes to 1 hour.

Cabbage 'n Noodles

3 c. cabbage, sliced
2 med. onions, sliced in half
  moons
¼ c. green peppers, chopped
1 c. vegetable broth
  (see Soups section)
1 c. grated cheese (Parmesan
  and cheddar)

3 T. tamari
2 t. curry
2 t. paprika
4 c. cooked noodles (Japanese
  udon are best)
½ c. melted butter
nuts (optional)

In a large, heavy skillet, sauté cabbage, onions, and green peppers about 5 minutes. Add 1 c. vegetable broth. Cover and cook 5 more minutes. Add seasonings, then mix with noodles and cheese. Serve hot.

For variety, sprinkle some chopped nuts on top, or try using Chinese cabbage in place of regular cabbage.

Cabbage and Corn Bread Pot

¼ c. oil
1 head cabbage
1 c. cheese sauce
1½ t. paprika
1 T. caraway seeds
1 t. thyme

1 T. tamari
1 c. cornbread crumbs
4 T. butter, melted
¼-½ c. Parmesan cheese
2 tomatoes, cut in wedges
parsley

Cut cabbage in quarters then slice in half-moons. Put oil in a large skillet and heat. Add cabbage and onions and sauté until tender (about 10 minutes) stirring occasionally. Mix in cheese sauce, spices, and tamari. Put in an oiled casserole dish.

Melt butter and mix in the cornbread crumbs. Put on top of casserole. Then top with tomato wedges, parsley and Parmesan. Bake at 400° for 20 minutes.

Sauerkraut

10 lbs. cabbage   7 lbs. sea salt

Grate cabbage, mix with salt, and put in jar or crock. Cover with cheesecloth and put weight on top. Spoon off "scum" daily, wiping rim, too. After 2 weeks, remove, put in glass jars, and process. (See Drying and Preserving section.)

Bobalkie

Make small balls (about ½-inch in diameter) from the dough of a French bread recipe. Bake at 350° for 15 minutes.

Melt butter in an iron skillet. Add well-drained sauerkraut and balls and fry until sauerkraut is warm.

Stroganoff

4 c. vegetables, chopped
　(broccoli, cauliflower,
　summer squash)
1 lg. onion, chopped
oil or half oil, half butter

1 c. mushrooms, sliced
2 t. basil
1 t. nutmeg
sea salt and pepper to taste
1½ c. sour cream

Sauté vegetables in butter and oil in a large skillet for about 5 minutes. Add mushrooms and sauté another minute or two. Add spices and sour cream and Worcestershire sauce. Heat, but don't boil. Serve over whole wheat, spinach, or soya noodles.

Ploughman's Share
(From our restaurant.)

This recipe needs no proportions; it all depends on your family's hunger!

First have ready:

baked potatoes
steamed broccoli, cut length-
　wise into small sections

steamed cauliflower, cut into
　small flowerettes
steamed onions, sliced in half-
　moons

(Toss vegetables with tamari and vegetable salt, or herbs of your choice.)

sliced cheese of your choice
　(cheddar is nice)
chopped green onions

sliced mushrooms
butter

Now, to assemble, cut baked potato in half and lay open on a plate. Place steamed vegetables, mushrooms, green onions on top, and cover with cheese. Bake until cheese melts. Serve hot, topped

Stuffed Tomatoes

¼ c. onion, chopped
1 c. fresh spinach, chopped
¼ c. bread crumbs
fresh celantro

½ c. grated cheese
dash hot sauce or cayenne
baco-bits
4-6 med. tomatoes

Wash and core tomatoes. Scoop out section from top of each; drain and salt. Combine stuffing mixture and fill each tomato. Place in a baking pan (uncovered) and bake at 375° for 20 minutes. Remove and top with grated cheese. Return to oven until cheese melts.

Udon Fun

8 oz. udon Japanese
 noodles
3 c. broccoli
1 t. fresh ginger, chopped
2 med. onions, sliced in half
 moons

6 cloves garlic, minced
3 T. tamari
1 t. sea salt
1 c. bean sprouts
½ c. sliced almonds
1 c. Parmesan cheese

Prepare noodles (follow package directions). Steam broccoli until tender; about 10 minutes. Meanwhile, sauté ginger, garlic, and onions until transparent. In a large pot, combine noodles, broccoli, and onions. Add remaining ingredients, toss. When heated through, serve. Be careful not to heat too long so your sprouts stay crisp.

Zucchini Boats

4 zucchini (about 8 inches in
 length)
1 c. onion, minced
¾ c. butter
1½ lbs. ricotta cheese

2 T. tamari
½ c. Parmesan cheese
½ c. chopped walnuts
sea salt and pepper to taste

Trim zucchini and slice in half lengthwise. Steam 10-15 minutes. Scoop out pulp. Sauté onion, butter, and tamari until transparent. Add zucchini pulp and simmer for 5 minutes. Remove from heat. Add cheeses, chopped walnuts, salt and pepper.

Stuff zucchini shells with this mixture. Heat in oven at 400° until hot. Optional: sprinkle top with Parmesan cheese.

Zucchini Burgers

1 lg. (or 2 med.) zucchini,
    sliced in rounds
6 slices light rye bread
6 slices jack cheese

butter
garlic powder
6 tomato slices

Follow the recipe for frying eggplant, only fry zucchini instead. Spread garlic, butter mixture on bread. Toast in oven or broiler. Top with zucchini, cheese, then a tomato slice, and return to oven until cheese melts.

Green Beans Sauté

Steam green beans about 5 minutes. In a skillet, with about ⅛-inch oil, combine chopped garlic and ginger and onion slices. When garlic begins to brown, add beans and sauté. Season with garlic, tamari. When almost tender, add mushrooms. Just before serving, top with chopped almonds and parmesan cheese.

Sweet 'n Sour Green Beans

3 c. green beans
1 c. salted water
1 med. onion, thinly sliced
    (or pearl onions)

½ c. baco-bits
½ c. vinegar
2 T. sugar or honey
1 c. mushrooms

Cook beans until tender. Drain* and add baco-bits. Sauté onion until transparent. Stir in vinegar and honey, add mushrooms. Heat briefly to blend all flavors. Mix well with beans.

* Save water for soup stock.

Yellow Wax Beans

3 c. beans
¼ c. butter

1 c. bread crumbs
sea salt

Steam beans. Melt butter. Add crumbs and brown well. Mix with beans and serve.

Stuffed Peppers

6 lg. bell peppers

Follow recipe for Hot Rice Stuffing (this section). Remove pepper tops and seeds.* Fill with stuffing and bake in a shallow pan (with a little water in bottom) at 350° for 20 minutes. Add grated cheddar cheese and bake until cheese melts. For variation, use cream cheese.

* However, I usually put the pepper seeds in my stuffing.

Fried Okra

Slice okra in ¼-inch rounds.

Follow recipe for fried eggplant. Heat an iron skillet with ¼-inch oil until oil is hot. Drop in okra and fry until brown. Serve with ketchup, hot sauce, or tomato sauce. This is a sure way to prepare okra without sliminess.

Okra

2 c. okra, sliced	1 med. tomato, cubed
1 c. zucchini, sliced	2 T. (4-5 cloves) garlic,
1 c. cucumbers, quartered and	minced
sliced	½ t. sea salt
¼ c. green pepper	½ t. whole thyme

Prepare okra and zucchini as in Fried Okra above, and set aside. In a large skillet, sauté onions, garlic, and green pepper (in ¼-inch oil) about 5 minutes. Add tomatoes and seasonings, okra, and zucchini. Serve with Golden Sauce and over rice or rice cakes.

Spaghetti Squash

We've just discovered this new squash and are really excited about it. True to its name, it is stringy like spaghetti after you bake it. Bake whole for 60-90 minutes, or cut in half, put a little water in the middle of each half and bake 45 minutes or until tender. Use instead of spaghetti noodles with tomato sauce or choose another tasty sauce. Or just try butter, honey, and a little cinnamon.

Cottage Cheese-Crookneck Casserole

2 lb. crookneck squash, thinly
  sliced
1 lg. onion, sliced in half
  moons
¼ lb. mushrooms, sliced
4 garlic cloves, minced
2 eggs, beaten
1 pt. cottage cheese

8 oz. jack cheese, grated
4 T. oil
thyme
garlic powder
kelp
Parmesan cheese
sea salt

Sauté garlic and onions in oil, about 1 minute. Add squash and lightly sauté. Remove from heat. In a casserole dish, spread a layer using half of the vegetables. Sprinkle with herbs and Parmesan. Then spread a layer using all the cottage cheese. Next, sprinkle on half of the grated cheese. Cover with remaining vegetables, then the rest of the cheese. Sprinkle with thyme and Parmesan. Bake in oven at 350° for 30 minutes.

Stuffed Acorn Squash

Cut squash in half. Remove inner pulp and seeds. Place in a baking pan with a little water in the center of each half, and a little water in the bottom of the pan. Bake at 400° for 20 minutes. While baking, prepare stuffing. After 20 minutes remove from oven and stuff. Return and bake until squash is tender; 20-30 minutes more.

Use Rice Stuffing, Bread Stuffing, Sour Cream-Rice Stuffing, Apple-Apricot Stuffing, Eggplant, or Apple-Nut Stuffing. (See recipes in this section.)

Sautéed Vegetables with Nuts

2 c. broccoli, quartered lengthwise
1 c. cauliflower, quartered lengthwise
¾ c. carrots, sliced in rounds
1 c. brussel sprouts, quartered
¼ c. green bell peppers, sliced thinly in rounds, then in half
½ c. onions, sliced in half-moons
4 cloves garlic, minced

½ c. mushrooms, sliced ⅛-inch thick
½ c. almonds, slivered
¼ c. walnuts, chopped coarsely
3 T. sesame seeds
3 T. poppy seeds
sea salt
tamari
basil, whole
1-2 c. bouillon in water

First, prepare Sour Cream Sauce (see Sauces section).

In a large skillet, sauté onions, garlic. Add carrots and peppers and cook until onions are transparent. Add bouillon water, cover and steam 5 minutes. Meanwhile, steam broccoli, cauliflower, and brussel sprouts about 5 minutes.

Mix vegetables together, being very careful not to break them apart. Add mushrooms and spices, a little parsley, and walnuts and almonds.

Top with sauce. Sprinkle with poppy seeds and sesame seeds, some fresh, chopped parsley, some cherry tomatoes, paprika. Not only is this good to eat, but it can look like a masterpiece.

May be served with fried bulghur or rice.

Raw Stuffing

Grate ¼ c. parsnips, ¼ c. onions, ⅛ c. parsley, and ¼ c. celery. Add ½ c. nut butter or Tahini and ¼ c. mashed avocado. Season with kelp, salt, garlic powder. *Yield: 1¼ c.*

Cream Cheese Stuffing

8 oz. cream cheese
¼ c. olives
¼ c. ground sesame

½ t. curry powder
1 well-beaten egg (optional)

Combine ingredients and mix well. Use for tomatoes, peppers, sandwiches. You can substitute ricotta or hoop cheese. Also try adding green onions, parsley, or corn. *Yield: 1½ c.*

Sour Cream Rice Stuffing

1½ T. butter
1½ T. oil
½ c. chopped onions
⅓ c. chopped celery and tops
3 garlic cloves, minced
¾ c. chopped mushrooms
¼ c. sliced almonds
1½ c. brown rice, cooked

¼ c. sour cream
¼ c. grated Parmesan cheese
1½ T. wheat germ
½ t. sea salt
1 t. whole thyme
¼ t. garlic powder
1 t. parsley

In a large skillet with butter and oil, sauté onions, celery and garlic until tender. When almost done, add mushrooms and almonds. Stir and cook 1 more minute. Remove from heat and add rice. Mix together sour cream, Parmesan and spices; then add to rice. A great stuffing for squash, fish, peppers, tomatoes, or as a dish in itself! *Yield: 4 c.*

Apple-Apricot Stuffing

1 c. apple juice
½ lb. dried apricots
1½ c. cooked bulghur
⅔ c. walnuts, chopped

¼ c. celery tops, chopped
½ c. onions, chopped
sea salt to taste
2 t. nutmeg

Let apricots sit in apple juice until they have absorbed it. Sauté onion and celery. Add to bulghur along with walnuts, seasonings, and apricots.

Great also in squash, fish, vegetables. Try shaping into balls and frying in butter. *Yield: 3½ c.*

Apple-Nut Stuffing

2 c. apples, sliced
⅔ to ¾ c. raisins
½ c. walnuts, coarsely
  chopped
½ c. sunflower seeds (or
  almonds)

½-¾ c. honey
1 t. cinnamon
½ t. nutmeg
⅛ t. cloves
¼ t. sea salt

In a saucepan combine apples and raisins—with a little water at first to prevent sticking. Cook about 10 minutes to soften. Remove from heat. Add the other ingredients. This stuffing is great in squash, crepes or pastries. *Yield: 3½ c.*

Potato-Cheese Stuffing

2 c. cooked potatoes
1 c. sour cream
1 c. grated goat cheese
½ c. crumbled bleu cheese
½ c. green onion

2 T. fresh parsley, chopped
½ t. sea salt
½ t. pepper
1 t. garlic powder
1 t. coriander

Mash the potatoes, mix in sour cream and cheeses. Add the rest of the ingredients. If you prefer a more moist filling, add more sour cream. *Yield: 4 c.*

Variations:

Try this filling in baked potato shells. Top with baco-bits and bake 20 minutes.

This is excellent inside pastry, baked.

Bread Stuffing

6 slices whole wheat bread
1 med. onion, cut in
  half-moons
½ c. celery, chopped
2 c. cooked potatoes
1 c. mushrooms, sliced
  thick

2 t. butter
½ t. sea salt
¼ t. sage
1 t. parsley
¼ t. rosemary
1 t. thyme
½ t. garlic powder

Toast bread so that it is dried out. Cut into 1-inch squares. In a skillet, melt butter and add onion and celery. Sauté until onions are transparent. Add potatoes and bread, and cook until heated. Add mushrooms and seasonings. Roll up in fish or put in squash or peppers. *Yield: 5 c.*

Eggplant-Squash Stuffing

4 c. acorn squash	1 c. tomato, chopped
1 med. onion	½ c. celery, finely chopped
1 med.-lg. eggplant	

Begin steaming squash. After about 15 minutes (when squash begins to soften), add onion and eggplant. Steam until all ingredients will mash well. Remove from heat and mash. Add tomato and celery. *Yield: 8 c.*

Add:

1 T. oregano	2 t. sea salt
1 t. coriander	2 c. bread crumbs
1 T. thyme	1 c. sesame seeds
½ t. marjoram	

Mix well. Try this mixture for stuffing eggplant or acorn squash—or wrapped in chard leaves.

Spanish Rice Stuffing

¾ c. onion, chopped	1½ c. rice, cooked
¼ c. green pepper	½-1 c. Hot Sauce
3 garlic cloves, minced	

In a skillet, sauté onion, green pepper, garlic.

Add rice, then Hot Sauce. The amount of rice and sauce depends on how moist you want your stuffing. *Yield: 2-2¼ c.*

Vegetable Bake

This is quick and easy. It's up to you which vegetables you wish to use. It may take some vegetables longer to bake than others so get those started first.

potatoes	turnips
medium onions	carrots
Jerusalem artichokes	

Wash vegetables, rub oil on their skins, place in a baking pan.

With these particular vegetables begin baking the potatoes and turnips first, then after about 15 minutes add the onions and Jerusalem artichokes. After another 15 minutes add carrots and bake another half hour.

Raw Seed Loaf I

¾ c. sunflower seeds
¼ c. sesame seeds
¾ c. walnuts
¾ c. almonds
1 c. red cabbage
¼ c. red onions
¼ c. green onions
1 c. carrots
1 c. spinach
¾ c. cucumbers

½ c. beets
1 c. zucchini
1 t. garlic powder
2 t. kelp
1 T. nutritional yeast
½ T. tamari
¼ c. lemon juice
¼-1 c. square tofu, cut in
    small chunks

Grind seeds and nuts in a blender or a hand mill. Put in a large bowl. Grate or dice remaining vegetables and add to the seeds and nuts. Add tofu and seasonings.

When mixture is combined, shape into a beautiful ring or design, garnish with fresh parsley, watercress, or sprouts. Lay on a bed of lettuce. Surround with fresh tomatoes. Prepare a sauce or dressing to go with it. Not only nutritious but delicious.

Raw Seed Loaf II

½ c. sesame seed
½ c. sunflower seeds
¼ c. almonds
¼ c. walnuts
¼ c. chopped green peppers
½ c. corn
2 med. tomatoes

¼ c. green onions
2 T. brewer's yeast
1 T. tamari
1 t. kelp
½ t. garlic powder
¼ t. sea salt

Prepare as in Raw Seed Loaf I above.

Vegetable Balls

½ head lettuce
½ large onion
½ bunch celery
1 tomato

1 c. peas
1 green pepper
1 or 2 carrots
½ c. nuts

Grind mixture and roll into balls. Serve on a bed of lettuce or with a grain. *Yield: 4 servings.*

Pierogge
(A Polish and Russian dish—also known as Varenky.)

Dough:

4 egg yolks
1 whole egg
1 T. sea salt

2 c. water (potato water may
  be used)
6 c. unbleached white flour

Beat eggs, salt, water, and flour to make a pliable dough. Roll out and cut in 4-inch rounds. Fill with 1-2 T. of either of the following fillings. Pinch the edges together. It is very important that the edges are well sealed. You can also seal them by pressing with a fork.

Drop pierogge in boiling water, and cook until they float to the top. Continue cooking 2 more minutes. Be sure not to crowd them, so they can rise.

Remove from water. You can either stop at this stage; or, if you prefer a more crisp outside, fry them in butter until browned. Serve with sour cream.

Fillings:

Cinnamon and Cheese

1 lb. hoop cheese or dry
  cottage cheese (put through
  a sieve)
1 T. bread crumbs (these
  absorb moisture in the
  cheese)

1 egg yolk
½ t. sea salt
1 T. honey
¼ t. cinnamon
1 dash nutmeg

Sauerkraut

1 2-lb. can sauerkraut
1 lg. onion, chopped
¼ c. mushrooms, chopped

4 T. butter
salt, pepper to taste

Rinse sauerkraut in cold water several times. Place in a saucepan, and cover with water. Cook 30 minutes and drain. Meanwhile, sauté onion, mushrooms, salt, and pepper in batter. Add to sauerkraut. This mixture must cool before filling dough.

You can also stuff pierogge with a potato stuffing or a sweet filling. (See stuffings in this section.)

Egg Rolls

Outer Shell:

2 c. pastry flour (unbleached flour)	2 eggs
	2¾ c. water

Beat eggs and water. Mix in pastry flour and beat with a whisk until smooth. Lightly grease a small fry pan. Heat and pour in 1 ladleful of batter, tilting pan until batter covers bottom entirely. (It is important to have a thin layer so it adheres to pan, so quickly pour any excess back into bowl.) Cook 1 minute on one side. Flip onto a plate, fried side up. (The reason you cook just one side at this time is that the outside will cook when you deep fry it with filling.) *Yield: 20-24 egg rolls.*

Filling:

1 c. bean sprouts	1 c. tofu
1 c. shredded cabbage	1 t. ginger
½ c. mushrooms, chopped	¼ t. tamari
6 green onions, chopped	

Combine ingredients. Spoon 3-4 T. of this mixture into the egg rolls. Fold one side over, then fold in the sides. Brush edges with a little egg, then roll the last side. Cook in hot oil (enough to cover) until crispy.

For variation, try adding water chestnuts.

Vegetable Pot Pie

1 c. chopped broccoli	½ c. diced carrots
1 c. chopped cauliflower	1 c. diced turnip
1 c. peas	1 cream sauce or gravy recipe
¾ c. corn	1 flaky pie crust recipe
¾ c. chopped onion	

Combine vegetables with sauce. Prepare a crust and line a 9-inch pie pan. Fill with vegetable mixture and top with crust. Bake at 425° for 5 minutes; turn oven down to 375° and bake 20 more minutes.

Add a slice of cheese when serving. You may also try millet crust.

Pizza

4 c. unbleached white flour (or whole wheat)	1 package yeast
	1⅓ c. water
2 T. oil	1 t. sea salt

Dissolve yeast in 3 T. of milk, then mix dough. Knead for 10 minutes. Let rise 2 hours.

Meanwhile, prepare the vegetables and sauce:

2 c. tomato sauce	1 c. mushrooms, sliced
1 c. broccoli, chopped	1 lb. mozzarella, sliced
1 c. onions, minced	1 c. Parmesan
1 c. tomatoes, sliced in half-moons	¼ c. sliced olives

Oil cookie sheet. Spread dough out, about ¼-inch think. Prick the crust and bake at 375° for 20 minutes. Remove from oven and spread tomato sauce on crust, then mozzarella cheese.

Sauté the mushrooms, onions, and broccoli about 3 minutes in a little oil. Spread on pizza. Then put on tomato slices and olives. Sprinkle with Parmesan cheese. Bake at 450° for 20 minutes or until crust is golden.

Chili Rellenos

12 Anaheim chilies	16 eggs
cheese (Monterey jack)	oil

To prepare chilies, dry-roast them in cast-iron skillet until blisters appear on both sides. Or lay them on a dry cookie sheet and place in hot oven until blisters appear on both sides. Submerge chilies in cold water and pull away the skin from chili meat, being careful not to remove any meat. Put cheese slices inside chilies.

To prepare batter, beat egg whites until stiff, then add half of the egg yolks and beat again, getting as close as possible to same consistency of whites.

To deep fry, heat cast-iron skillet, half-full with oil. To test for proper heat, drip in a little batter. If batter floats to surface, oil is ready. Spoon enough batter into oil to hold a chili, then place chili in center. Spoon enough batter over chili to cover it entirely.

With a flipper or spoon, splash oil on top of chili, and watch it rise. When the relleno turns golden brown, remove from oil, and lay on absorbent towel, and cover with toweling.

To dry fry, moisten paper towel with oil, spread oil around in iron skillet. Heat skillet to medium-high heat (point of cooking an omelette). Spoon in batter. Place chili on top, and spoon the batter over it. When bottom is cooked, turn relleno over (it shouldn't stick). Cook until brown. Serve with guacamole sauce and rice.

Precooked fish, shrimp, mushrooms, and slightly steamed vegetables can also be cooked the same way.

Enchiladas

1 pkg. of 12 corn tortillas   2 c. enchilada sauce

In a pan, heat enchilada sauce. In a skillet, heat oil. Dunk tortillas first into oil to soften them, then dip into sauce when they are somewhat soft. Fill with one of the following:

Filling I:

1 onion, chopped
2 garlic cloves, minced
1 c. mushrooms, sliced
2 bunches fresh spinach, chopped

½ t. sea salt
½ t. garlic powder
½ pkg. tofu, chopped
grated cheese

Heat skillet, with ⅛ cup of oil. Add garlic cloves and onions, and sauté until onions are transparent. Add mushrooms, tofu, and seasonings, and cook 1 minute. Remove from heat and stir in spinach. Fill each tortilla with grated cheese and vegetable filling. Roll and put into a baking pan. Cover with remaining sauce and sprinkle with cheese. Bake 20-30 minutes or until aroma drives you crazy!

Filling II:

1 onion, chopped
1½ c. soybeans or pintos, cooked

grated cheese
¾ t. turmeric
½ t. sea salt

Sauté onions until transparent. Add soybeans and seasonings. Fill each tortilla with grated cheese and beans, and proceed as in Filling I. (You can use rice instead soybeans.)

Filling III:

1 onion, sliced
1 c. mushrooms, sliced
4 mild chilies, chopped
  (Anaheim)

1 med. tomato, chopped
¾ c. sour cream
¼ c. green onions, chopped
grated cheese

Heat skillet. Sauté onions until transparent. Add mushrooms and chilies. Remove from heat and mix with sour cream and tomatoes. Fill each tortilla with vegetable mixture and proceed as in Filling I.

Vegetable Burritos

1 c. zucchini, diced
½ c. broccoli, diced
½ c. mushrooms, sliced
¼ c. onions, chopped
6 flour tortillas

¼-½ c. grated cheese
½ c. tomatoes, chopped
dash sea salt
dash cayenne

Heat iron skillet with ⅛-inch oil. Add zucchini, broccoli, mushrooms, and onions, and sauté 5 minutes. Add tomatoes and spices. In another skillet, heat flour tortillas in a little melted butter with cheese in each one, until cheese is melted. Put in vegetables and serve with hot sauce. *Yield: 6 burritos.*

Chop Suey

1 recipe for Chinese Sauce
  (doubled)
2 c. broccoli, chopped small
3 c. mushrooms, sliced

4 c. mung sprouts
1 c. carrots, grated (optional)
1 c. jicama or water chestnuts

Prepare Chinese Sauce and when sautéing onions and celery add the broccoli and carrots. When thickening is added, also add mushrooms and bean sprouts. Turn off and cover. It's ready to serve with rice or noodles. It is important to serve immediately so your vegetables remain crisp.

Variations:

Substitute or add other vegetables.

Try some chopped walnuts or almonds on top, with chives or scallions.

Try some different Chinese and Japanese vegetables available at specialty and many large supermarkets: Chinese cabbage, lotus root, bamboo shoots, and bok choy.

Tempura

When tempura is prepared correctly it is not a very greasy food. There are some simple procedures that will give you good results.

The batter should remain cool during the entire cooking process. It helps to keep ice cubes in the batter, or keep only a little out and refrigerate the rest until you need it. Keep your vegetables and/or fish cold so they do not heat up batter.

Dusting the food with flour before dipping in batter helps batter to stick.

Heat your oil to 375° or a little hotter. When you begin your tempura remember the importance of maintaining the temperature before adding your next batch.

If you cannot serve it immediately (which is when it is best) keep it warm in the oven; but do not cover it, for the heat causes it to absorb moisture and become soggy.

Basic Recipe:

1-1¼ c. flour (whole wheat* or unbleached)	1 c. ice water 1 large egg

Combine egg and water. Sift in flour, stirring. Batter will be thin and lumpy. Heat oil; to test, drop in a little batter—it should sink, then rise again to top.

Cook tempura until golden. Drain on an absorbent surface.

* When using whole wheat flour you will use less (about 1 c.).

Eggs

We have had much discussion about eggs—the cholesterol question being the main topic. Pros and cons. Still we feel that eggs are valuable in our diet for they contain the 12 mineral salts our bodies need. Chickens are able to obtain them from the soil. When we don't have enough eggs produced by our own hens we purchase fertile eggs. Fertile eggs are higher in nutrients than eggs laid by caged hens. We eat an average of two eggs every other day.

Omelettes

Omelettes are so much fun because there is no limit to what you can do with them. You can be as simple as you like; or as creative. Omelettes are also the kind of thing that goes well any time of day.

The following recipe has been tested and proven (used in our restaurant) and we've found it to be the best.

Preheat oven to 400°.

Whip 3 eggs and 3 T. water (with a little salt) in a bowl, with a hand mixer or a whisk, until light and fluffy. Meanwhile, heat the omelette pan with very little oil. Sprinkle Parmesan on the bottom and as it begins to brown, *slowly* pour in the eggs. Cook over medium-high heat.

As the eggs begin to set up, insert a fork in different places and lift up so that some of the uncooked egg may run underneath and the cooked part you are lifting may fall back in place without breaking. Also, run your fork along the edges, and swirl pan so uncooked egg may also run underneath.

When your egg has set up and is no longer very runny on the top, place pan in oven so it may rise; 2-5 minutes.

To remove, run a rubber spatula along the sides, then slip it underneath and help the omelette slide onto the plate. Serve immediately or it will fall.

Omelette Fillings:

Vegetables, onions, tofu—sautéed until tender.
Cheese, grated.

Chilies, tomatoes.

Peaches, cinnamon, nutmeg, honey and sour cream. (Try using some of the chutneys or preserves.)

Zucchini, sour cream, mushrooms. (Sauté zucchini and mushrooms.)

Ricotta, fresh garlic, and onion sautéed; tomato sauce.

Sour cream with green onions, tomatoes, mushrooms, basil, thyme, oregano, artichoke hearts. Top with cheese sauce.

Sauté sliced water chestnuts, mushrooms, sunchokes, fresh peas, broccoli flowers. Top omelette with ginger sauce.

When using precooked fillings, you can just add them to the omelette before serving, but it is usually best to warm most of them. After your omelette begins to rise, spoon on filling and return to oven until warmed (or until cheese melts, if using cheese).

Chili Quillies from Nidia

2 small onions
1 green pepper
2 chilies (Anaheim)
1 small jalapeno
6 corn tortillas
2 medium tomatoes, firm
5 cloves garlic, minced
1½ dozen eggs (beaten with ⅓ c. milk)

3 pinches tarragon, basil, chili powder
2 pinches garlic powder and oregano
3 c. cheddar cheese (medium-sharp)
1 dozen tortillas
⅔ c. oil

Dice the first set of ingredients. In the second set, beat eggs with milk and spices. Set both mixtures aside.

Grate 3 c. medium-sharp cheddar.

Now you are ready to cook. Crisp fry 12 corn tortillas* in an iron skillet, with ⅓ c. oil. Heat oil until it smokes slightly, and keep at that temperature to keep tortillas from soaking up oil. Slide whole tortilla into oil and fry until crisp. Drain, and keep warm in oven.

In an iron skillet with ⅓ c. oil, add chili powder and diced tortillas. Sauté until soft, then add onions, green peppers, and garlic. Stir around, then add tomatoes—and ½ c. hot sauce, if you're daring. Stir a little.

Now is the time to add the egg mixture and cook, stirring occasionally until eggs aren't runny.

Last, but most important—assembling: Put some grated cheese on a crisp-fried tortilla, then some of the egg mixture. Top with some hot sauce or tomato sauce and serve.

* You can use flour tortillas instead. Separate and warm in a dry skillet. Assemble the same way, or roll like a burrito.

Chili Quillies — Susan's Oven Method

(This version came from watching Nidia's method and shortening the process.)

12 corn tortillas	¼ c. oil
2 med. onions, sliced in half-moons	10 beaten eggs
	2 t. sea salt
1 can chopped chilies (not hot) or 4 fresh Anaheim chilies, diced	2 t. cumin
	1 t. garlic powder
	¾ c. grated jack cheese
1 lg. can enchilada sauce	½ c. Parmesan cheese

Mix eggs, salt, cumin, and garlic powder.

Cut tortillas into 16ths. Put ⅛ c. oil into an iron skillet. Heat oil and drop in the tortillas. Stir until all are evenly coated with oil. Cook over medium heat until browned, but not crisp. Pour in half of the enchilada sauce. Stir until tortillas are well-coated. Cook 2 minutes and remove from heat.

Heat another skillet. Add ⅛ c. oil and mix in onion and garlic. Cook until onions are transparent. If you are using fresh chilies, cook along with onion.

In a small baking pan, line bottom with half of the tortilla mixture, then half of the onions and chilies, then half of the egg mixture, half of the grated cheese, and half of the Parmesan.

Repeat layers and bake at 375° for 40 minutes.

Heat the remainder of your enchilada sauce and pour over each serving.

I like to remove casserole after 20 minutes and quickly put fresh tomato slices on top and return to oven for remaining 20 minutes.

Late Morning Filler

6 eggs
1 med. onion, diced
½ c. chilies or green peppers
¼ c. mushrooms
1 tomato, cut in wedges

½ c. jack cheese, grated
1 c. sour cream
salt or kelp to taste
paprika

In a skillet (about 9″ diameter) sauté onions and chilies for about 3 minutes. Add mushrooms. Push the onion mixture to the sides of the pan. In the middle, put in eggs one at a time. Be careful not to break the yolks.

Cover and cook over low heat until whites begin to set up on top. Put sour cream around the edges of the eggs. Sprinkle with cheese and seasoning. Cover and cook until cheese melts. Serve with hot tortillas and hot sauce, or English muffins.

For variation, try adding sauerkraut with caraway seeds and eliminate the chilies.

Egg Lasagne

6 eggs, well-beaten
　(8 if small)

6 T. water

Filling:

½ c. ricotta
¼ c. cottage cheese
¼ t. oregano
⅛ t. thyme
½ t. garlic powder

1 oz. fresh parsley, finely
　chopped
½ c. mushrooms, sliced
2-3 c. tomato sauce
1 c. grated cheese

In this recipe the eggs replace the traditional pasta. Pour eggs into a large, lightly oiled frying pan. Let them firm up like an omelette. Remove from pan into a baking dish or pan. Meanwhile, mix the filling together, fill egg, roll, and pour tomato sauce over the top. Sprinkle with cheese. Heat in oven at 375° for about 20 minutes.

Quiche

4 c. broccoli, cauliflower, or
　summer squash (or some of
　each)
1 med. onion, sliced
3 cloves garlic, minced
6 beaten eggs
½ c. milk

2½ c. grated cheese
　(try Swiss)
½ t. sea salt
1 t. thyme
1 t. cumin
1 t. basil
2 t. garlic powder

Lightly sauté garlic, onions, and broccoli. Meanwhile, mix eggs, milk, and cheese; then add seasonings. Mix in vegetables and pour into an oiled casserole dish. Bake at 350° for ½ hour.

Egg Foo Yong

⅓ c. onion, chopped
⅓ c. celery, chopped
½ c. mung bean sprouts

1 t. sea salt
1 t. kelp
8-10 eggs

Sauté until tender the onions and celery. In last minute of sautéing, add bean sprouts. Remove from heat.

Beat eggs, adding salt, kelp. Add vegetables to beaten eggs. Pour spoonfuls of batter into hot oiled frying pan. Brown on both sides like pancakes. Serve with Chinese Sauce.

Cheese-Egg Timbale

4 T. butter	1 T. sweet basil
2 c. milk	2 t. sea salt
2 T. flour	dash cayenne
1½ c. cheese, grated	

Sauté flour in butter. Slowly stir in milk, and remove from heat. Add grated cheese, salt, sweet basil, cayenne.

Beat eggs. Add to the cheese mixture and pour into an oiled casserole dish. Sprinkle with baco-bits. Bake at 350° for 30 minutes or until set.

Variation:

Chop and sauté 1 c. zucchini, or your favorite vegetable, and add to the cheese mixture along with the eggs.

Vegetable Ideas

Here are some special ideas on the preparation of various vegetables.

Artichokes

Steam sitting upright, 30-40 minutes; or in a pressure cooker, 10 minutes. When leaves remove easily, the artichoke is done. Serve with sauces, mayonnaise, or stuffed. You can tie the leaves together to keep artichoke in shape.

Asparagus

Remove tough, lower end of stalk, or just bend asparagus; it will break naturally at its tender point. Steam 15-20 minutes. Bake, prepare tempura style, serve with sauce, or serve cold with dressing. Dip cooked asparagus in batter and fry.

Beets

Slices or chunks. Steam 20-30 minutes. Bake, or boil in soups. Serve with butter or sauce. Cook, then serve chilled in salads. Or grate raw in salads.

Beet Greens

Steam until tender; 5 minutes. Younger plants are better.

Serve plain or with butter. Use in soups, adding near the end. Or in salad dressings (pureeing first).

Bok Choy

An oriental vegetable. See cabbage.

Broccoli

Use whole, trimming off bottom of stalk, slice lengthwise, or chop into flowerettes. Steam, sauté, or prepare tempura style. Serve hot with butter, tamari, sauces, cheese. Use in casseroles, or raw in salads or as an appetizer. Lightly steam and chill then use in salads.

Brussel Sprouts

Whole or halved. For cooking, see broccoli. Serve as broccoli; also serve chilled.

Cabbage

Whole, chopped, shredded, sliced. Steam, sauté, boil, bake. Serve with sauces, in casseroles, stuff the leaves, sauerkraut. Cold, raw in salad.

Carrots

Slice in rounds, quarter lengthwise, in curls, or grated. Steam, bake, sauté (when in rounds), stews, soups, cakes, puddings, juiced. Serve with butter, honey glazes, sauces, creamed. Raw in salads as an appetizer.

Cauliflower

(See broccoli.)

Celery

Use whole, sliced, chopped. Steam, sauté, boil in soup or stews. Serve with other vegetables, with sauce, in casseroles, stuffings, raw in salads, stuffed as an appetizer.

Chard

Cook leaves and stalks whole, or chop. (See cabbage.)

Chestnuts

Use whole, chopped, or sliced, fresh, dried, or canned. Roast, steam, sauté, boil. When dried, soak overnight, then steam about 60 minutes. Serve hot with other vegetables, particularly those with oriental influence. Serve cold with dessert recipes. To shell and blanch, cut a gash into each one and place in a pan. Mix with a little oil and bake in the oven for 20 minutes.

Corn

Use on the cob or as kernels cut from cob. Steam, boil, wrap and bake whole in husk (400°, 25-35 minutes). Serve on cob with butter, or in combination with other vegetables; in casseroles, puddings, and soups. Raw in salads and relishes.

Cucumber

Slice, chop, quarter lengthwise. Steamed or sautéed. Serve hot with sauce, in soup or in fillings. Raw in salads, sandwiches, soups, as appetizer garnish.

Eggplant

Use whole, halved, sliced, chopped. Steam, boil, bake, as tempura, breaded, broil. Serve stuffed, baked, with sauces, with other vegetables, a la parmigiana, in casseroles, stuffing. Precooked and chilled, marinated or plain, in salads.

Endive

Use leaves whole or chopped. Steam, wilt, sauté, bake. Serve hot in casseroles, sauces, with hot marinade poured over to wilt. Raw in salads.

Green Beans/Yellow Wax

Use whole, removing tips, slice or chop. Steam, sauté, boil. Serve hot with butter, sauce, as tempura, in soups, or casseroles. Serve chilled in salads, raw in salads, appetizers.

Jicama

Use chopped, sliced, grated, sautéed or steamed. Great with Chinese vegetables, raw in salads.

Kale

(See chard.)

Kohlrabi

Use whole leaves and bulbs. Slice, chop, grate bulbs. Steam sauté, boil, bake. Serve with sauces, mashed, in soups. Precooked, chilled in salads, raw in salads.

Leeks

Use white tops and green part, about one-fourth of the way up. Chop or slice. Steam, sauté, boil in soups. Serve in potato soup, with oriental or other vegetable combinations, in soups or with sauce. Serve cooked and chilled or raw in salads, in cold soup.

Lettuce

Use leaves, whole or chopped. Steam, sauté, wilt. Serve in soup, hot marinade, raw in salads.

Lima Beans

Shell. Steam or boil.

Mushrooms

Use whole, caps, sliced, or chopped. Sauté, steam, bake, broil, as tempura. Serve hot with any of the vegetables, stuffings, casseroles, in soups, gravies, or stuffed. Serve cooked and chilled in marinade, raw in salads.

Okra

Chop, slice. Steam, boil, dry. Dip in egg and corn or cracker meal and fry; in sauces, in soups and stews.

Onions

Whole, sliced, chopped, grated. Steam, sauté, bake, as tempura, boil. Use in sauces, gravies, soups, with any vegetables, stuffing, casseroles. Raw or marinate for salads.

Parsnip

(See kohlrabi.)

Peas

Shell. Steam, sauté, bake. Serve in soups, stews, with vegetable combinations (peas, mushrooms, onions), in fillings. Especially good with potatoes. Raw in salads. Good in seafood salads.

Peppers (Bell) Red or Green

Whole, sliced, chopped. Steam, sauté, bake, broil, as tempura. Sauces, soups, stuffed, with vegetables. Raw, alone or in salads. (Use seeds in recipes—they contain lots of vitamin C.)

Potatoes

Whole, sliced, diced, grated. Steam, boil, sauté, fry, bake, as tempura. Serve in casseroles, with sauces, fried with onions, in stuffings and fillings, mashed. Great as leftovers, stuffed (save potato water for bread and sourdough starter). Cooked and chilled in salads.

Pumpkins

Use whole, sliced, chopped, grated. Steam, sauté, bake, boil. Save seeds—great roasted. Serve hot with butter, sauces, in soups and stews, mashed in stuffings, in pies, with yoghurt, casseroles, pudding. Store whole pumpkins in dark, cool place.

Radishes

Chop, slice. Raw in salads, appetizers, juiced.

Seaweed

The seaweeds readily available include:

Nori-thin sheets which you toast 4-6 inches above flame. Crumble in salads or soups. *Hiziki* you can serve as a vegetable. To prepare, rinse with cold water, changing water twice, then soak for 15 minutes. Remove from water, saving water. Cut into small strips. Sauté in oil. Add water and some tamari. Cover and simmer 1 hour. *Wakame* you can use in soup. Soak for 10 minutes in water, chop and cook with tamari or miso and a little water. *Dulse* can be used in soups, salads, or as a snack. *Kombu* should be boiled in 3-inch pieces in 6 c. water for 5 minutes. Use stock for soup making.

Spinach

Use whole, leaves or chopped. Steam, sauté. Serve with sauce, soufflé, pudding, stuffings, fillings, pies. Drop in soups, hot with butter. Raw in salads, juiced. Good pureed in salad dressing and noodles.

Squash

Summer squash, chayotte, crookneck, Italian, spaceships, zucchini. Slice, quarter lengthwise, chop, grate. Steam, sauté, bake, as tempura. Serve hot with other vegetables, soups, stews, stuffed, stuffings, fillings. Raw or marinade in salads.

Sunchokes

(Jerusalem artichokes). Whole, sliced, chopped, grated, steamed. Sauté, bake, boil, fry, as tempura. Serve hot with butter, sauces, fried and topped with nutritional yeast, soups, stews, casseroles. Serve chilled in salads; raw, grated in salads.

Tomatoes

Whole, sliced, chopped, quartered. Steam, sauté, stew, bake, broil, as tempura. Hot with other vegetables, stuffed, shish-kabobs, glazed, soups, stews, casseroles. Green—sliced, battered and fried. Cold in salads, relishes, dressings, juice, garnish.

Turnips

(See kohlrabi.)

Watercress

Use whole or leaves only. Steam, sauté. Sauces, soups (especially cold), salads, sandwiches.

Winter Squash

(See pumpkins.) Acorn, butternut, banana, spaghetti. Save seeds—they're good roasted.

Yams

(See potatoes and pumpkins.)

Fish

Fishing takes patience, luck, and a love of the water. We often fish on the sea in small boats known as dories which seem to react to every whisper of wind and every ripple water.

Our interest is sparked by the desire to experience the limitless wonders the sea has to offer.

We are careful to catch only what we need, wasting nothing.

On our hikes in the mountains we've caught many a trout to be prepared over the camp fire.

Fish is a complete protein food and it also supplies many minerals and vitamins. The flavors vary according to the species and can be prepared in many pleasing ways.

Don't accept the statement, "I don't like fish." Try the different suggestions in this section until you find some your family will like.

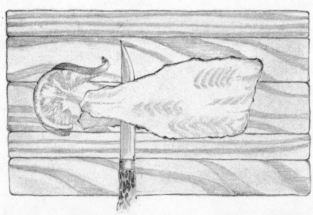

Fileting a Fish (See P. 103.)

Cleaning and Preparing the Fish

Cleaning fish requires the virtue of perserverence. Clean them as soon after they are caught as possible.

The first step is to scale the fish (not necessary if fileting). We use a knife—a dull one is best. Begin at the tail and scrape scales against the grain. (With some fish like cod or snapper remember that some of the fins are mildly poisonous and can give you a reaction like a bee sting—so be careful.)

Cut off the head (unless you choose to leave it on) and cut through the pectoral fin. Then cut the belly open, starting at the tail. Remove the "innards" and wash fish thoroughly. With some fish, like trout, it is necessary to work along the backbone with your finger to get out the bloodline.

If you prefer the fish to be whole, leave the head and fins intact. If you want to remove just the fins, cut along either side of the fin and pull sharply forward to remove the small base.

To filet a fish, lay it flat on your cutting board and with a sharp knife make a cut straight down, just behind the pectoral fin—clear to the backbone. Then, turning the knife towards the tail and keeping the blade against the backbone, begin cutting with a slow, sawing action, cutting down to the tail. Repeat on

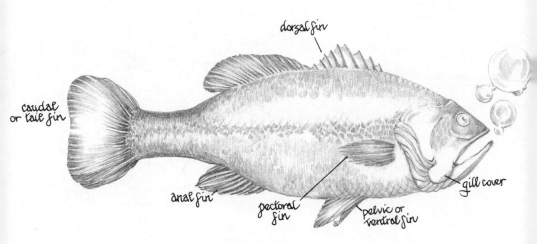

other side. To skin, start at the tail and work your knife blade carefully in between skin and filet. Hold onto the skin and pull as you cut. The skin should separate in one piece.

In "steaking" a fish, remove head and entrails, and scale. Then you just cut the size steak you desire in cross-wise sections. We usually cut ¾ - to 1-inch thick.

When cleaning fish, save the heads and tails and, in the case of fileting, save the backbone to boil in water for broth. (Also, fish heads make good fertilizer—especially when buried around rose bushes!)

(After cleaning fish you can get the fishy odor off your hands by squeezing a little lemon juice on them.)

Storing Fish

Refrigerator

Wrap well and store in coldest section of your icebox. It is best to store for just one day, three at the most.

Freezing

Fat or oily fish have a fairly short freezer life (oils in flesh tend to go rancid). (Fat is usually dark-tinted flesh; lean is white, sometimes with red patches or streaks.) Fish must be wrapped well or it will get "freezer burn." It is best to freeze fish in water—use coffee cans, milk cartons, ice tray; metal can is the best because it won't puncture.

When storing in a plastic bag, you must be careful to expel the inside air that would dry out the fish. Water pressure will force air out of bag. After inserting fish, hold mouth of bag open and dip three-fourths of the way into water. (Be careful not to get water inside bag.) Close bag and freeze.

Thawing

A day ahead (or overnight) before you plan to use frozen fish, put it in refrigerator for slow thaw. For a quick thaw, put fish in plastic bags and immerse in cold water. To thaw fish frozen in a can, run cold water over the can until the chunk of fish slips out easily; hold the chunk under water until surplus ice melts—put the solid fish back in the can and set in cold water until the fish thaws; 2-3 hours.

If baking, boiling, broiling, it is not necessary to completely defrost. If frying, thaw completely.

When fish is left over, wrap well and refrigerate immediately. Use it the next day—or you can freeze it for 7 to 10 days.

Kinds of Fish
(Kinds we are familiar with.)

Cod, red snapper, ling cod, perch, butter fish, flag fish, bass: medium-flesh fish. Good fried, baked, poached, sautéed.

Trout, sole: soft flesh. Best fried, baked, sautéed.

Salmon, bonita, halibut, calico bass, sea bass, swordfish: heavier flesh. Great steaked and broiled, or baked, fried, skewered, poached, steamed.

Catfish: flavor like ling cod.

Abalone, mussels, oysters, clams, squid (see recipes in this chapter).

Scallops: great in seviche.

Lobster, shrimp.

Ways of Cooking Fish

Whatever method you choose, don't overcook fish; just enough to remove "rawness" and heighten flavor.

Poached
I usually poach in a skillet because not much water is needed (enough to come one-fourth way up on fish). Bring water to a boil. Cut fish in fourth-inch chunks. Add to water. Turn down temperature so water remains hot but not boiling. Cover skillet and cook about 5 minutes.

Sautéed
Cook in skillet with a little oil, or dip in batter first.

Broiled
Baste with butter or herb-butter. Broil first side about 3 minutes, turn.

Grilled
Brush with oil to prevent sticking.

Skewered and roasted

A method that may be used for firm-fleshed fish.

Baked

Cook 10-15 minutes. You can use a Dutch oven to bake fish outdoors.

Steamed

Lay on a steam rack with a little water underneath.

Outdoors

No pan? Try using just a flat rock large enough for your filets to fit on top. The rock sits right in the middle of your fire until it's sizzling hot. Pull the rock out to the side and cook your fish 10-15 minutes or until it flakes easily (you can cook eggs and many other things this way, too!).

Or, wrap fish in an aluminum package with salt, pepper, lemon and/or butter. Place on a bed of coals to cook. Turn frequently or cover top with coals. Cooks in 15-20 minutes. Test for doneness (flakes easily; not pink in middle).

Fried

Dip fish in egg and batter. It is important to wait until oil gets hot, then add fish. Keep temperature at 375° to 400°.

A test for doneness: flesh starts to flake when pulled with a fork.

Smoked

A little time and energy put into constructing a smokehouse will reward you with some very tasty products.

A smokehouse can be a small wooden building with only a dirt floor. It should not be totally airtight. Install hooks or nails inside to hang the fish on.

To prepare fish for smoking, scale and remove "innards" and gills, but leave skin on. Soak fish for 12 hours in brine.

If you want a drier fish—one that will last 6-9 months—prepare it this way: when cleaning and scaling, salt the meat side of the fish and lay two such salted meat sides together (skin down, meat up; meat down, skin up). This begins the process sooner.

After all the fish are cleaned, put them in brine. Add spices if desired. Let set 12 hours. While preparing your fire, remove fish from brine and salt again. Then smoke for 3 days. This gives you a drier fish, but one that lasts.

Start your fire on the dirt floor. When a good bed of coals has been built up, add a good smoking wood like apple, green hickory, or oak. Fish must be hung high enough so it doesn't cook from the fire. Let the wood smoke the fish for 12 hours. This particular method doesn't preserve fish for longer than 2-3 days, refrigerated, but you can freeze it.

Another smokehouse method: Set up an old refrigerator (latches removed) equipped inside with racks and hooks. Next to it, set up a 25- or 50-gallon drum, or a small wood-burning stove. Run a pipe into a hole in the refrigerator to send the smoke in.

Fish in Other Dishes

You can include fish or shellfish as an addition to many of the recipes we have in this book. Here are some ideas.

Beans 'n Pasta

Add shrimp to Lasagne. Add shellfish to Udon Fun. Add fish or shellfish to Quik Noodle Dish.

Sauces and Gravies

Add fish and/or shellfish to Curry Sauce. Serve with a grain. Add shrimp to Black Bean Sauce—it's great! Or, shellfish in Tomato Sauce. Try Fish Cakes and gravy, or fried fish and gravy.

Vegetable Dishes

Egg Rolls and shrimp. Cabbage and Noodles with shellfish. Sautéed vegetables and nuts with fish or shellfish. Egg Foo Yong with shrimp or fish. Omelettes or Quiche with a shellfish.

How Much Fish To Cook

To figure quantity per person, use ¼ lb. per person, if filets; ½ lb. per person, if steaks.

Fish Broth

Use heads, fins, tails—even frames if they've been fileted and there is meat left on them. Cook in just enough water to cover. Cover pot and simmer 45 minutes. Strain off the broth. Use in soups and chowders.

Servings in Recipes

The following recipes will yield 4-6 servings unless otherwise indicated.

Baked Fish in Herb-Butter Sauce
(From our restaurant.)

1½-2 lb. fish filets or steaks	¼ t. thyme
1 stick (½ c.) butter	½ t. rosemary
3 T. tamari	¼ t. tarragon
1 t. garlic	¼ c. mushrooms, sliced
½ t. basil	¼ c. green onions, chopped
1 t. oregano	1 lemon, sliced (optional)

Lay filets in baking pan. In a small pan, melt butter, add tamari and spices. Pour over the filets and bake at 375° for 8 minutes. Remove and put mushrooms and green onions and lemon slices on top of fish. Baste until mushrooms and green onions are well-coated. Return to oven and bake 5 minutes.

Fish Parmesan

1½-2 lbs. fish filets or steaks	1 t. kelp
2 eggs, beaten	2 t. sea salt
2 c. bread crumbs (fine)	thyme
4 oz. Parmesan cheese	tomato slices
1 t. garlic powder	fresh parsley, chopped

Cut fish into portions. Four-ounce portions are good. Combine bread crumbs with garlic, kelp, and salt and half of the Parmesan. Dip fish in egg, then in crumbs until well-coated. Lay in a baking pan well-coated with oil. Bake at 400° for 5 minutes. Remove; top each portion with tomato slices and sprinkle with Parmesan and fresh parsley. Return to oven and bake for 5-10 minutes. Serve with lemon wedges.

Baked Fish in Milk

2 lbs. fish filets or steaks	2 T. butter
½ c. milk	¼ c. celery, finely chopped
½ onion, sliced	¼ c. potatoes, cut small
¼ c. carrots, sliced in thin rounds	1 t. sea salt
	½ t. paprika

Steam carrots, celery, and potatoes in very little water for about 5 minutes. Lay filets in a baking pan, pour over them milk and any water from vegetables. Dot with butter and put vegetables along the sides. Season. Bake at 375° for 8-10 minutes. You may baste the fish after about 5 minutes. If steaks are thick, it may take a little longer.

Variations:

Try various sauces.
Use different or a greater variety of vegetables.

Sweet 'n Sour Fish

Prepare recipe for Sweet 'n Sour Sauce (see Sauce section).
Prepare fish as in Simon's Catch but instead of placing on a bun, put on rice then pour sauce over.
Bake fish with sauce at 375° for 8-10 minutes.
Broil fish with a little sauce and serve more sauce on the side. Baste fish when broiling.
Baste raw fish with a little sauce, broil for 3-5 minutes each side. Serve with extra sauce.

Whole Baked Fish with Stuffing

1 6-10 lb. fish	recipe for Herb-Butter Sauce
lemon or lime juice	1 lemon, sliced thin
recipe for Apple-Apricot or Sour Cream Stuffing	1 med. red onion, sliced thin into rings

Two hours ahead of time brush inside of fish with lemon or lime juice and refrigerate.
Meanwhile, prepare stuffing and Herb-Butter Sauce.

Place the fish in a large roasting pan (you can line with foil to prevent sticking). Stuff the inside and close with toothpicks. Baste with Herb-Butter Sauce. Bake at 350° for 1½ to 1¾ hours. After 1 hour, remove and top with lemon and onion. Return to oven, basting occasionally. When fish is done, lift out to a platter. Slide foil out. Try decorating your platter with fresh parsley, purple grapes, nuts, cranberries. Don't forget to remove the toothpicks!

Fish Roll-Ups

Instead of baking a whole fish you can use filets. Spread stuffing on a filet, roll it up and stick in a toothpick. Place in an oiled baking pan or casserole. Baste each roll-up with butter and lemon. Bake at 375° about 30 minutes. Also, try sprinkling with herbs or put onion rings and mushrooms on the top and baste.

Broiled Filets or Steaks

2 lbs. filets or steaks   1 recipe Barbecue Sauce
½ c. onion, chopped

Prepare Barbecue Sauce. Lay filets on a cookie sheet, put onions on top and cover with Barbecue Sauce. Put under broiler and cook about 3-5 minutes on each side. Cooking time depends on thickness of fish. It is best to have a thicker filet or steak—⅜-inch to 1½ inches. Broil 3-5 inches from heat. If it is a thicker fish, cooking will take from 8-15 minutes.

Fish Creole

1½ lb. fish (white), cut in
  2-oz. squares
1 c. red onions, sliced in
  half-moons
1 c. zucchini, sliced in rounds
¾ c. green pepper, sliced in
  half-moons
1 c. fresh corn, cut from the
  cob
2 c. fresh tomatoes, diced
1 c. celery, diced

1 c. eggplant, cut in small
  chunks
4 garlic cloves, minced
2 c. tomato sauce
1½ c. tomato juice
2 t. garlic powder
2 t. rosemary
1 T. oregano
1 t. tarragon
1 t. sea salt
Parmesan cheese

In a large pot, heat tomato sauce and juice with seasonings. Cook until thoroughly heated. Meanwhile, in a large skillet, sauté onions, garlic, green pepper, and celery until onions are transparent. Add the rest of the vegetables and simmer. Pour half of sauce over the vegetables. Leave the rest in pot. Add fish to pot and cook about 3-5 minutes—until pink is gone. Mix with vegetables and sauce. Serve. Sprinkle top with Parmesan cheese.

When adding the rest of the vegetables, make sure that total cooking time before sauce is added doesn't exceed 5 minutes.

Fish Kabobs

2 lbs. fish
2 med. onions (or 12 small
  pearl)
2 green peppers
1 basket cherry tomatoes

1 pineapple (cut in chunks)
12 mushrooms
1 recipe for Marinade
  (see Salads)

Cut fish into 2-inch squares. Put in a bowl and cover with marinade. Stick in refrigerator for 45 minutes. Preheat broiler at 350°. On skewers alternate fish and vegetables until full. Baste with remaining marinade or with barbecue sauce or your choice of sauce. Put kabobs under broiler and broil for 5-8 minutes until nicely browned. Serve with rice and remaining sauce. It is best to use meaty but lean fish.

Variation:

Try using large shrimp.

Boiled Fish Dinner

2 c. potatoes, cut in large
  chunks
1 large carrot, cut into sticks
2 c. onions
2 c. beets, cut into chunks
½ c. celery, diced
2 ears corn, cut from cob

6 4-oz. portions fish or 6 c.
  fish cut into chunks
6 c. broth
10 T. oats, ground
2 t. oregano
1 t. basil
2 T. tamari

In a large pot put broth, oats, spices, potatoes, onions, carrot, beets, and celery. Cook until potatoes and beets are tender; about 30 minutes. Add corn, cook an additional 5 minutes then add fish and cook until fish is done; about 5 minutes. Serve sprinkled with Parmesan cheese or nutritional yeast.

Batter-Fried Fish

2 lbs. filets (no more than
  1-inch thick)
1 c. whole wheat flour
  (or corn, corn and rye,
  unbleached white, or millet)

¾ to 1 c. milk (or water for
  crisper batter)
sea salt
seasoning to taste

Prepare batter. Some flours may be a little heavier than others, requiring a little more liquid. Dry fish on an absorbent paper towel or a lint-free cloth.

In selecting your cooking pot, keep in mind that deep ones prevent grease from spattering too much. Of course, a deep-fat fryer is ideal but not necessary. Fill a deep, heavy pot a little less than half full of oil, heat until just before the point of smoking (350°-375°).

Use a strainer that will fit to lower fish into oil (if you're more daring just cook fish in the oil). If you cook fish in a strainer it may be necessary to turn them. Cook 3-5 minutes.

I usually use a heavy skillet with ½- to ¾-inch of oil. If cooking more than one batch, be sure the oil heats back up to 350°-375° before starting another batch.

Variation:

Another quick and easy batter is ordinary pancake batter, perhaps some left over from breakfast.

Creamed Fish

6 T. butter
¾ c. flour
6 c. milk
1 t. celery salt
½ t. dry mustard
1 t. sea salt

2 c. onion, sliced
2 c. mushrooms, sliced
1 c. carrots, sliced in rounds
1 c. cauliflower or fresh peas
1 c. fresh corn

In a large cooking pot melt butter and stir in flour with a whisk to a smooth paste. Add milk and seasonings. Meanwhile, Sauté at medium heat until golden brown on both sides. Mix sour creamed mixture, then add rest of vegetables. Cut fish into 1- to 2-inch strips and add to creamed mixture. Cook about 5 minutes. Serve with toast, rice, noodles, or rice cakes.

Sautéed Fish with Almond Sour Cream

2 lbs. fish cut into 4-oz.
   portions
1 onion, sliced thin
¼ c. almonds, coarsely
   chopped

1 garlic clove, minced
¼ c. butter
1 c. sour cream
½ t. rosemary, crushed

In a large skillet sauté onions, garlic, and almonds in butter until almonds are lightly browned. Dust fish filets with flour. Sauté at medium heat until golden brown on both sides. Mix sour cream with onions, garlic, and almond mixture. Add rosemary to mixture and cover fish with it. Cover skillet and cook over low heat about 5 minutes. Serve with a grain or pasta.

Simon's Catch
(From our restaurant.)

6 filets, cut into 4-oz. portions
1 c. cornmeal
½ t. garlic powder
1 t. sea salt

1 t. kelp
1 t. thyme
1 egg, beaten
oil

Dip filets into beaten egg then into cornmeal mixture. Put about ½-inch of oil in skillet. Heat until almost smoking. Carefully drop in fish and cook until browned and crisp. Drain.

Toast sesame bun and lay fish on one side. Lay lettuce, sprouts, tomato on top side of bun. Serve with tartar sauce and lemon wedges.

Fish Cakes
(This recipe is a good way to use leftover fish.)

3 c. fish, cooked
2 c. millet, cooked
1 c. onion, chopped small
1 t. sea salt
1 t. kelp

1½ t. tamari
1 t. dry mustard
1 t. powdered bouillon,
    vegetable broth, or season
    with herbs of your choice

Mix ingredients in a bowl. Shape into patties and fry until crisp. Top with cheese and melt if desired. For variety add mushroom slices.

Seviche
(Raw fish.)

2 lbs. fish
1¾ c. lemon or lime juice
1 med. onion, chopped or
    finely sliced

1 small green pepper, chopped
1 tomato, chopped
1 fresh garlic clove, minced
¾ c. oil (preferably olive)

Cut fish into strips, add onions, green peppers, tomatoes and fresh garlic. Pour lemon juice and oil over fish (make sure it covers the fish). Let sit 2-3 hours in refrigerator. Serve on a bed of lettuce.

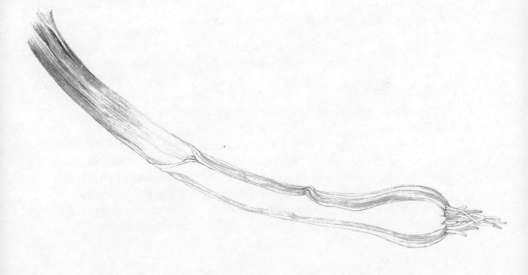

Seafood Salad

1½ c. fish* cut in 1-inch
   squares
1½ c. shrimp,** chopped
¼ c. celery, chopped fine
1 t. basil

¼ c. green onion, chopped
½ c. mayonnaise
1 t. kelp
2 t. tamari
1 t. dry mustard

Poach fish and boil shrimp. Allow to cool. Add celery and green onions. Mix in mayonnaise and spices.

This is good in sandwiches or stuffed in tomatoes or avocados.

* Tuna or salmon are great!
** Or use all fish.

Seafood Filling

1 c. fish
1½ c. shrimp
¼ c. green onions

¼ c. celery
½-¾ c. recipe for Cream
   Sauce

Prepare as in Seafood Salad and pour Cream Sauce over mixture when ready. Use in crepes, tarts, pies.

Lobster

There is a difference between east- and west-coast lobsters. Many prefer the east-coast variety because of their claws (considered the best part). The west-coast lobsters are spiney with no claws.

Steaming a lobster live is the best way to prepare it. Put enough water in a large pot to cover lobster. Add a little salt. Bring water to a boil. Drop in lobster head first (or you can kill lobster by laying on its hard-shell back and inserting a knife tip between the head and body, severing the spinal cord).

Cover pot, return to boil. Simmer about 10-15 minutes for first pound and 2 minutes for each additional half-pound. The shell will be bright red.

Remove and clean, or serve and let each person break his own apart. Twist off claws and crack them open. Use a nut cracker, pliers, rock, hammer or anything that works. Next you can separate the tail from the body by arching the back until it cracks. Break flippers from the tail, insert a fork and push out the meat.

Unhinge the back from the body. This is where the liver is—which many people like better than the meat. Crack apart rest of the body. (The small claws have a meat which can be removed by sucking.)

The lobster is so rich and tasty on its own that anything more than drawn butter almost detracts from its flavor.

Abalone or Conch

We're very lucky to be on the California coast where we can obtain fresh abalone. This is a somewhat threatened species and their shipment to other parts of the country is prohibited. Besides, fresh abalone is very perishable and must be eaten within a day.

This leaves the possibility of obtaining fresh abalone to the area they happen to inhabit. Canned abalone is available in other parts of the country and can be used as you would fresh.

Here's how to clean abalone. When you're holding an abalone shell there is an obviously heavier end. This is where you begin. Run your knife in between the shell and the meat and remove it. Attached to the meat will be the "innards"—they are between the meat and the shell. Make sure they are cut away.

On the edges of the white flesh are dark outer edges. Trim these away for they are very tough. All you will have left is a white piece of flesh.

The abalone usually contracts when it is caught, so once you have the flesh trimmed out you will usually have to pound it to tenderize it. It is easier to pound when left whole or at least in large pieces. Pound it as little as you can and still make it tender (try to use an implement that is larger than the piece of abalone).

Abalone Steaks

2 lbs. abalone steaks
   (½-inch thick or less)
2 eggs, beaten
1 c. flour

1 t. sea salt
½ t. kelp
¼ c. butter

Dip steaks in beaten eggs, then in flour mixture. Melt butter in large, heavy skillet. Sauté steaks 2 minutes each side.

Sautéed Abalone

2 lb. abalone steaks
1 c. butter
2 c. celery, finely chopped
1 c. onion, finely chopped

juice of 3 lemons
1 c. Parmesan cheese
1 t. sea salt

Prepare steaks as in Abalone Steaks. Sauté the above ingredients. Pour over steaks and serve.

Abalone Tempura or Fritters

Cut abalone into small strips. Prepare as for Tempura or Fritter recipe.

Abalone Burgers

4 oz. abalone steaks
1 egg, beaten
1 c. cornmeal
½ t. garlic
1 t. kelp powder

1 t. sea salt
oil
½ c. mushrooms
½ c. onions
1 recipe for gravy

Dip abalone steak in egg, then in cornmeal mixture. Heat oil in skillet until almost smoking. Fry steak until crisp and brown. Meanwhile, prepare a gravy recipe adding mushrooms and onions. Pour over steak and serve.

Shrimp

Here is how to peel and devein shrimp. Rinse shrimp. Bring a pot of water to a boil and drop them in. Cover and return to boil. Reduce heat and cook 5 minutes. Remove shrimp and put in collander. Rinse under cold water to prevent any further cooking.

To peel, begin lifting one side where the tentacles and feelers are. Pull across, removing whole shell at one—or one side at a time. You have a choice of either leaving the tail on, if needed, or removing it. Clean away any remaining shell parts or feeler bits.

Make a shallow cut lengthwise along the back and with your fingers or a knife tip, remove the vein. Rinse shrimp again. Now it's ready to serve cold or hot in many ways.

Great chilled and served as shrimp cocktail; see Seafood Filling; see Salads (The Farmer and The Fisherman); use in kebobs; see Eggs (Omelette Cordelia or Quiche); follow recipe for Egg Foo Yong, adding shrimp; tempura—see Vegetarian Main Dishes; pizza—see Vegetarian Main Dishes.

You can also use shrimp in Fish Creole with fish and/or oysters, scallops, mussels, crab or clams; or in Black Bean Sauce.

Broiled Shrimp

1 lb. shrimp   recipe for Fish Marinade

Prepare marinade in a large bowl, add shrimp and stir gently until all are well-covered. Preheat broiler. Place shrimp on a broiler pan. Baste again with marinade. Place about 4 inches below broiler and broil 3-4 minutes. Then turn and repeat. Serve with marinade from the pan.

Baked Shrimp with Tomato Sauce

1½ lb. med. shrimp (or small)   1 c. broccoli, chopped
1 recipe Tomato Sauce   ½ c. green olives, sliced
cooked spaghetti for 6   (optional)
1 c. mushrooms, sliced   Parmesan cheese, grated

Prepare tomato sauce. It is best when prepared the night before. Put spaghetti in an oiled casserole dish. Top with sauce, saving out ½ c., then with mushrooms. If you use broccoli, mix in with the sauce. Put shrimp on top. Drizzle with rest of sauce and top with green olives and Parmesan. Bake at 375° for 10 minutes or until Parmesan begins to brown.

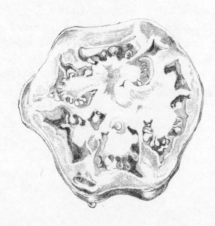

Shrimp in Black Bean Sauce

1½ lb. med. shrimp
1 recipe Black Bean Sauce
¼ c. walnuts, finely chopped

¼ c. scallions and tops, finely chopped

Prepare Black Bean Sauce. (See Sauce section.) Precook shrimp. Add to sauce and serve with rice or udon noodles. Top with walnuts and scallions or chives.

Squid

Squid is related to the clam, oyster, scallop, and mussel family. Virtually the entire squid is edible.

If you are purchasing squid, it will usually be cleaned for you. If you've caught your own the first step is cleaning. We've had experience mostly with the small squid which are about 3 to 4 inches long. All that is necessary is to rinse them up and down until the "ink" stops coming out. Then we either barbecue or cook tempura style. After cooking them, pull the tentacles and head and the cuttlebone comes out easily. Discard the cuttlebone and eat the rest.

With larger squid, a more complex process is involved in cleaning and preparing.

First it is necessary to slice the squid lengthwise, starting at the end of the body and moving towards the top. This will enable you to grasp everything inside the body; and, with a slight pull, it should all come free. Set aside. If not, clean out any remaining pieces with your fingers.

Next peel away the purplish layer over the skin. You can get a grip on it by rubbing the edge a little. The skin will just peel away.

Next cut away the "innards" from the head and tentacles and discard them. Squeeze end of tentacles and discard the creamy-yellow meat that comes out. Rinse them and cut them according to recipe.

Squid cooks fast because it is so thin. If cooked properly it will be tender and not rubbery.

Sautéed Squid

1½ lb. squid
¼ c. butter
4 garlic cloves, minced

1 t. sea salt
1 lemon juiced

Cut squid into rings or pieces. Put in a large skillet with just enough water to cover bottom. Cover and simmer about 15 minutes over low heat until tender. Test it with a fork to make sure. Drain water from skillet and add butter, garlic, salt and lemon. Cook over high heat and fry until squid are crisp. Serve.

Fried Squid

1½ lbs. squid, cut in slices or
    chunks
lemon wedges

1 recipe batter for fish or
    tempura batter

In a large, deep pot or skillet, heat oil to a point just before smoking. Dip squid in batter and drop into oil. The pieces cook quickly and rise to the top when done. Serve with cocktail sauce.

Corn-Fried Squid

1½ lbs. squid cut in slices or
    chunks
1 egg, beaten

1 recipe for cornmeal mixture
    (Simon's Catch)
lemon wedges

Follow cooking instructions in above recipe. Prepare squid by dipping in egg, then in cornmeal mixture, and frying until crisp.

Barbecued Squid

Dip pieces of squid in Barbecue Sauce and cook on grill.

Oysters

To clean oysters, follow directions for cleaning clams. If you buy oysters they are usually cleaned. You merely have to run them under cold water and rinse the shell with a cloth.

To open oysters, follow the same procedure as for clams, except that to get them started you may have to chip off the thin end of the shell. Use a hammer or something similar.

Oysters are excellent raw with lemon or lime or cocktail sauce. If you cook, be careful not to overcook; just until warmed through.

You can broil oysters on the half shell and baste with sauce of your choice or garlic butter. Broil about 3 inches below broiler for 5 minutes, turning once. Try sprinkling with Parmesan cheese or bread crumbs.

To fry oysters in batter, drain and pat dry with lint-free towel. Dip in batter as for fish. Serve with garlic butter, tartar sauce, or cocktail sauce. Use in creoles or sauces.

For Oysters Creole, follow recipe for Fish Creole, substituting oyster juice for tomato juice. Sauté in butter 3-5 minutes.

For oysters sautéed in almond sour cream, follow recipe for sautéed fish, substituting oysters.

See also fish and shellfish suggestions.

Clams

Since clams feed themselves by pumping sea water into one side of the shell and out the other (to trap the plankton) you can clean them using the same principle. Fill a pot with salted water and put in the clams. They will pump in clean water and pump out any internal sand. Change the water once or twice. The process takes about 45 minutes. You can also add cornmeal as an extra precaution; it tends to absorb any poisons taken in from the algae clams eat.

Opening clams is no real problem. The soft-shell variety will break apart easily. Hard-shell clams require something like an "abalone bar," a flat piece of iron—or, use a clam knife, which is made on the same pinciple. You can also use a strong, thin knife with a rounded tip.

Lay the clam in the palm of your hand. There is an obviously stronger side of the shell. This is where you want to begin.

Insert knife blade between the two shells and begin prying up to force the shells open. Be careful not to poke the large (abductor) muscle because it will cause the clam to tense up. Run the blade around the clam until the halves open up. Next, insert the blade between the thin membrane which runs around the perimeter of the shell and the shell it is attached to, and separate. Next, the large abductor muscle must be set free from the meat. Run knife between it and shells.

Now your clam is ready to serve on the half-shell.

To open clams for chowders and soups or creoles, just put in a pot with a little water, cover and steam until shells pop open. Save the liquid to use in other recipes.

Clams, oysters, scallops, and mussels can be cooked the same way. They all cook very fast so be careful not to overcook.

Follow recipes for oysters.

Scallops

To clean scallops insert your knife and twist to break open the shell. Cut around the meat in the center. The whole piece will come out. Cut away "innards" to get to the marshmallow-like meat at the center. It is now ready to prepare.

If you buy already cleaned scallops just rinse under cold water before cooking.

Scallops are great in seviche. They cook very fast. Follow recipes for oysters; be careful not to overcook. Also follow recipe for Fish Parmesan and either bake or broil. We also dip scallops in an egg yolk batter and fry.

Mussels

Mussels are found along the coasts. They cling to rocks or anything protruding from the water. You can remove them by pulling them quickly from the rock before they have a chance to tense their abductor muscle. If your grasp was a little slow, you'll have to pry the mussel off with an abalone bar—a flat piece of iron or steel.

A note of caution: unless you know that mussels are located in an area where they are safe to eat, it is better to purchase them from a fish market.

To clean mussels, scrub shells well with a brush to remove mud and waste matter. Then you can place them in a pot of cold water and let them stand for a couple of hours. Dead mussels will float to the top. Discard them.

To open the good ones, insert knife between shells and run around the edge. Remove meat from shells and trim the remaining whiskers.

To steam mussels open, follow method for clams.

Avoid overcooking mussels; follow recipes for oysters.

Beans and Pasta

I have really attempted to write about beans in such a way that you may realize how good they are for you and how good they can taste! Sometimes people are turned off by the very name, "bean"; they won't even try them. But we can't disguise them, so I decided my approach would be the simple truth—because "We Love Beans."

When properly cooked, and when correctly combined with other foods containing the several amino acids that beans lack, they are a good source of protein, a good meat substitute, and a hearty meal. We usually serve cornbread or tortillas with our beans, as a nutritional supplement. You can also serve eggs, milk products, fish, or various grains to make a complete protein.

In the bean or legume family the soybean is unique, with the highest nutrient value. Unlike other beans, soybeans are a complete protein (see Soybeans) and many food products are made from them.

The second half of this chapter is about pasta. Pasta immediately makes us think Italian because it is one of the basic Italian foods. Creative Italians have spent many an hour in the kitchen devising delicious ways to serve this staple food. The recipes in this chapter have been inspired by their efforts.

Tips on Cooking Beans

There are a few tricks and shortcuts to cooking beans. (Remember that ¾ c. of dried beans, peas, or lentils will make 2 c. of cooked beans.)

Soak the beans before cooking, rinsing them first. You can either soak them overnight (which cuts the cooking time by 45 minutes), or do the quick-soak method.

To quick-soak, put dry beans in a pot (¾ c. beans to 2½ c. water), and bring to a boil. Continue boiling for 2 minutes. Remove from heat and let sit, covered, 2 hours. In the same water, simmer beans 1½ -3 hours, depending on the beans.

Do not add salt or tamari (soy sauce) until beans are tender. (Salt draws out moisture, which will prevent beans from cooking.)

We like to add a bay leaf during cooking. It helps digestion. We also add onions, spices, and tomatoes for flavor. If pressure cooking, bring to full pressure then turn down to a slow simmer at 15 pounds pressure. Time varies 45 to 90 minutes. It will cut cooking time by an hour or two.

A Good Pot of Pintos or Any Ole Bean

1½ c. water
1 c. pintos

1 c. chopped onions
1 t. sea salt

Cook pintos in water, simmering 1½ hours. Add onions and cook ½ hour or until done. Add salt. The reason we add onions in the last 10 minutes is to prevent them from overcooking. However, for added flavor, you may add onions to beans and cook the whole time.

If pressure cooking, use 2½ c. water to 1 c. beans and cook 45 to 60 minutes, or more as needed.

Refried Beans

Mash cooked beans. Add onions if desired and fry on an oiled skillet until hot.

Beans with Tomato

1 c. pintos
1 c. limas
2 c. whole, fresh, chopped
    tomatoes (or canned)

2 c. onions, chopped
2 t. garlic powder
2 t. sea salt
2 T. tamari

Cook presoaked beans 1 hour, then add tomatoes, garlic powder, and continue cooking for another 50 minutes. Add onions and cook until tender; about 10 minutes. Add tamari and salt. Mix well and serve, or cook a little longer if desired.

Yield: 5-6 c.

Chili Beans

Follow recipe for Beans with Tomato. Add:

½ t. cayenne
1½ T. cumin

1 t. chili peppers, ground

Tamale Pie

(This is a good way to use extra beans, or prepare new beans as Beans with Tomato.)

4 c. beans, cooked
¾ c. green peppers, chopped
1 t. cayenne
2 t. cumin

¾ c. celery, diced
1 c. corn, cut from cob
1½ c. cheese, grated

Crust:

3 eggs
¼ c. oil
dash sea salt

1 c. milk
2 c. cornmeal

To prepare the crust, separate egg yolks and set whites aside. Beat yolks with oil. Add milk, cornmeal, and salt. Spread half of mixture in bottom of a casserole dish or baking pan. Bake in a 350° oven 10 minutes. Remove and spread in the bean mixture. Sprinkle cheese on top, then cornmeal. Return to oven and bake until top is browned.

For a different texture you can beat the egg whites and pour on top of crust. *Yield: 4-6 servings.*

*W*e dig in our Mother Earth and plant the seed.

To the seed we give drink from the waters;

the sun doth nourish and give it life.

As it grows it becomes full of life more abundant.

When it reaches its full height this plant doth give

to us of its life-giving properties,

from the air and earth and water and sun.

We do eat, consume, to become this life;

in turn giving to one another and also giving back

to our mother that which we did not use.

So is the completion of a cycle of life.

Black-Eyed Peas

Follow recipe for Beans. It's best to cook on top of the stove, not in a pressure cooker—the peas can clog the vent. Cooking time on top of the stove: 1 hour.

Garbanzos

Cook as Beans. Takes 2-3 hours on top of stove.

Garbanzo Spread

3. c. cooked garbanzos	lemon juice
1 c. sesame seeds	garlic powder
3 T. sesame oil	basil
onions, chopped	

Mash garbanzos. Add rest of ingredients. Season to taste.

Black Beans

½ lb. black beans	1 c. sugar or ¾ c. honey
water	1 T. chopped ginger

Soak beans overnight. Drain and place in a saucepan. Add water to half-way level in pan. Add sugar and ginger, and cook until tender, not mushy—about 1½ hours.

If pressure cooking black beans, be careful that they do not clog vent. Pressure cooking requires 1 hour; top-of-stove, 2-3 hours.

Soybeans
(Or: How to get protein without really trying.)

"Soybeans" and "protein" have become almost synonymous. Soybeans are not only rich in protein, they also contain many vitamins and minerals.

They can be used in many, many ways. Besides as just plain beans, you can make soy cheese, tofu, soy milk, flour, oil, tamari, miso, imitation meat, soy grits, flakes, nuts.

To cook, soak 1 c. soybeans overnight in 3 c. water, or use the quick-soak method (see Beans). Don't drain. Bring water to a boil for a few minutes, and skim off foam that collects on top. Reduce heat and simmer 2-3 hours until beans are very tender. It is important that you cook soybeans well to aid in digestion. Also add a bay leaf or two when cooking.

When cooking in a pressure cooker,* use slightly less water and first bring to a boil, skimming off foam. Then cover with pressure lid and cook 1 hour or until done.

If you want to add onions, remove the beans from heat after 55 minutes. Check to see if beans are nearly done, then add onions and continue cooking for a few minutes until onions are of desired tenderness. If you prefer, for added flavor, add onions when you begin to cook beans.

* (Be careful, because even soybeans can clog vent.)

Soybean Loaf

Soak 2 c. soybeans overnight, or use quick-soak method (see Beans). Cook in 6 c. water for 2 hours or use a pressure cooker.

Sauté: 1 chopped onion and 3 chopped carrots until tender; add to soybeans.

Mix in:

4 beaten eggs	½ c. wheat germ
2 c. bread crumbs, or 1 c. cornmeal mixed in 2 c. water	½ c. sesame seeds
	1 T. kelp
	2 t. cumin
1 c. whole canned tomatoes, or whole chopped, fresh tomatoes	1 t. sea salt
	⅓ c. oil or melted butter
	2 t. garlic powder

Mix well and put into two oiled loaf pans. Bake at 375° for 1 hour.

Variation:

Bind with 2 c. cheese sauce, in place of tomatoes.

Soyburgers

4 c. cooked soybeans*
3-6 eggs, beaten
½ c. wheat germ or bread crumbs
1 stalk celery
1 c. grated carrot

2-3 cloves garlic, minced
¾ c. chopped onion
1 T. poultry seasoning, sage, marjoram, savory, thyme
¼ t. pepper
1½ t. sea salt

Mix well and shape into patties. Either fry, or bake in 400° oven. Top with cheese, onions, and mushrooms. Serve on sesame buns. *Yield: 10-12 patties.*

* Try using sprouted soybeans, steamed, or soy grits or flakes.

Soy Milk

Soak soybeans overnight. Grind beans or crush with a mortar and pestle. Put in a pot and pour boiling water over them to cover. Add 1 inch of cold water. Stir and let sit 5 minutes.

Squeeze through a cloth bag. Pour the bean "remains" into the pot again with hot water, using only half as much water. Stir, let sit 5 minutes, and squeeze through cloth again. Heat milk to just before boiling.

Tofu

After soy milk is heated, add lemon juice or vinegar to curdle (2-3 lemons for a gallon). Let sit to cool. Separate curds from whey. Add salt to taste.

Tamari

Tamari is naturally fermented soy sauce. It is made from wheat, soybeans, water, and salt. It is the liquid which comes to the surface after miso has aged in wood for 2 years. It is a great flavor accompaniment to many foods; especially grains, vegetables, and sauces. You can use it instead of salt.

Miso is rich in protein, natural sugar, oil, vitamins, and minerals. It is made from soybeans and aged in wood for 2 years.

Cheese-Soybean Soup

Soak 2 c. soybeans overnight. Cook as in Soybean recipe. When done, mash together with 1 large can of v-8 juice,* or put through a blender.

Sauté and add to the soybean mixture: 3 T. oil, 1 small onion, chopped; 1 clove garlic, minced; 1 clove; 2 stalks of celery, with leaves. Then add 1½ c. grated cheese (cheddar or jack). Simmer for 30 minutes.

* Or use fresh tomatoes, pureed, and add a few spices.

Soy Nuts

Soak soybeans overnight. Roast in the oven for 45 minutes with a little tamari. You may like a little garlic added.

Soy Grits

Soy grits are coarsely ground soybeans. They cook in less time than whole beans and contribute a different texture to some foods.

Soy Flakes

Soy flakes are made by a process that partially cooks and compresses the whole bean into flakes.

Soybean Cheese Spread

3 c. soybeans, soaked   sesame oil
1 c. sesame seeds, ground   sea salt
1 T. caraway seeds

Grind soaked beans and steam for 20 minutes. Mix ground sesame seeds and caraway seeds, using enough sesame oil to make a pasty mixture. Add salt to taste. Add this paste to soybeans and mix well.

Lentils

2 c. lentils   4-6 c. water

Soak lentils overnight or use the quick-soak method (boil 2 minutes, soak 1 hour). Cook in a pot with water. Bring to a boil then cook over medium-low heat for 45 minutes. Add some onions and carrots. Season to taste. (I like garlic and tamari.) Serve hot.

Lentils can be prepared and used like Refried Beans. Roll in a tortilla with cheese.

(Lentils are dangerous to pressure cook; they may clog the vent.)

Lentil-Nut Loaf

2 c. lentils   1 c. chopped walnuts
2 small onions, chopped   1 c. chopped almonds
4 cloves garlic, minced   6 eggs, beaten
6 celery ribs, chopped   2 t. sea salt
1 c. bread crumbs   1 T. basil
2/3 c. rolled oats   2 t. thyme

Follow cooking method for Lentils. Sauté onions, garlic, and celery in a little oil until tender. Mix with lentils. Add seasonings and other ingredients. Mix well and put into two oiled loaf pans and bake at 375° for 1 hour or more. Serve plain, or with tomato sauce or hot sauce.

Variations:

Add 1 c. chopped tomatoes and 1½ c. cheese.
Add 2 c. chopped, hard-boiled eggs. Serve with hot gravy.

Lentil Burgers

2 c. lentils, cooked   ¼ c. carrots, grated
½ c. onions, chopped   ½ c. wheat germ or bread
¼ c. celery, chopped fine   crumbs
½ c. sunflower seeds (raw or   2 t. sea salt
   toasted)   2 t. thyme

Mix well and shape into patties. Fry in a little oil in 400° oven. Serve plain or top with cheese or gravy.

Pasta

Well-cooked pasta is tender, yet firm; not sticky. To cook pasta, follow the package directions for each kind of noodle. One standard method is to bring water to a boil, add noodles, salt, and oil (oil prevents noodles from sticking together); and return to a boil. Reduce heat to medium-low and continue cooking 7-10 minutes, until tender. Drain immediately and rinse with cold water to remove excess starch to prevent sticking. Shorten cooking time slightly if pasta is to be used in a combination dish or casserole that will be cooked longer. The less water used, the more vitamins. Or, make your own noodles (below). It's not as difficult as it may sound.

Homemade Noodles

4 c. flour	4 T. oil
2 t. sea salt	⅓ c .water
4 eggs	

Put flour in a bowl or on a floured board. Make an indentation, or hole, in the middle. Mix egg, oil, salt, and water. Pour into hole. Work the mixture until flour forms a ball of dough. Knead the dough 10 minutes. Cover and let sit 1 hour.

Roll out the dough on a floured surface, flouring your rolling pin to prevent sticking. Keep turning dough over and roll as thin as you can get it. Cut into noodles of desired width. Let dry 30 minutes. Then cook. If noodles are to be stored, let them dry thoroughly and place in a covered jar. *Yield: 4-6 servings.*

To Cook:

1 t. sea salt	1 t. oil
4 c. water	8 oz. Homemade Noodles

Bring water to boil; leave pan uncovered. Add sea salt, oil, and noodles. Cook until done. To test, press a piece of noodle against side of pan. It should break—clean and easy.

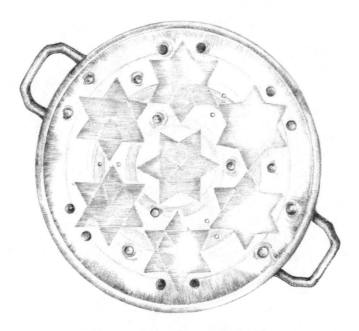

Pancake Noodles and Broth

2 eggs, separated
sea salt
1 c. flour
1 c. milk

oil, butter, or margarine
(to grease pan)
6 c. broth

Blend yolks, salt, flour, and milk. Stir well and fold in egg whites. Grease the pan lightly, and drop mixture in 1 T. at a time, tilting pan in all directions to spread batter very thin. Fry on one side 2-3 minutes, or until done. Drop gently onto a board, cut into thin, noodle-like strips and drop into hot broth. Serve with chives sprinkled on top.

Spinach Noodles
(Or other vegetable noodle.)

Prepare as Homemade Noodles, omitting water. Add 2 to 4 T. spinach, either pureed in a blender, or steamed for 30 seconds then chopped very fine. Add with other ingredients. If dough isn't wet enough, add more puree; or, if using chopped spinach, add more water. You may also use other greens.

Seven Quick Noodle Dishes

4 c. cooked noodles	⅔ c. basil
⅓ c. butter	1 c. ground almonds
2 T. tamari	

Melt butter and add remaining ingredients. Stir into noodles.
Yield: 4-6 servings.

Six Variations—Add:

Cream, olives, mushrooms, cheese.

Butter, garlic, Parmesan cheese.

Bleu cheese, dry mustard, chopped onion, croutons.

Sunflower seeds, chopped green peppers, minced garlic,
cumin, curry, tamari.

Cream cheese, cinnamon (mix in when noodles are still hot).

Scalded poppy seeds (scald with boiling water or scalded
milk). Soak 3 hours and put through a blender or food mill. Mix
into noodles with butter and poppy seeds.

Udon Noodles

These are hard-wheat noodles you can purchase in oriental
food sections or stores. Cooking directions are on the package.
The noodles are a little thicker than spaghetti and taste so good!
(See Udon Fun in section on Vegetarian Main Dishes.)

Soba

Soba is a buckwheat noodle, stronger in flavor; used in many
Japanese dishes. I like it with spaghetti sauce. You can use soba in
any of the Quick Noodle dishes above.

Noodle Puddin'
(A sweet treat.)

5 c. broad noodles, cooked
  (or shell macaroni)
1 c. cottage cheese
2 c. (16 oz.) cream cheese
1 c. ricotta cheese
1 c. whipping cream
4 eggs
½ c. orange juice

1 T. grated orange peel
Mandarin oranges
1 t. nutmeg
½ t. cinnamon
½ t. sea salt
8 T. honey
¼ c. dry bread crumbs
4 T. melted butter

Mix cream cheese with whipping cream until smooth and creamy. Add other cheeses. Separate eggs and add beaten yolks. Mix in orange juice with oranges. Mix with noodles and add spices. Pour into an oiled baking dish and top with bread crumbs and melted butter. Bake at 375° for 50 minutes. Cool.

Yield: 15 servings.

Noodles Parmesan

4 c. cooked noodles
½ c. butter
1-2 t. garlic powder
1 c. cream

½ c. Parmesan cheese
2 T. fresh parsley, chopped
1 t. kelp
sea salt to taste

Melt butter in a large pot, add garlic powder. Add noodles and toss. Add other ingredients. Garnish with paprika *or* cayenne, *or* chopped almonds. *Yield: 6-8 servings.*

Fried Noodles

4 c. cooked noodles
¼ c. butter
2 t. garlic powder

½ c. bread crumbs
sea salt to taste
1 t. kelp

Melt butter and add garlic powder. Add noodles and bread crumbs. Mix gently but well and fry until crisp.

Yield: 6-8 servings.

Mannicotti

Pasta:

1½ c. unbleached flour
1½ c. water
½ t. sea salt

Beat eggs until smooth. Add other ingredients and let stand ½ hour or more. Put 2 oz. of batter into an 8-inch skillet. Cook over medium heat until top is dry, but bottom is not brown. Cool and stack between wax paper. *Yield: 12.*

Filling:

2 lbs. ricotta (or ½ ricotta, ½ cottage cheese)
8 oz. mozzarella cheese, diced
8 oz. mozzarella cheese, grated
⅓ c. Parmesan cheese
2 eggs, beaten
1 t. sea salt
¼ t. pepper
1 T. parsley

Mix all ingredients. Spread 2 oz. of mixture down the center of each manicotti. Roll and seal with egg yolk. Lay side-by-side in a casserole dish. Cover with tomato sauce (see Sauces and Gravies), and sprinkle with grated mozzarella cheese. Bake ½ hour at 375°. *Yield 4-6 servings.*

Lasagne

6 lasagne noodles
5 c. tomato sauce
1 lb. ricotta cheese
1 lb. cottage cheese (farmers or hoop)
1 lb. mozzarella, sliced
1 t. garlic (granulated)
1 t. oregano
t. thyme
2 eggs, beaten
¼ c. finely chopped fresh parsley
2 c. chopped spinach
2 c. mushrooms, sliced
1 c. Parmesan cheese
½ c. green olives, sliced
½ c. green olives, sliced

Cook noodles until tender; 10 minutes. (It's best to prepare tomato sauce the night before.) Combine ricotta, cottage cheese, spices and eggs. In baking pan, lay down 3 noodles, spread with half of the cheese mixture—2 cups. Add 1 c. mushroom and 1 c. spinach; top with 2 c. tomato sauce and ½ c. Parmesan. Make a second layer the same way. On very top place olive slices and mozzarella.

Bake at 400° for 20-30 minutes or until mixture bubbles and cheese browns. Cool 10 minutes before cutting.

Lasagne freezes well either before or after baking. (Be sure to thaw frozen lasagne slowly in a refrigerator, so that the mixture doesn't become watery.) *Yield: 6-8 servings.*

Milk

What a joy it is to have our herds out in the mountains every day, moving across the hillsides, eating from the meadows, drinking from the streams, and lying in the sun.

The herders keep a watchful eye over their flocks, singing as they busily spin wool or make baskets.

From the tasty brush and grasses of the wilderness, blended together in harmony with Mother Earth and Father Sun, our goats form milk. In its essence of purity, the milk is an elixir of health, giving to our bodies many of the essential vitamins, minerals, and proteins.

There are many ways we have found to use this milk. In the following recipes we offer you those things we have developed with much patience and practice. Either goat's or cow's milk can be used in the recipes, keeping in mind that cow's milk has a much higher cream content than goat's milk. Goat's milk has a stronger flavor (not always favorable) the longer you process it.

Cheese is one of the most ancient of foods. Like bread, it was a practical way of carrying milk on a journey. It is an almost perfect whole food, rich in protein, fat, vitamins, and minerals. Decorated and festively wrapped, cheese also makes a beautiful gift.

Yoghurt

1 qt. milk	2 T. culture
½ c. nonfat dry milk powder	1-2 T. honey (optional)

Heat milk to scalding.* Set aside to cool. Mix milk powder into ¾ c. milk, whisking until it becomes a smooth paste. Add the rest of the milk.

After milk has cooled to wrist temperature (100°), add culture.** At this point, especially when we use goat's milk, it's nice to add 2 T. honey. It helps the yoghurt to grow and prevents it from having such a strong taste.

Put yoghurt into jars, turn lids all the way, then turn back an eighth of a turn.

To keep your yoghurt at a warm, steady temperature, you have several choices:

Put into a thermos chest with hot water and leave overnight.

Put into a thermos bottle and keep in a warm place overnight.

Put jars in a pan of hot water and cover with a towel.

Leave in a warm oven or on the back of the stove—or in the sun during the day and in a warm spot at night.

Let yoghurt set until it reaches the desired thickness. Remove and chill. Serve with fresh fruit or add preserves. And don't forget to save some yoghurt for culture.

If yoghurt doesn't turn out, it is usually because of the culture. If you add it to the milk too soon, it will be killed. Overuse can also destroy its action.

If you desire acidophilous, add it at the same time you add the culture.

* You scald the milk to kill the lactic acid, which makes cheese.

** We usually use "store-bought" culture to begin, then we save yoghurt from each batch we make as a culture for the next batch.

Yoghurt Cheese
(Texture like cream cheese.)

Follow yoghurt recipe. When it reaches the desired consistency, pour into cheesecloth (of a tight weave). Tie and hang up about 15 hours or until it reaches a creamy spread state. Be sure to put a container underneath to catch the whey.

You can add honey and cinnamon and serve with your favorite quick bread.

The whey, which is also very nutritional, can be used in baking or in salad dressings.

Soft Cheese

Raw milk (cow or goat) has all the ingredients you need for making good soft cheese. If the milk is left in a warm location, its lactic acid will cause it to separate into curds and whey. The amount of time varies with the temperature. It can take anywhere from 12 to 36 hours to curdle in 70°-100° weather, depending on the constancy of the temperature.

If the milk is overheated, the lactic acid is killed, and the milk is prevented from separating.

To tell when the cheese is ready to be harvested, put your finger into the curd at an angle and lift. If the curd breaks clean over your finger it's ready.

Sun Cheese

This is the easiest way to make cheese, and a great way to use up milk that is starting to turn. All you have to do is place your milk in a glass jar and cover. Put it in the sun for a few days until it separates into curds 'n whey.* To quicken the process you must keep it at a steady temperature; so, bring it in at night, moving carefully so you don't mix the curds 'n whey, and leave it in a warm place.

This particular cheese, especially when made with goat's milk, is a bit tart, so you may want to add seasonings: caraway, salt, and parsley; honey and cinnamon; ground, roasted sesame seeds; crushed garlic, parsley, and salt; basil, rosemary, and garlic.

Be careful when removing curds. It is best to try to scrape them from the top and not mix in with the whey, or they will be too soggy. Try a strainer.

* To speed up the process you may add lemon juice or vinegar (2-3 lemons per gallon, or ¼ c. vinegar).

Another help in speeding up the process and using the sun's energy all year 'round is a Sun Cheese box. We built a rectangular-shaped box with glass sides and top, and set the jars inside.

Rennetless Top o' Stove Cheese

This is another easy way to make soft cheese. Put milk in a pot and place over medium heat. Add lemon juice or vinegar. Stay close and stir frequently to prevent sticking and scorching. When milk curdles and separates, it is done. Skim off top curds, salt and serve.

If a drier cheese is desired, hang in a cheesecloth (fine-weave) bag for a couple of days, or press. An easy way to press this cheese is to put it in a cheesecloth bag and set it in a collander. Place a rock or other heavy object on top of the cheese to weight it down. This will press the cheese. Make sure there is a pan underneath to catch the whey. After 2-5 days, when the desired amount of liquid is removed, you may serve the cheese or dry it out still more by hanging it up for a day, or until of the consistency desired.

Season as in Sun Cheese or use in salad dressing.

If you scorch the milk—but catch it before the flavor gets too bad—add some hickory seasonings and fool 'em with smoked cheese!

Mock Cream Cheese

Follow Sun Cheese recipe. Do not add lemon or vinegar. When ready, hang curds in a cheesecloth bag 6-12 hours, and there it is!

Cottage Cheese

Follow Sun Cheese recipe. You can use rennet to quicken the process. Gently break the curds with your hands. Then heat the curds 'n whey to 90° for half an hour or until curds are of desired firmness. Salt and drain.* Chill curds, add a little milk or cream, and serve.

* For small curds pour ice-cold water over the large curds and they will separate. Chill.

Kefir

Proceed as in yoghurt recipe, using kefir culture instead of yoghurt culture.

Cream

To separate cream, pour milk into a shallow pan, let set until cream rises and skim off. Of course, if you have a cream separator, that's the thing to use.

Butter

Separate cream and put into a jar. Should be fairly cool (50-60°). Shake jar for 35-50 minutes. (This is a good time to have a friend or two around to take turns!) When the cream forms a large lump (which happens rather suddenly), pour through a strainer, reserving the liquid as buttermilk for cooking or drinking.

Pour a small amount of cold water over the butter and drain off. (This may be repeated if necessary. Butter may even still be creamy enough to put back into buttermilk, add more cold water, and rework.)

Work finished butter with a spoon or paddle and mold to desired shape; store.

Sour Cream

Combine 1 c. sweet cream with 1½ T. lemon juice or 1⅓ T. vinegar and let set.

Hard Cheeses

To make milk into hard cheese, you must add something that will coagulate and separate the curds from the whey. Rennet is usually used. Rennet is an animal product made from the stomach acid of an unweaned calf or other animal, or from the lining membrane of the stomach (especially the fourth stomach) of a cud-chewing animal (goats and calves).

Certain extracts of wild thistle, wild artichokes, or stinging nettles, will also coagulate the milk.

Tools and supplies you will need include a cheese thermometer, a large kettle, a knife, cheesecloth, a cheese press, and rennet tablets or powder.

Basic Hard Cheese

Be sure to use milk that is of good quality. Sour milk makes a sour, tart cheese, To make 2 lbs. of cheese you will need 8 qts. of milk. We have had our best results using 4 qts. from our evening milking and 4 qts. from the morning milking.

Heat milk on the top of your stove at medium heat until it is lukewarm. Remove from heat and add half a rennet tablet. Let stand until curd forms. This takes about 45 minutes.

Cut curds into small chunks with a knife and gently stir with your hands.

Now slowly heat the curds 'n whey, letting temperature rise about 1½° every 5 minutes until temperature has reached 102°. It is best to use a double boiler. Be very careful that you do not heat the curds past 102°. Use a cheese thermometer.

The temperature is important because it determines the texture. If the temperature is too hot the cheese will be rubbery.

It is also important to keep stirring to maintain an even, constant temperature and to keep curds from sticking together.

When firm curds form, remove pan from heat and put aside to cool, stirring occasionally. When cold, salt and pour curds into a cheesecloth bag. Hang it up to drain for a few days; or you can press out liquid.

You can add some spices if you wish. (See suggestions for Sun Cheese.)

Feta

Follow the recipe for Basic Hard Cheese. After it has hung for a few days, take it down and roll it in salt. Put in a press and resalt it every day for seven days (the salt removes some of the liquid), keeping the press tight in between saltings. When the cheese is thoroughly drained, store until ready to serve.

I have made this cheese by just salting it and putting it in a gallon jar, wedging in the cheese so it doesn't touch bottom. The whey drains into the bottom of the jar and I pour it out every morning when resalting the cheese. The method is not as effective.

Bleu Cheese Culture

Take a culture of mold from aged bleu cheese and insert it into a loaf of bread. Keep in a moist, dark place for six weeks. When the bread has crumbled completely and the mold has separated, dry the mold into a powder. Bottle and cork tightly.

To use, sprinkle dried mold on fresh cheese. You can pierce the cheese with the head of a needle in several places. Salt lightly and let rest several days. When mold has had a good start, pierce the cheese in at least 60 places to let air reach the mold deep inside the cheese. Keep in a cool, dark place. Age 2-5 months.

Sea Cheese

Heat milk to 85°. Add 1 rennet tablet. Let stand until a firm curd forms (45 minutes). Break up curd with hands. Heat slowly, stirring constantly to as high a heat as the hand can stand. Gather curd in the hands and knead to a firm ball. Return to whey and set aside to cool. Drain, press, wax, and store.

Ricotta

Follow recipe for Sea Cheese. Before returning cheese to whey, heat the whey until a coat of cream rises to the top. Add 1 qt. milk (per 10 qts. whey). Stir, heating until almost boiling. When curd rises, add 1 c. strong vinegar. Stir well; curd will come together. Drain curd. Salt to taste; serve fresh.

Homemade Rennet from Goats

The goat has four stomachs. The fourth of these (boda bag stomach) contains an enzyme that curdles milk. The goat should preferably be unweaned, although goats up to six months old and weaned can be used. When the goat is butchered, the fourth stomach is cut open, cleaned out, salted, and dried. Once dried, the stomach is made into a powder, using a food grinder or a mortar and pestle. Store in an airtight jar until needed.

Using Homemade Rennet

We use about ½ t. of our homemade rennet powder for every 1-3 gallons of milk. It is hard to specify an exact amount of powder, because that from the stomach of a younger, unweaned animal tends to be stronger than that from an older one. A good guideline is that the curds should be firm (not too soft or hard).

Put the powder in a small square of cheesecloth and tie it up. Soak the bag in 1 c. warm water. Let sit 12-24 hours. Remove bag and use water in place of rennet tablets.

Of course, you can buy rennet tablets and with them will come very thorough directions for use.

Pressing Cheese

The easiest method of cheese-making is simply hanging the curds in a cheesecloth bag and letting them drip until dry. This makes a soft, creamy cheese.

If you would like a little harder cheese, there is a fairly easy method. Put the cheesecloth bag, after drying, into a colander, and press it with a "follower" such as a plate, or a piece of wood.

Put a rock or other weight on the "follower" to keep the cheese under pressure.

The very best method for making blocks of hard cheese requires the use of a cheese press. You can make such a press just as we did, if you wish.

We first made a round metal mold, 8 inches in diameter and 4 inches deep. (This makes blocks of cheese weighing from 5-10 lbs.) A wooden "follower" was cut the same diameter as the mold and sanded and oiled.

To use the press, line the mold with cheesecloth, with enough surplus to pull over the top of the cheese. Place the salted, seasoned curds in the mold, and press firmly to fit. Fold the cheesecloth over the top of the curds and smooth it out to prevent your final cheese block from cracking. Insert the "follower" and put 10-15 pounds of weight on it.

After a few hours, when whey has stopped draining, the weights should be removed and the cheese turned over and pressed again from the other side. Leave like this 12-24 hours.

Remove cheese from the mold and remove the cheesecloth from the cheese.

Cheese Press

The next step is to allow the cheese to form a rind. The cheese should be salted all over. This will help to form a rind by removing any excess moisture. If there are any cracks, it is important to get them out now. Dip your finger in warm salt water and rub cracks until smooth. The rind is very important if the cheese is to be aged.

The first day after removing cheese from the mold and salting, it should be turned 2-3 times to prevent moisture build-up underneath. It takes 2-5 days to form a rind, so each day following the first, the cheese should be salted and turned twice.

If any deep cracks appear, the cheese should not be aged for any great length of time. If small cracks appear, try the "warm salt water'n finger" method (above).

Aging Cheese

One of the most important factors in aging cheese is the place where you age it. (A spring box is an ideal place.) Your cellar or cheesebox must have a constant temperature of 50°-55° and be well-ventilated to prevent mold growth. It is nice to have removable shelves so they can be aired in the sunshine now and then and kept very clean.

The quality of the milk used should be good, for aging will make the flavors stronger. Sour milk, for example (especially goat), makes really sour, tart cheese.

Be sure the cheese has a good rind on it before beginning to age.

Once you begin the aging process, check the cheeses every few days, turning them and scraping off any mold. We let our cheese age 4-6 weeks. After 2 weeks it begins to have a distinctive, yet still mild flavor. Experiment—your own tastebuds will tell you how long it should be aged.

When the cheese is properly aged you can either eat it immediately or wax it and store it.

Homemade Ice Cream
(Using ice cream maker.)

To start ice cream making you need lots of ice (8 trays of cubes if your ice is from the refrigerator). The more ice you have, the harder and thicker the ice cream will become as you churn it. Pour the batter into the middle container of the ice cream maker. Insert container into outer tub. Pour a layer of rock salt on the bottom of the tub, add a layer of ice, then alternate salt and ice layers to the top. Then get in there and turn that crank! It usually takes about 20 minutes to make thick ice cream.

Basic Vanilla Ice Cream Mix

1 gal. milk	1 t. sea salt
2 eggs (optional)	1 t. vanilla
2 c. honey	

Kelp powder added to this or any of the following ice cream recipes will help to stabilize the mixture (4 t. kelp to 1 gal. milk). This amount won't alter the flavor. With Basic Vanilla as a starting point, try some of the following suggestions. *Yield: 1 gallon.*

Maple-Walnut

Substitute 2-3 c. maple syrup for honey. Add 3 c. broken walnuts.

Orange-Banana

Grate 4 or 5 oranges, add 3 c. honey, and soak for 2 hours. Mash 3 cups bananas, add 1 t. sea salt and 1 c. milk, and combine this mixture with orange mixture. Be sure it is all well-mixed. Add to a gallon of milk and churn.

Carob-Burnt Almond

Beat together 1 c. milk, 1 c. roasted carob powder, 1 c. honey, and 1 t. sea salt.

Add 1 c. honey; 2 c. roasted, chopped almonds; and 2 t. cinnamon.

Mix with a gallon of milk and churn.

Fresh Fruit

Add 3-4 c. fresh fruit.

Fig

In the gallon of milk to be used in the Basic Vanilla recipe, soak 3 c. figs overnight.

Mint

Add 1 c. fresh mint or ½ c. dried mint, or equivalent mint extract.

Frozen Treats

(Ice creams without an ice cream freezer.)

Frozen Treat with Eggs

4 eggs, well-beaten
½ c. honey

4 c. cream
2 t. vanilla

In a double boiler, cook eggs, honey, and 2 c. cream until it starts to thicken. Remove and chill. Meanwhile, whip remaining 2 c. cream and vanilla until stiff. Add to egg mixture. Put in freezer until mixture is frozen.

Frozen Treat with Gelatin

2 t. gelatin
¼ c. water (cold)
½ c. milk
½ c. honey

⅛ t. sea salt
2 t. vanilla (vanilla bean)
2 c. cream

Dissolve gelatin in ¼ c. cold water. Meanwhile, scald milk together with honey and salt, then add vanilla (or, if you're using vanilla bean, scrape out beans into the milk when cooling). Add gelatin. Whip cream until stiff and fold into chilled mixture. Put into freezer until frozen. Try adding 1½ c. carob chips.

Blender Quick Sherbet

2 c. water (or half water,
    half juice)
1 c. honey
2 T. lemon juice

3 t. gelatin
¼ c. cold water
2 qts. strawberries
4 egg whites

Bring water, honey, and lemon juice to a boil and continue boiling for 3 minutes. Add 3 t. gelatin dissolved in ¼ c. cold water. Blenderize strawberries, then mix into the gelatin mixture. Chill until nearly firm, then beat egg whites until stiff. Add fruit mixture slowly, beating well. Freeze. You may use ripe raspberries, peaches, or apricots in place of strawberries.

Lime or Lemon Sherbet

2 t. gelatin (dissolved in ¼ c.
    water)
2 c. water

¾ c. honey
1 c. lime juice
3 egg whites

Boil water and honey. Add gelatin and cool down until mixture is lukewarm. Add lime juice. Beat egg whites until stiff and fold in fruit-juice mixture. Beat well. Freeze.

Pineapple Sherbet

2 t. gelatin
3 c. crushed pineapple
½ c. honey
¼ c. cold water

1 c. orange juice
⅓ c. lemon juice
3 egg whites

Dissolve gelatin in water. Combine fruit, juice, and honey and add to gelatin. Freeze until nearly firm. Beat egg white until stiff. Add fruit mixture slowly and beat until fluffy. Return to freezer until frozen.

Sour Cream or Yoghurt Freeze

2 c. sour cream or yoghurt
2 bananas, mashed
2 papaya, mashed
6 T. honey

1 c. juice (lemon and honey)
1 c. other fruit of your choice
　(persimmons)
1 c. milk powder

Blend all ingredients until smooth. Freeze. If you like this mixture thick, try adding milk powder.

Corn

(From the Mother to us all.)

Corn is one of the most ancient of foods, and is important in America's culture.

We feel especially blessed that the Brotherhood of the Sun was given the Hopi corn seed by White Bear, beloved friend and Chief of the Hopis. He explained to us that this seed was brought to our continent in ancient time from the previous world, or Motherland.

This corn produces seed in four colors: white, red, blue, and yellow, symbolizing the four races of man, the four directions, and the four elements—air, earth, fire, and water. The Hopis were instructed to keep each seed pure to maintain the sacred truths, which they have done to this day.

White Bear gave us special instructions on how to plant this vital seed, emphasizing that it should not cross-pollinate and become like the mixed corn, commonly known as "Indian" corn, which resulted from improper planting by tribes in the past.

The Hopi corn is filled with life-force. When you eat it you can somehow "feel" it nourishing your body! It is one of our main staples, used daily. We give thanks to our red brothers for their gift to us, and to our Creator for this gift of life.

We are also blessed to be able to grow good sweet corn. It is so delicious that many times it is eaten even before it reaches the stove!

Although we use Hopi corn, the recipes that follow can be made with any dried corn or cornmeal sold in the markets.

Storing, Husking, and Shelling

We let our corn dry on the stalk until we harvest it sometime in November. Even then it is left on the cobs and stored in burlap bags or onion sacks. We keep the best corn for seed and use the rest to shell.

There are several methods of shelling corn. One is to simply rub two ears together. There is also a small hand tool that runs over the ear and shells it. Because we have to do a large quantity, we use a hand-cranked husker and sheller into which we feed the cobs and just turn the crank!

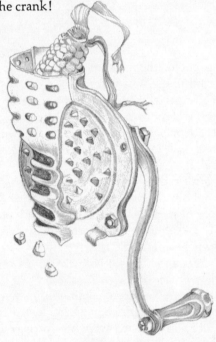

Grinding

The mortar and pestle has come from the original way of grinding employed by our red brothers. They used a long, cylindrical stone to grind the corn against a hard surface, such as a big rock. After a time, the grinding process would develop "bowls" in the rock.

We have since "advanced" to the use of Corona hand grinders and electric grinders. At the ranch, we have a stone grinder—bicycle powered!

Whatever equipment or method, grind the corn to desired fineness or consistency and use your favorite recipe!

We have found that corn has a sweetness of its own and can be used with or without sweetening.

Corncob Ash as a Leavening Agent

Corncob ash was long used as a leavening agent. You can still do it. Substitute equal amounts of ash for baking powder.

To make the ash, dry fresh cobs in the open air for two weeks, or use already dried corn and remove kernels. Ignite cobs and burn them in a heavy, open skillet. (They are slow to start; be patient!) Don't burn any paper, wood, or matches with them. When cobs are completely burned, cool and put through a fine strainer to remove large particles. Store in an airtight jar.

Another way to make ash is to wrap cobs in foil and leave in an oven overnight or until charred.

Cornmeal Mush

6 c. water   2 c. cornmeal
2 t. sea salt

Bring water to a boil. Meanwhile, mix cornmeal with just enough water to make a paste and remove all lumps. When water boils, add paste and salt. Mix in well with a whisk. Cook for 45 minutes to 1 hour on very low heat, stirring occasionally.

Fried Mush

When you have leftover mush, put it in a loaf pan in the icebox or just leave at room temperature until it "gels." Slice it and fry in a little oil until golden brown on the outside. Serve with butter and maple syrup.

Mush Crackers

You can make good crackers with leftover mush. Add flour to make a good, stiff dough. It's nice also to add rye flour and caraway seeds. Add oil.

When dough is of a good consistency for rolling, put on a floured board and roll to ⅛- to ¼-inch thickness. Cut in desired shape. Sprinkle pieces with sesame seeds and put on a well-greased cookie sheet. Bake at 450° for 20 minutes or until golden brown.

Corn-Rye Crackers

3 c. cornmeal
2½ c. rye flour
½ c. Tahini
¼ c. oil

1 c. water
1½ t. caraway seed
1 t. garlic powder
1 t. sea salt

Mix flour and cornmeal. In another bowl, mix oil and Tahini, then slowly add water. Combine the two mixtures and knead to be sure they are well-mixed.

Roll out on a floured board as thin as you like. We make it ¼-inch thick. To make round crackers, cut with cup or a mug upside down. You can have a saucer of water handy to dip the rim of the cup into—it prevents sticking.

Put on a well-greased cookie sheet and bake at 450° for 20 minutes or until golden brown and not moist. If you are making thinner crackers, baking time will be less.

This recipe makes 40 crackers. Serve what you need and store the rest for later use.

Corn Dumplin's

1 c. flour
½ c. cornmeal
2 eggs, beaten

¼ t. sea salt
1 t. baking powder
1 c. warm water

Mix dry ingredients. Add water and beat well to keep from lumping. Add eggs. Mix until smooth and thick. Drop by rounded teaspoonfuls into boiling broth. Cook 3-5 minutes, or until dumplings rise to surface. Remove and serve.

Corn Cakes

2 c. cornmeal
½ t. sea salt
4 eggs, separated

molasses (optional: add with
  egg yolks)

Barely moisten the cornmeal and salt with water. Beat in egg yolks. Fold in stiffly beaten egg whites. Spoon onto hot griddle and treat as pancakes.

Cornmeal Soup

¼ c. cornmeal

½ c. cold water

Mix and add to 1 qt. boiling vegetable broth. Add some fresh vegetables.

Corn Nuts

Soak whole, dried corn overnight. Drain on absorbent toweling or paper towel. Put a little oil in a fry pan. Heat and add corn. Cover and roast until golden brown. Salt and serve.

(Be careful when removing lid because some of the corn will pop.)

Apple-Corn Cookies
(From our bakery.)

¾ c. honey
¾ c. butter
2 eggs, beaten
1¾ c. cornmeal

1¼ c. soy flour
¼ t. sea salt
1 T. baking powder

Cream honey and butter. Add eggs and mix. Add cornmeal, soy flour, salt, and baking powder.

Now mix together as a filling: ⅜ c. applesauce, ¼ t. cinnamon, ¼ t. lemon juice, 2 t. honey.

Press out cookies, making an indentation in the middle of each. Fill with ½ t. filling to each cookie. Bake at 350° for 10 minutes.

Pinole

2 c. blue or white cornmeal   ½ t. cinnamon
½ c. sugar

Brown cornmeal in a hot (425°) oven, 8-10 minutes. (Spread a thin layer on a cookie sheet and stir several times to prevent scorching.) Add sugar and cinnamon (use like cocoa in about the same proportion) to hot milk, and simmer 15 minutes.

Indian Puddin'

1 c. cornmeal   ¼ t. nutmeg
1 c. molasses   1 t. vanilla
4 c. milk   1 egg, beaten
¼ c. butter   ½ c. raisins
1 t. cinnamon

Scald 3 c. milk. Meanwhile, mix cornmeal with remaining cup of milk to a smooth paste. Mix in with scalded milk. Bring to a boil, stirring constantly. Reduce heat to low and cook for 5 more minutes, stirring occasionally. Remove from heat. Add butter, spices, vanilla, and raisins and mix. Add egg.

Pour into greased casserole dish and set in a baking pan with hot water in it. Bake, uncovered, in slow oven (275°), 3 hours.

Basic Corn Bread

3 c. cornmeal   2 c. water
1 t. sea salt

Corn bread can be simple or extravagant. Use well-ground corn. Mix ingredients well, removing all lumps. Either bake in an oiled bread pan; or—if you desire a thinner, crunchier bread—bake in a larger, square pan. Bake at 375°, 1 hour. Time depends on the cornmeal. You don't want batter to be too dry. A variation on this recipe is to soak the cornmeal in liquid overnight. When you use milk, it's sweeter. You can also add ¼ c. oil if you wish.

Fluffy Corn Bread

Use Basic Corn Bread recipe but use 2 c. milk instead of water. Separate 3 eggs; mix in yolks. Add ¼ c. oil. Beat egg whites until stiff and fold into bread. Bake as for Basic Corn Bread.

Sweet 'n Fluffy Corn Bread

Follow the Fluffy Corn Bread recipe and before you fold in the egg whites, mix in ¼ c. honey or molasses.

You may also try adding rye flour, or fresh corn and green chilies; or substitute vegetable broth for water; or sprinkle top with sesame seeds!

If you really want a light, fluffy bread, use 2 t. baking powder.

Pan Bread

Use any of the corn bread recipes. Pour mixture ¼-inch thick into a hot skillet, lightly coated with oil. Cover and cook over medium heat about ½ hour. Turn bread over after 15 minutes. For variation, try adding kelp and some fresh greens.

Spoon Bread

2 c. milk	¾ c. butter
1½ c. yellow cornmeal	3 eggs, separated
1 t. sea salt	

Heat 1½ c. milk to scalding. Mix the remaining ½ c. milk with cornmeal and salt to make a smooth paste. Beat into scalded milk. Add butter and beaten egg yolks. Stir into cornmeal mixture. Beat egg whites to soft peaks and fold in batter. Pour into a greased 8-inch pan and bake at 350° for 45 minutes.

It's best when served with honey or maple syrup.

Corny Custard Bread

1 c. cornmeal	1 t. sea salt
1 c. whole wheat (or oatmeal, millet, or rice flour)	2 T. baking powder
	½ c. honey
2 c. milk	¼ c. oil
1 or 2 well-beaten eggs	

Mix together cornmeal, flour, salt, and baking powder. In a separate bowl, combine milk, eggs, honey and oil. Combine both mixtures and bake in a well-oiled pan at 375° for about 1 hour.

Northwind Corn Bread
(From our bakery.)

1¾ c. cornmeal	½ t. sea salt
1½ c. whole wheat flour	⅓ c. oil or melted butter
3 eggs	½ c. molasses
2 t. baking powder	2 c. water

Beat eggs. Add oil, molasses, and water and mix. Add dry ingredients. Pour into oiled bread pans. Bake at 400° for 1 hour.

Corn-Chia Bread
(From our bakery.)

¼ c. warm water	2½ t. sea salt
1 pkg .yeast	2 T. butter
1 T. honey	1½ c. whole wheat flour
1 c. milk	1 c. unbleached white flour
2 c. cornmeal	¾ c. sunflower seeds
¼ c. molasses	poppy seeds

Dissolve yeast in water. Add honey and let sit. Mixture will foam in 10 minutes.

Meanwhile, scald milk and add half of cornmeal and the molasses, salt, and butter. When lukewarm, combine with yeast. Add rest of cornmeal, other flours, and sunflower seeds. Knead for about 10 minutes.

Put in a greased bowl, cover and let rise in a warm place until double in volume—about 1 hour. Punch and shape into round loaf.

Put on greased cookie sheet. Baste top with egg white and sprinkle on poppy seeds. Let rise until double in volume. Bake at 375° for 40-45 minutes.

Corn-Rye Bread

4 c. cornmeal	4 egg yolks, beaten
2 c. rye flour	4 egg whites, beaten stiff
8 c. milk	1 t. sea salt
6 T. butter, melted	2 T. caraway seeds

Heat milk to scalding and pour over cornmeal. Mix well and let sit overnight. In morning, add rye flour, butter, egg yolks, salt, and caraway. Fold in egg whites. Pour into oiled baking pan and bake at 350° for 1 hour or until knife comes out clean.

Acorn-Corn Bread

3 c. cornmeal	2 c. milk
1 c. rye flour	1 t. sea salt
1 c. acorn meal	½ c. honey
3 eggs, separated	1 t. baking powder

Combine cornmeal, acorn meal and rye flour. Add oil, yolks, milk; then, salt and honey. Beat egg whites until stiff and fold into bread. Bake at 375°.

Corn-Cheese Muffins or Quick Bread

1 c. whole wheat pastry flour	2 eggs, slightly beaten
1 c. cornmeal	1 c. milk
1½ T. honey	¼ c. butter, melted
4 t. baking powder	½ to 1 c. grated cheese of
1½ t. sea salt	your choice

Sift dry ingredients together in a bowl. Make a well in the center and pour in eggs, milk, butter, and honey. Stir to a smooth batter and add cheese. Fill well-oiled muffin tins or loaf pans. Bake at 425°. Muffins for 15-20 minutes; bread for 45 minutes.

Corn Tortillas I

1 qt. dry corn   4 qt. water
1 T. lime (or 1 c. wood ashes)

The night before, put corn and lime into a large pot with water. Bring to a boil, and continue boiling for 2 minutes. Let stand until the next day. Wash the corn well and put through a grinder.

An alternate preparation: instead of letting it sit overnight you can boil the corn and lime until the covering of the corn looks loose and swollen. Wash until lime or wood ash is removed and hulls are loose enough to float away. Then grind.

Add enough water to ground corn to form into a ball. Be careful not to make the mixture too sticky. Pat out into thin tortillas. You can do it between your hands, roll them in between wax paper or in plastic bags with a rolling pin, or use a tortilla press. (See illustration next page.)

Cook on dry, unoiled skillet or griddle until flecked with brown on both sides. If you want a soft tortilla, you must keep turning every 20 seconds. *Yield: 18-24 tortillas.*

Corn Tortillas II

5 c. corn flour   sea salt
½ c. oil   warm water

Add enough warm water to form a dry dough. Be careful not to make it too sticky. Roll into balls 1¾ inches in diameter to desired thickness. *Yield: 24 tortillas.*

Cooked Whole Corn

Soak whole corn overnight. Cook the next day until soft. You can use a pressure cooker.

Sweet Corn

Put unhusked corn in water enough to come up to one-fourth depth of corn. Bring to a boil. Remove from heat and let sit, covered, 5 minutes. Serve. Leaving on husks retains more nutrients and flavor. If you husk corn first, steam for 8 minutes.

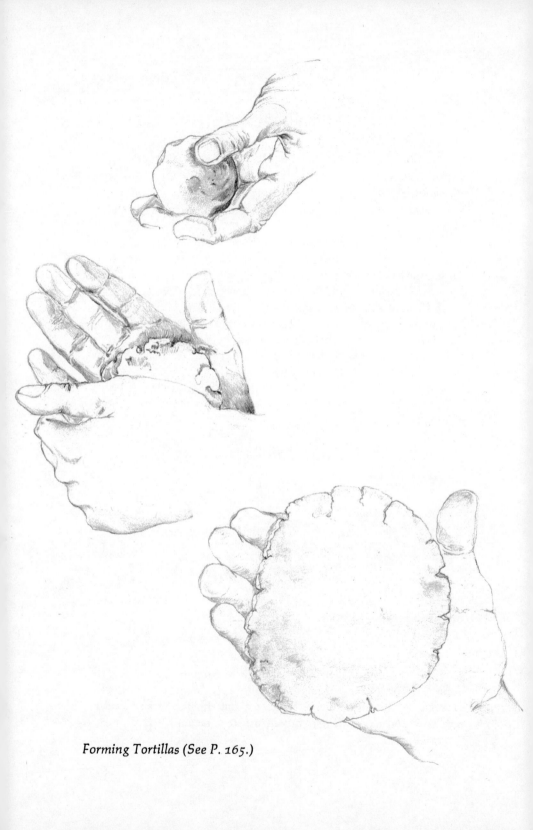

Forming Tortillas (See P. 165.)

Barbecued Corn

Soak corn in husks 2 hours. Put in hot coals and cook about 5 minutes or bake in oven.

Corn and Vegetables Sautéed

1 c. celery, chopped
1 med. onion, chopped
1 c. sunchokes, sliced
2 t. tarragon
1 T. Worcestershire sauce
1½ t. sea salt
2 T. flour

1½ c. cucumbers
3 c. fresh corn or whole boiled corn
1 c. tomatoes
2 t. cumin
2 t. paprika

Sauté in a skillet with oil, the celery, onion, and sunchokes, until onion is transparent. Add tomatoes, cucumbers, and corn. Add seasonings and continue sautéing on low heat about 5 minutes. Sprinkle with flour and mix well. Cook 5 more minutes. Serve hot. *Yield: 4-6 servings.*

Corn Chowder

2 c. corn
¼ c. celery, chopped
1 med. onion, chopped
¼ c. water

4 c. milk
4 T. butter
1 t. sea salt
pepper

Sauté corn, celery, and onion for 3 minutes. Add water and cover. Cook for 10 minutes. Meanwhile, scald milk and add butter, seasoning, and vegetables. Serve with a dash of paprika. *Yield: 4-6 servings.*

Creamed Corn

3 c. corn
1 c. milk
2 T. butter

½ t. sea salt
2 dashes pepper

Steam corn 5-8 minutes. Add remaining ingedrients. Serve hot as a side dish. *Yield: 4-6 side dish servings.*

Corn Pudding with Baco-Bits

3 c. fresh corn (about 6 ears)	2 eggs
4 T. butter	1 t. sea salt
3 T. unbleached white flour	2 t. parsley
1½ c. milk	¼ t. cayenne

Melt butter. Sauté flour until browned. Slowly add milk, stirring constantly until you have a thick sauce. Beat eggs and add to some of the sauce. Add salt, parsley, and cayenne. Scrape corn off cobs and add to mixture. Place in a casserole dish. Mix in the rest of the cream sauce. Sprinkle top with baco-bits. Bake at 350° for 20-30 minutes. *Yield: 4-6 servings.*

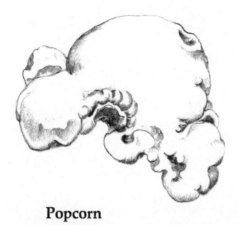

Popcorn

In the evenings we may find ourselves on the way to our lodge for a story reading. From the kitchen there come strange, popping sounds. As we come a little closer, our noses tell us that it's time for popcorn—and the story!

If we didn't know better, we would call popcorn a staple! Here is one of our favorite popcorn-popping methods. Place a pot over a high flame. Cover the bottom with oil. Put in just 3 or 4 kernels of popcorn and cover until they pop. Now be quick—it's time to put in the rest of the corn—not too much! You want all the kernels to be covered with a bit of oil. Put on a lid.

When the kernels begin to pop, begin shaking the pot over the flame. When the kernels are through popping, remove from heat and pour into a bowl. Add salt.

The next decision is whether to "dive in" or try variety seasoning. Here are some: butter; garlic powder and nutritional yeast; cayenne; powdered herbs; kelp; melted butter with fresh, minced garlic and Parmesan.

Remember the good old carmel corn? Well, just melt butter and add honey and/or molasses and pour over the popcorn until it's well-coated.

It is also possible to pop corn without oil, or with hardly any oil. I usually do put just a little oil in and heat the pan, following the method above. It is really important to continuously shake the pan to keep kernels from burning on the bottom.

Grains and Cereals

When winter has come and the north wind blows, our bodies need extra fuel for energy and warmth. Whole grains and freshly ground cereals help to provide this fuel. Many times we have reflected on the spring planting of many rows of seed. We had watched them grow. We remembered the joyous time of harvest.

An Aztec Indian brother came and taught us many simple ways of the land, one of them being the harvesting of wheat. We went out into the shining sun, sickle in hand, and cut the matured wheat. We bound the bundles with some of the wheat itself. It was satisfying to stand back after a hard day's work and see all those bundles, neat and tall.

The bundles were brought in from the fields and we prepared to separate the wheat from the chaff. On a windy day we beat the wheat from the stalks and winnowed it in the air. Then we gleaned the remainder so that all was saved.

These are the whole grains, available to you at natural food stores wherever you live.

Whole Grains

When choosing grains for your cooking needs it is best to buy whole grains. When grains are cracked or ground, much of the nutrient value is lost.

Think of what "whole grain" means. Whole, as defined in a dictionary, means having all its proper parts, without subtraction, organic unity. The various nutrients are reliant on each other in providing balance and "wholeness" in nourishing your body. If you eat truly whole foods in adequate variety you don't have to worry about vitamins and other nutrients.

You may use several methods in preparing whole grains in order to provide a variety of tastes and textures.

Whole Grain and Cereals

When cooking whole grain and cereals, first wash the grains. Possibly two rinses will be necessary (although the more washing, the more nutrient loss). Bring water to a boil, add the grain and salt, cover and return to a boil. Reduce heat to low, keep pan covered and continue cooking. The amount of time needed will vary (see Cereals), or you can often tell just by listening or smelling when all the water has been cooked out. That's the time to remove from heat, lift up the lid and check. If your grain is cooked, give it a stir to moisten the top grains. Keep covered until ready to serve.

You can, if you wish, put the water, salt, and grain in a pot of cold water and bring to a boil. From that point, follow method outlined above.

Most of our cookware is preseasoned which helps to keep the grains from sticking to the sides and bottom.

For pressure cooking, decrease proportions to 1½ c. water to 1 c. grain. Bring to full pressure. Reduce heat and cook 45 minutes.

Many Ways with Many Grains

Try sautéing grains first in a large skillet with a little oil. When the grain has browned add water (2 c. water to 1 c. grain). Cover and simmer about 30 minutes or until fluffy.

You can also sprout the grains first, then steam them or use in casseroles, burgers, or breads.

Remember that 1 c. uncooked grain equals 2 c. cooked grain and serves 2-5 persons.

Buckwheat groats and bulghur wheat cook in the same amount of time, about 25 minutes. Use 1 c. grain to 2 c. water. Both grains are best when sautéed, then steamed.

Millet is sometimes substituted for rice. It is good in casseroles, refried, in loaves, or as cereal. Use 1 c. millet to 2 c. water. Cooks in 30 minutes. Easily digested.

To cook barley use 1 c. barley to 2 c. water. Cooks in about 90 minutes.

For rye use 1 c. rye to 2 c. water. Cooks in about 60 minutes. Great in casseroles, sprouted, or in cereals.

Whole wheat "berries," or kernels, also require 2 c. water to 1 c. berries. Cook in 60 minutes. Good in cereals or casseroles.

Oat groats, 1 c. groats to 2 c. water. Cooks in 60 minutes. Corn—see Corn section.

If you have your own grinder you can coarsely grind these grains into grits, which cuts cooking time and can add a different texture to breads and burgers.

All of these whole grains (except bulghur) make a great flour, especially when freshly ground.

You can also buy flakes, whole grains prepared in a process that partially cooks and compresses the whole grain into a flake. It gives the grain a different texture and makes it cook faster.

Vegetable-Bulghur or Buckwheat Groats

2 c. bulghur
1 med. onion, chopped

4 c. vegetable broth
3 T. tamari

Sauté bulghur or groats in a large skillet with oil and chopped onions. Cook until browned. Add some vegetable broth and Tamari and cover. Simmer 30-45 minutes until tender. Season to taste. *Yield: 4-6 servings.*

Kasha

1 c. groats	6 c. water
1 c. cornmeal	sea salt
½ c. rice	tamari (optional)
¼ c. sesame seeds	garlic powder

Boil, then turn down heat. Cook over medium-low heat for about 25 minutes. Season to taste. *Yield: 5-7 servings.*

Sprouted Rye Burgers

2 c. sprouted rye	1 egg
¼ c. bread crumbs	½ t. garlic powder
¼ c. carrots and zucchini, grated	1 t. kelp
¼ c. onion, grated	¼ t. cayenne

Steam rye sprouts for 15 minutes. Allow to cool. Mash or grind them and add rest of the ingredients. Shape into 4 patties and fry or bake on a lightly oiled surface until browned. You can also use any of the other grains. *Yield: 4 servings.*

Meat Substitute

1 c. millet, roasted and ground	1 T. kelp
1 c. rye flakes, ground	1 t. celery seed
1 c. soy flakes, ground	2 t. garlic powder
½ c. minced, dehydrated onion	1 t. thyme
½ c. parsley	⅓ c. tamari
1 T. oregano	2¾ c. bouillon broth

Mix all ingredients and pour hot bouillon over mixture. Stir and let sit until all liquid is soaked in.

Ways To Use:

Shape into patties and fry.
Meat balls or loafs.
Use in casseroles as an alternating layer.
Serve with cream sauce.
Add nutritional yeast.

Millet Mixture

3 c. cooked millet
2 c. onion, chopped
1 c. celery, chopped fine
1 c. almonds, ground
1 c. sour cream (optional)
¼ c. butter

2 T. tamari
1½ t. garlic powder
1½ t. rosemary
1 t. oregano
1 t. thyme
1 t. curry (optional)

In a large skillet, melt butter and add onions, celery, and almonds. Sauté until almonds are browned. Add millet, seasonings and, if desired, sour cream. This recipe can be used with barley, rye, rice, buckwheat, groats, or bulghur.

Yield: 10-12 servings.

"Where's the Meat" Loaf

4 c. cooked barley
3 eggs, beaten
5 slices whole wheat toast, crumbled
½ lg. onion
3 green onions

½ c. mushrooms, sliced
1 T. tamari
1 T. dry mustard
1 t. thyme
1 t. sea salt
1 t. garlic powder

Combine ingredients. Put in an oiled loaf pan and bake at 350° for about 45 minutes. Top with tomato paste halfway through baking, if you like. We made this recipe larger, because the leftovers are great the next day in sandwiches with ketchup.

Yield: 2 loaves.

Mock Meatballs

2 c. cooked grain
¼ c. sunflower seeds, ground
½ c. onion, finely chopped

1 egg (optional)
season to taste
whole wheat pastry flour

In making meatballs the main idea is to combine ingredients that will bind well together. So when making these meatballs you can use any of the ingredients mentioned in "Where's the Meat" Loaf. If your mitxure is sticky enough you can omit the egg.

Combine ingredients. Shape into 2-inch balls. Roll in flour and fry until golden brown. Serve with some gravy.

Yield: 4-6 servings.

Brown Rice

1 c. uncooked rice   sea salt, if desired
4 c. water

Wash rice and prepare by cold water or boiling water method.
Takes 1 hour. Be sure not to stir it or it will become gummy.
Yield: 2 c. cooked rice

Steamed (Fluffier) Rice

Cook rice until the water is absorbed. Remove immediately
and put in a collander. Place collander in a pan with boiling water.
(Don't let water touch rice.) Cover and steam until tender; 15-20
minutes.

Rice can be served plain or with vegetables and/or a sauce, in
casseroles, as rice cakes, refried, or in soups or stew.

Refried Rice
(Or any grain.)

2 c. cooked brown rice
1½ c. onions, chopped
1 T. tamari
3 eggs, beaten

1½ c. mushrooms, sliced
1 t. sea salt
1 t. garlic powder or fresh
cloves, minced

Put oil in a large frying pan over medium heat. When oil is hot, add onions and garlic and cook 2 minutes. Add rice and Tamari, and cook until it begins to brown. Add mushrooms and seasonings and mix well. Move rice to one side of the pan. Pour in half of the eggs and cook until not so runny. Mix in with rice. Cook rest of the eggs and mix in.

Serve plain with Chinese vegetables, Chinese sauce, or Sweet 'n Sour Sauce. *Yield: 4-6 servings.*

Rice Casserole

2 c. cooked brown rice
1½ c. chopped vegetables

1 c. cheese sauce
¾ c. chopped nuts

Bake at 375° until bubbling. See Rice Cakes. *Yield: 4-6 servings.*

Rice Salad

1½ c. cooked rice
⅓ c. Clipper Belle Dressing
¼ c. yoghurt
¼ c. scallions, finely chopped

¼ c. green pepper, finely
chopped
1 T. parsley or watercress

Toss and serve. You can use other dressings and you can substitute bulghur or rye for the rice. *Yield: 3-4 servings.*

Rolled Oats

1 c. oats
2 c. water

⅛ t. sea salt

Bring water to a boil. Add oats and salt and bring to a boil again. Reduce heat to low and cover. Continue cooking 10 minutes or, if you like your oatmeal heavier (stickier), cook longer. *Yield: 2 c.*

Cream of Wheat, Rice, Rye

Toast grain first, then grind (1 c. ground grain to 3 c. water). Bring water to a boil. Add salt and cereal and stir. Return to a boil and turn to low heat. Cover and cook 1 hour, stirring occasionally.

Variations:

Serve with honey, molasses, or syrup.
Top with fruit.
Mix in some dried fruit during cooking.
If you're not into a sweet taste, try Tamari and some nutritional yeast.

Whole Grain Mush

3 c. water	¼ c. wheat berries
¼ c. whole oats	¼ c. buckwheat groats
¼ c. barley	¼ t. sea salt

Bring the water to a boil. Add grains and salt and return to boiling. Lower heat, cover, and cook 90 minutes, stirring occasionally. *Yield: 2 c.*

Cornmeal Mush and Fried Mush

(See Corn section.)

Acorn Meal

You can add ground acorn meal or grits (see instructions) to any of the cereals.

Sprouted Grain Cereal

Wheat, rye, oats, sunflower seeds, corn, or millet can be used. After sprouting (see sprouting time in Sprout section), steam sprouts 15-30 minutes, until tender.

Millet

1 c. millet   ¼ t. sea salt
2 c. water

Bring water to a boil and add millet and salt. Return to boiling, then reduce heat to medium-low and cook for 30 minutes. If you want it creamier, use 1 c. millet to 3 c. water and cook 45 minutes.

Add dried fruit, if desired, or try cinnamon or nutmeg.
Yield: 2 c.

Rye or Barley

These grains make a great cereal. They take a little longer to cook, about 90 minutes. Use 1 c. grain to 3 c. water.

Granola I

4 c. oats   ¾ c. almonds, slivered
¾ c. sunflower seeds   1 T. cinnamon
¾ c. coconut, shredded   ⅔ c. molasses or honey
½ c. sesame seeds   ⅓ c. oil

Oven Method:

Mix dry ingredients. Mix honey with oil. Combine wet and dry ingredients. Spread granola over cookie sheet. Bake at 325° for 30-40 minutes, stirring often for even baking. When cool, mix in ¾ c. raisins. *Yield: 5-7 servings.*

Skillet Method:

Combine ingredients in a heavy skillet. You don't want to fill the skillet too full; if it isn't big enough, make the granola in batches. Cook over medium heat, stirring constantly to cook evenly and prevent burning. Cooks in about 10 minutes.

Granola II

1 c. oats
1 c. rye flakes
1 c. soy flakes
1 c. wheat flakes
¾ c. squash seeds
¾ c. pumpkin seeds
½ c. wheat germ (optional)
⅔ c. molasses or honey

⅓ c. oil
½ c. sesame seeds
½ c. walnuts, coarsely
  chopped
½ c. cashews
½ c. coconut, shredded
1 t. coriander
1 t. allspice

Prepare as in Granola I.

Muesli
(*Energy-packed cereal.*)

1 c. oats
⅔ c. dried apricots, chopped
¼ c. dried apples, chopped
⅛ c. sesame
¾ t. cinnamon
¼ t. sea salt

1½ c. milk
⅛ t. nutmeg
1½ t. vanilla
½ c. almonds, slivered (or half
  almonds, half walnuts)
½ c. sunflower seeds

Soak oats, apricots, apples, and spices in milk or water overnight. Next morning, add nuts and sunflower seeds. Serve raw.

If there is leftover cereal, add flour, eggs, and honey and/or date sugar to make some good tastin' cookies for lunch.

Variations:

Try adding figs, currants.
Grind chia seeds and add.
Sprinkle with bee pollen.

Ground Seeds

Try grinding any of the following seeds: sesame, sunflower, pumpkin, squash, flax, chia.

Mix with carob, coconut, ground raisins, honey, or molasses, and serve.

Also try some Tahini and mashed banana—it's a real energy boost and a sweet treat, too!

Breads

What a feeling of love comes from the kitchen where the aroma of freshly baked bread fills the air!

Bread—ancient food—it is one of man's main staples, and is carried along on many a journey.

And many are the health-giving properties in freshly ground flours. Ideally, having your own stone grinder would be the best way by far to preserve the nutritive value of grains.

With the convenience of bakeries today many people find it easier to purchase bread than to bake it themselves. But don't let the amount of time it takes to make yeasted breads keep you away. You'll find that most of the time is in allowing the bread to rise. During that time you can be doing something else creative.

We enjoy baking so much that at our ranch we have built an outdoor oven. The oven has proved its worth for it bakes bread to perfection.

By experiment and experience in our bakery and restaurant we have learned some hints and shortcuts in bread making that we are happy to share.

Bread Baking Hints From Our Bakery
(If you're having trouble.)

Yeast

Use up to 1½ T. per loaf if your bread is slow in rising.

Mix yeast and sweetener with warm water until it foams before mixing it with other ingredients (about 5 minutes).

Be sure yeast is fresh; that is, has been kept airtight and cool—not necessarily in refrigerator. Yeast shouldn't be much over a month old.

All ingredients should be at room temperature or warmer. 75° is a good temperature. Water or milk should be at 90° or so; too cold, and the yeast goes to sleep.

You can use malt or yeast food to replace some of the sweetener—about ¼ oz. per loaf, maximum. You can get malt or yeast food from your local bakery. They are natural ingredients . and give yeast "grow-power" and bread a good flavor.

Try the sponge method: mix water or milk, sweetener, and yeast together with just enough flour to form batter. Let sit for 45 minutes or so. Then mix oil, salt, and other ingredients and the rest of the flour until it hangs together and pulls away from the sides of bowl. Let sit another ½ hour (warm room, with cover), then mix remaining flour, and knead.

If your whole wheat flour is of a coarse grind (that is, you can see large particles of bran—the dark-colored part), the sponge method is good because it takes longer for the gluten to develop. Finer grinds take less time so rarely need a sponge.

Remember that dough works best when used fresh. Once you have mixed and kneaded the bread it should be watched carefully and let rise until only double in bulk, then put in loaf pans and let rise less than double—then bake! Too much rising and bread will be dry and possibly taste yeasty or like alcohol vapor. So watch the dough because it may rise slowly (for reason given later) or very, very quickly.

Sourdough is a yeast substitute. It has a stronger flavor.

Moistener

Butter, margarine, shortening, oil, vegetables, potatoes, potato water, tomatoes, milk, or water are all moistening agents. If your bread fails to rise or rises slowly, check the amount you use.

Sometime flour itself is moist and needs less oil or other moistening ingredients. So if your bread fails, experiment with the moisture.

Oil is the heaviest moistener and imparts a very soft texture; and it will help bread stay softer longer. Butter is the lightest of the oils and develops a more "cakey" texture.

Vegetables or tomato sauce for specialty breads should always be added last in the mixing process. It is well to use a sponge when making these specialty breads.

Sweetener

Sweeteners help bread to rise by feeding the yeast.

The amount of sweetener helps to determine the final color of the bread. With more sweetener, the bread will be dark-crusted; with less, a tan crust.

When using honey, chances are your bread will be lighter in color, but don't increase the quantity to get a darker-crusted bread. Honey is very heavy and inhibits rising (the major reason, along with its cost, that most professional bakers do not use it). Honey also comes in varying densities; some are lighter, so watch it. Honey is an inconsistency factor. It can help the process to work one time and make it fail another. Keep to the amount in the recipe—never more than ¼ c. per 2 loaves.

Molasses is lighter than honey and can be used more easily.

Brown sugar is the sweetener most conducive to even, consistent bread making. However, in our bakery honey is used—excluding heavy, dense honey—and the bread works, better some times than others. If you substitute honey for sugar, reduce liquid by ¼ c.

Flour

More than anything else, flour can make or break the bread-making project. It is the prime inconsistency factor, and the most difficult to predict. Bad flour looks just about like good flour!

The gluten or protein in flour gives it is rising properties. High-protein, hard spring wheat is best, depending on when and where it is grown. Montana wheat has a good reputation. Winter wheat is less glutenous and rougher in texture when baked.

Experiment with different kinds of wheat flour. Even unbleached white flour can vary in gluten content. When you find a good flour you'll know by the texture of the dough. It will be springy and rise quickly when poked with finger. It is best, of course, to grind your own wheat.

Tests for Doneness

Bread will shrink from sides of pan. It will sound hollow when tapped. Color will be golden brown. Let bread cool on its side; preferrably on a rack. Don't wrap bread before it is cool.

To keep bread from drying out and becoming moldy it is best to use it right away (within 3-4 days). Wrap breads to retain moisture. Store in a cool, dry place. You can freeze it also. It will keep for several months.

Flavor

Fruits, nuts, nutritional yeast, and protein powder give flavor but should be added after the first rising because they can slow the rising process. Herbs and spices also give flavor.

Salt adds flavor, controls fermentation. Too much salt can retard rising.

Eggs add color, flavor, and lightness.

To Freshen Stale Bread

Put bread into a glass baking dish that has been rinsed with water. Cover and put into a cold oven. Turn oven to 250°-300°. Leave bread in for 10-15 minutes. This replaces the lost moisture.

Croutons

Let bread dry out at room temperature for a few days or put in the oven at 250°-300° until dry and crisp. Cut into 1-inch cubes. Toss with oil, garlic powder, and herbs of your choice. Parmesan cheese is good, too. Bake at 400° until golden and crisp, about 10 minutes. Cool and store until ready to use.

Bread Crumbs

Let bread dry out at room temperature for a few days or put in the oven at 250° until dry and crisp. Break up and either grind in blender, put through a food mill, put in a bag or between waxed paper and roll with a rolling pin, or roll between palms of your hands.

Corn Bread

Because corn is such a major part of our diet we have set aside a whole chapter to talk about the many things we do with it. Please refer to the Corn section for the many unusual corn bread recipes.

Whole Wheat Bread

1 pkg. active yeast	1½ c. milk
1½ c. lukewarm water	2 t. sea salt
5 T. honey	7 c. whole wheat flour
4 T. butter or margarine	

Dissolve yeast in water. Add 1 T. of honey (honey will make mixture foam in about 10 minutes).

Scald milk and add butter, honey, and salt. Let mixture cool to lukewarm, then add to yeast mixture.

Gradually add whole wheat flour, beating well. Turn out on a lightly floured board (let rest 10 minutes or so, optional), and knead until smooth and elastic. Place in large, well-greased bowl. Cover with damp cloth or towel and place in a warm place, undisturbed, for about 1½ hours. (Dough will be double in bulk.)

Turn out on a floured board. Punch down, and knead, knead, knead. When you are tired, divide dough into 2 equal loaves. Place in greased loaf pans (sprinkle with sesame seeds if desired), covered with a damp cloth and set in a warm place to let rise again until almost double in bulk.

Bake in a preheated oven (350°) about 1 hour, or until done. When it is done, it will sound hollow if tapped on the bottom.

For a variation, add sunflower seeds or sesame seeds to the mixture when adding flour.

Sponge Method Whole Wheat Bread

The sponge method is often preferred over the one used in the recipe above. It makes a lighter textured bread.

2 T. yeast	¼ c. oil
2 c. lukewarm water	½ c. milk powder
¼ c. molasses	2 t. sea salt
¼ c. honey	7 c. whole wheat flour

Dissolve yeast in lukewarm water, add honey and molasses, and enough flour (about 2 c.) to form a batter. Cover and let sit in a warm place for 45 minutes to an hour. Then mix in rest of the ingredients and just enough flour so that the dough hangs together and pulls away from the sides of the bowl.

Let sit another half-hour (covered, in warm place) then mix in remaining flour and knead, knead, knead. Divide in half and place in 2 oiled bread pans. Cover and let rise again until double in bulk. Bake in a preheated oven (350°) about 1 hour or until done.

Katie's Sourdough Bread

Starter:

2 c. warm potato water	1 t. honey
1 T. active yeast	

Mix and let stand in a warm place 48 hours.

The Bread:

6 c. unbleached white flour*	½ c. oil
2 c. warm water	1 T. sea salt

This recipe is a sponge, so you let it rise only once. To make the sponge, mix together and beat thoroughly: 2 c. of the whole wheat flour, warm water, and 2 c. starter (above). When well-mixed, let sit 12 hours. Remove 2 c. of the dough as a new starter and store in the refrigerator for the next time.

To your sponge, add the remaining flour, salt, and oil. Knead for 5-10 minutes. Let mixture rise until doubled, then punch down. Divide dough in half, and place in 2 oiled bread pans; then let rise again.

Bake at 400° for 10 minutes, then reduce heat to 350° and bake an additional 50 minutes.

*You can taste the sourdough better if you use unbleached white flour than if you use whole wheat.

Cheese Bread

4½-6 c. unbleached white flour	2 c. milk
2 T. yeast	2 T. butter
4 T. honey	2 c. cheddar, grated (or jack for milder flavor)
1 T. sea salt	1 egg, beaten

Mix milk, honey, butter, and yeast. Heat in saucepan until about wrist temperature. It is not necessary to completely melt butter. Set aside. Combine 2 cups of flour with salt and add to liquid mixture, then add cheese and egg. Continue mixing in flour ½ c. at a time until dough is stiff.

Knead until smooth and elastic. Shape into a round loaf. Let it rise in a warm place, covered with a damp cloth, for 40 minutes. Bake loaf in *center* of your oven at 375° for 40-50 minutes.

French Bread

1 pkg. active yeast
1 c. lukewarm water
2 T. honey

1 t. sea salt
2 T. butter
7 c. unbleached white flour

Dissolve yeast in ¼ c. of lukewarm water, and mix in the honey. In remaining water, add butter and salt, and mix until butter is melted. Proceed as in whole wheat bread recipe.

When it is time to shape into a loaf, roll dough into one long piece, pinching ends and stretching. Make diagonal cuts and let rise in a warm place until almost double. Brush top with egg white and water. Put on a buttered baking sheet sprinkled with cornmeal.

Bake at 425° for 10 minutes. Brush again with egg white, reduce heat to 375°, and bake an additional 35 minutes. You can brush it 1 or 2 more times with egg white. For a crustier loaf, place a pan of boiling water in bottom of oven.

Slovak Easter Paska

7-8 c. unbleached white flour
1½ c. milk, scalded
½ c. lukewarm water
½ c. honey
1 T. dry active yeast

4 eggs, beaten
⅓ c. butter, melted
1 c. raisins (optional)
2 t. sea salt

Dissolve yeast and 1 T. of honey in water. Scald milk and add honey, butter, and salt. Cool to lukewarm then add to yeast mixture. Add eggs, then gradually mix in flour. Don't use 8 cups unless you really need to. Knead, and as you do you can mix in raisins. Knead until smooth and elastic.

Place in a large, well-greased bowl. Cover and let rise in a warm place until double in bulk. Punch down. Bake this bread in 2 lb. coffee can or a No. 10 can or in a tube pan with removable center. Fill only ⅓ full. Bake at 350° for 1 hour. Serve with Honey Butter. *Yield: 2 loaves.*

Challah

2 T. yeast
¾ c. honey
7-8 c. flour
2¼ c. lukewarm water

½ c. oil
2 T. sea salt
3 eggs
poppy seeds

Dissolve yeast in ¾ c. of the lukewarm water. Add ¼ c. of the honey. In another bowl, mix 4 c. flour, remaining water, oil, honey, salt, and eggs. Mix well, then add 3 more cups of flour and still more if needed. Put in an oiled bowl. Cover and set in warm place until double in size.

Punch down, knead, and cover again until double in size. Punch down again and divide and shape. Cover and let rise again. Brush with a mixture of beaten egg and a little honey. Sprinkle with poppy seeds. Bake at 325° for 45 minutes.

Multi-Grain Bread
(From our bakery.)

2 T. yeast
2 c. lukewarm water
¼ c. molasses
¼ c. honey

¼ c. oil
½ c. milk powder
2 c. multi-grain cereal*
5 c. whole wheat flour

Dissolve yeast in water and let sit. Add all ingredients except cereal and flour and beat well. Gradually add flour (follow whole wheat bread recipe).

*Multi-grain cereal is basically a mixture of coarsely ground grits. So you can combine different grains and grind your own.

Dyan's Buckwheat Soda Bread

2 c. buckwheat flour
2 c. oatmeal flour
5 c. unbleached white flour
3 c. toasted wheat germ
4 eggs

5 T. soda
1 T. sea salt
5 c. sour milk
1 T. sugar
1 T. butter

Mix together flours and wheat germ, soda, and salt. In a small pan heat milk, add butter and melt. Add to flour and mix well. Add eggs and sugar. Mix and pour into 2 oiled loaf pans. Bake at 375° for 40-50 minutes.

Potato Bread

5 c. boiled potatoes	1 t. sea salt
12 c. unbleached white flour	1 c. milk
1 pkg. active yeast	1 T. butter
¼ c. warm water	1 c. onions, chopped fine
1 T. honey	poppy seeds

Dissolve yeast in water and add honey. Mash potatoes, leaving peelings on. Add flour to potatoes and mix the two together well. Melt butter. Take the chill off milk and mix together with salt and onion, then with yeast mixture. Mix with dough, then knead, knead, knead (try 15 minutes if you can) until dough is soft and pliable. Put in a well-greased pan, cover with a damp cloth, and let rise 1 hour. Punch down and knead again. Shape into 3 loaves any way you like. Cover again, and let rise until almost double. Bake at 425° for 1 hour.

Bible Bread

*(This is a yeast version of the original unleavened bread —
see Chapatis.)*

Prepare recipe for whole wheat bread. After the first rise, punch down, knead, and return to bowl. Let rise again. Roll out into pieces about ¼-inch thick and about 6-8 inches in diameter.* Put them on a cookie sheet that has been sprinkled with cornmeal to prevent sticking. Bake at 400° for 10 minutes or until they have "poofed up." Remove and cool.

* After cutting into rounds you can sprinkle with sesame seeds.

Oat Bread

1 c. rolled oats	1 T. butter
2 c. soy flour	¾ t. sea salt
2 c. whole wheat or	2 T. active dry yeast
unbleached white	2¼ c. boiling water
¼ c. molasses	

Boil 2 c. of water. In a bowl put oats, molasses, butter, and salt. Pour the boiling water over this mixture. Stir in soy flour while mixture is cooling.

Meanwhile, dissolve yeast in remaining ¼ c. warm water. Let

set 10 minutes. Add yeast to oats and mix in the whole wheat flour. Allow to rise in bowl until double in bulk. Then divide into 2 loaves and let rise again. Bake at 375° for 40 minutes.

Sprouted Wheat Bread
(This is the simplest and most basic of all recipes.)

Wheat berries or kernels   sea salt

Fill a gallon jar half full of wheat berries. Soak overnight in water. Drain, rinse, and drain again. Put the jar of berries in a dark place at 60°-80° for 3 days, rinsing 3 times a day.

After 3 days, put sprouts through a food mill. Add salt to taste, and shape into loaves. Put in oiled loaf pans and bake at as low a heat as possible (down to 250°), until browned.

Corn Bread can be made the same way from whole corn, but it takes 5 days to sprout.

For variation, add ⅓ c. sesame seeds for every 2 c. wheat sprouts.

Chumash Fry Bread

3 c. flour   1¼ t. baking powder
1⅓ c. warm water   ½ t. sea salt

Combine ingredients to make a soft dough. Pat out dough with hands until thin and shape into patty about ¼-inch thick. Fry in hot oil 1 inch deep in a large pan. Brown on both sides, and serve hot with honey or jelly.

You may omit baking powder; adding 2 t. oil and ¼ c. milk powder.

Chapatis

2 c. whole wheat flour   ¼ t. sea salt
¾ c. water

Mix ingredients into dough. If it is too dry, add more water. Knead 10 minutes or until smooth and elastic. Cover with a damp cloth and set aside for 25 minutes. Divide into 12 balls. Flatten and roll out.

Heat a lightly oiled pan. Put in chapati and move it around a little. Cook 2 minutes or until bubbles appear on top. Flip over and repeat. If you want it to puff up, hold it over an open flame. They are ready to serve. *Yield: 12 chapatis.*

Acorns

Acorns have a strong, rich taste and can be served alone, but are best when mixed into your favorite recipe as grits, flour, or meal.

When you're ready to begin processing them, be sure you allow yourself plenty of time to complete the entire process. Once you crack the acorn it begins to harden.

To Leach Acorns:

Leaching is a process that removes the tannic acid that causes the bitter taste.

Begin by cracking the acorns with a nutcracker or a rock. Now boil acorns in water for 15 minutes. Remove from heat and leave in water overnight. Then chop and grind as you would any grain and it is ready to use in cereals or breads.

Water from the leaching is saved and used as a tanning agent for hides.

Acorn Bread

1 c. acorn meal, leached	½ c. raisins or dried apricots
3 c. cornmeal	5 eggs, separated
½ c. oil	1½ c. milk (use more or less
½ c. molasses	to have a medium-thick
½ t. vanilla	batter)

Mix all together, except egg whites, then add vanilla and raisins or dried apricots. Last, add beaten egg whites. Bake at 325° for 30 minutes.

Acorn-Corn Bread

(See corn section.)

Steamed Acorn Black Bread

1½ c. acorn meal	½ c. sugar
1 c. white flour	1 t. sea salt
½ c. acorn grits	1 t. baking soda

Mix all ingredients well. Add ½ c. dark molasses, 1½ c. sour milk, and 2 T. oil.

Wring out pudding cloth in boiling water. Spread cloth in a round-bottomed bowl and turn batter into it. Tie up corners and suspend bag over boiling water in a closed kettle for 4 hours. Serve hot.

Sesame Buns

8 c. whole wheat pastry flour	1½ c. sesame seeds
3 c. very warm water	2 T. active yeast
¼ c. molasses	1½ t. sea salt

Mix 5 c. of the flour with water, molasses, and yeast. Add rest of the flour, sesame seeds, and salt. Knead until pliable. Let rise in a warm place for 1 hour. Punch down, separate into buns, and let rise again. Bake at 350° for 15-20 minutes.

English Muffins

5 c. whole wheat pastry or unbleached white flour	3 t. honey
2 c. milk	3 T. oil
2 t. active yeast	2 t. sea salt

Scald milk and cool to lukewarm. Add yeast and set aside for 5 minutes. Meanwhile, mix oil, honey, and salt, and combine with yeast mixture.

Slowly add flour and knead 10 minutes. Cover with a damp cloth and let rise in a warm place until double in bulk, about 1 hour.

Roll out to ¼-inch thickness. Cut into ¾-inch circles. Cover with a damp cloth and let rise again, ½ hour.

Bake on an open, ungreased frying pan, 10-15 minutes on each side.

If you want herb muffins, add ¼ t. each of rosemary, thyme, marjoram, nutmeg, and sage.

Steamed Brown Bread

1 c. whole wheat flour	1 t. baking soda
2 c. cornmeal (finely ground)	3 c. milk
1 c. rye	1 c. molasses
1½ t. sea salt	1 c. raisins
1 t. cinnamon	1 c. walnuts, chopped
1 t. cloves	(optional)

Combine dry ingredients, add milk and molasses. Mix in raisins. Pour into 2 1-lb. coffee tins or No. 10 vegetable cans,* greased. Fill ⅔ full. Place foil very tightly over the top (or use the plastic lid that sometimes comes with coffee tin). Put in a large pot, fill with water half way up sides of cans and cover pot tightly. Bring water to a boil. Turn down and steam for 3 hours.

Variations:

Use 1 c. whole wheat and 1 c. rye.
Substitute soy milk, buttermilk, or soured milk.

* You can get such cans from restaurants.

Cinnamon Rolls

Dough:

3¾ c. whole wheat pastry
flour
1½ t. sea salt
1½ T. active yeast
2 T. lukewarm water

2 beaten eggs
¼ c. melted butter
½ c. honey
1 c. warm water

Dissolve yeast in water. Mix eggs, butter, honey, and salt with yeast. Slowly add flour, alternating with water. Mix well and knead.

Cover with a damp cloth, and put in a warm place. When dough has doubled, roll out on a floured table into an oblong shape 1¼-inch thick.

Filling:

⅓ c. melted butter
1 c. honey
2 T. cinnamon

1 c. chopped walnuts
¾ c. raisins

Mix filling ingredients together and pour over rolled-out dough, then roll the dough up lengthwise, and cut into 1-inch sections. Place on a greased cookie sheet, leaving a little room in between pieces. You may sprinkle on a little more melted butter, honey, and cinnamon, if you wish.

Let rise again in a warm place about ½ hour. Bake at 350° for 30-45 minutes.

Apricot Bread

1 c. dried apricots*
½ c. water
½ c. butter or margarine
¾ c. honey
3 eggs

1 c. apricot or apple juice
2 c. flour
2 t. baking powder
½ t. sea salt
1 c. walnuts, chopped

Bring water to a boil and pour over apricots. Cover and let set. Cream butter, honey, eggs and juice. Slowly add flour, baking powder, and salt. Mix well. Add apricots and walnuts. Bake at 350° in a greased and floured pan (9"x5") for 1 hour and 15 minutes. Leave in pan to cool.

* Soak dried apricots in 1 c. apricot juice for a few hours.

Peach Bread

3 c. fresh peaches	½ t. sea salt
3 T. orange juice	⅔ c. oats
2 c. whole wheat pastry	½ c. walnuts, chopped
1 c. soy flour	⅔ c. honey
1 t. baking powder	⅓ c. butter
½ t. soda	2 eggs

Puree 1 c. of the peaches in blender with orange juice. Mix together flour, baking powder, soda, salt, oats, nuts. Cream honey and butter. Beat eggs and add to peach puree. Then mix in flour and add remaining 2 c. peaches. Bake at 350° for 50-60 minutes.

Banana Bread
(Quick 'n easy.)

1¾ c. flour	½ c. honey
2½ t. baking powder	2 eggs, beaten
1 t. sea salt	2 c. mashed, ripe bananas
⅓ c. butter	¾ c. chopped walnuts

Mix flour, baking powder, and salt. Cream butter with honey, then add eggs and bananas. Mix with flour and add walnuts. Bake at 350° for 1 hour.

Cranberry-Nut Bread

¼ c. butter	1 t. grated orange peel
½ c. honey	2 t. baking powder
2 beaten eggs	1½ t. sea salt
½ c. orange juice	¾ c. chopped cranberries
1½ c. whole wheat pastry flour	½ c. chopped walnuts

Cream butter and honey. Add eggs, orange juice, and peel. Mix flour, baking powder, and salt. Combine the two mixtures ⅓ at a time. Add cranberries and walnuts.

Bake in an oiled, floured loaf pan at 350° for 50-60 minutes.

Punkin's Braided Bread

Dough:

2 c. milk
2 T. active yeast
½ c. honey
10 c. unbleached white flour

1 c. butter
2 t. sea salt
6 beaten eggs

Scald milk. When it cools to 100°, add yeast. Let it sit 3 minutes, then add ¼ c. of the honey, the butter and salt. Slowly add 4 c. of the flour to make a sponge. Let rise 10 minutes.

Meanwhile, beat eggs with remaining ¼ c. honey and add to sponge. Slowly add remaining flour to make a soft dough. Knead it until it is soft and pliable. Let it rise until double in bulk, then punch down.

Roll out to ¼-inch thick, shaping into a square, then cut into 3 strips.

Filling:

2 c. steamed, mashed pumpkin
(go ahead and use whole
pumpkin—it's really a
treat!)
1 c. raisins
1 c. honey (if strong-tasting
honey, use less)

1 c. chopped walnuts
6 egg yolks
1 orange peel, grated coarsely
dash sea salt
nutmeg (don't be shy)
1 t. cinnamon
2 t. vanilla

Mix pumpkin, yolks, honey, walnuts, and raisins. Cook over medium heat for 5 minutes or until yolks thicken. Remove from heat and add rest of the ingredients.

Roll 3 strips out longer and fill each with filling mixture. Pinch up along the edges to form a seam, then braid the 3 resulting rolls together. Brush with an egg wash and bake at 350° for 30 minutes.

You can also use the Whole Wheat Bread recipe instead, but it is better if you substitute unbleached white flour for extra lightness.

Poppy Seed Rings

Prepare the pastry for Nut Pastry (see Cakes and Cookies). This recipe makes enough for 2 rings.

Filling:

1½ c. poppy seeds	1 c. raisins
¾ c. milk	1 c. almonds
¾ c. honey	1 t. vanilla
6 egg yolks	½ t. sea salt
¾ c. date sugar	

In a double boiler, combine blenderized poppy seeds, milk, honey, egg yolks, and date sugar. Cook until mixture thickens, then remove from heat. Add vanilla and salt. Grind raisins and almonds,* add to poppy seed mixture, and let cool.

Divide dough in half in an oblong shape. Spread half of filling in each one. Roll up and brush with an egg wash. Bake at 350° for 1½ hours.

* This can be done in a blender. Just add a little liquid to keep blade moving.

Basic Muffins

2 c. whole wheat flour	½ t. sea salt
3 t. baking powder	½ c. butter
2 eggs, beaten	½ c. honey
¾ c. milk	

Mix dry ingredients. Cream butter and honey, then add eggs and milk. Combine wet and dry ingredients, being careful not to overmix the batter. Pour ⅔ full into oiled muffin tins. Bake at 400° for 20-30 minutes. *Yield: 24 muffins.*

Variations:

Add 1 c. blueberries.
Add 1 c. chopped dates, ½ c. walnuts.
Add 1½ c. banana mush, ½ c. walnuts.

Bran Muffins

1½ c. flour
1½ c. bran
2½ t. baking powder
1 t. sea salt
1¼ c. milk
¼ c. butter or oil

⅓ c. honey
⅓ c. molasses
1 egg, beaten
¾ c. raisins
¾ c. chopped walnuts

Combine bran and milk. Let stand 10 minutes. Cream butter or oil with honey, then add molasses and egg. Add to bran mixture, then mix with dry ingredients ⅓ at a time. Bake in oiled muffin tins at 400° for 20-30 minutes. *Yield: 30 muffins.*

Cheese Muffins

2 c. flour
3 t. baking powder
1½ t. sea salt
3 eggs, beaten
1 c. milk

¼ c. melted butter or oil
1 T. honey
1½ c. grated cheese (Swiss, jack, sharp cheddar, or a combination)

Mix dry ingredients. Cream butter and honey. Add eggs and milk. Slowly add dry ingredients, ⅓ at a time; then add cheese. Pour into oiled and floured tins and bake at 400° for 25 minutes. *Yield: 24 muffins.*

Herb and Cheese Muffins

Follow Cheese Muffin recipe. To dry ingredients add: 2 t. marjoram, 2 t. thyme, 2 t. sweet basil.

Cheese 'n Jam Muffins

Follow Cheese Muffin recipe. Fill tins half full. Tablespoon your choice of jam into the center, then cover over jam with more muffin mix.

Coconut-Fruit Muffins

1⅓ c. dried figs, chopped
1 c. buttermilk
1¾ c. whole wheat pastry
   flour
½ c. wheat germ
3 t. baking powder
½ t. sea salt

3 eggs, beaten
¼ c. melted butter, margarine,
   or oil
½ c. honey
¾ c. sunflower seeds
¾ c. shredded coconut

Soak figs in milk for 2-3 hours. Mix dry ingredients. Cream butter with honey and add eggs. Mix with flour, then add figs, sunflower seeds and coconut. Pour into oiled and floured muffin tins, ⅔ full. Bake at 400° for ½ hour. *Yield: 24-30 muffins.*

Cakes
Cookies and Candies

Cakes and cookies and candies speak for themselves. A hand quickly going into the cookie jar; a finger into the frosting! A birthday means what kind of cake? Who gets to lick the bowl? There seems to be a universal feeling of excitement when it's time for dessert. Here is our contribution to the celebration!

The cakes in this section are among our favorites. Some of them are made with honey while others are made with sugar—because sugar proved to make a lighter cake. But don't let that keep you from using any recipes specifying sugar—because *honey will work*. We also use *date sugar* with honey added, because it isn't sweet enough by itself.

Many of these recipes are used daily in our bakery. And our restaurant has featured the Poppy Seed Cake, Chocolate Fudge Cake, and Froggy's Famous Cheese Cake. Our customers were so crazy about them that our cake pans barely had time to cool before they were in the oven again!

Cookies are great to have on hand and are so easy to prepare that those little "cookie munchkins" should never find the cookie jar empty. Honey cookies are usually softer and lighter than sugar cookies.

In these recipes make your own choice between *sugar* and *honey*. If a recipe calls for sugar and you would rather use honey you can make the adjustment by referring to the sugar information below.

Sugar

What can we say about sugar that hasn't already been said and debated innumerable times.

The facts are that it is a food product that offers us nothing nutritionally; and, contrary to popular belief, really does nothing to raise our energy level. In fact, it can cause fatigue, tooth decay, and depression because it robs us of the B vitamins.

Is there a difference, nutritionally, between raw or natural sugar and refined sugar? Not very much, really.

So why do we have any sugar in our book? First, you will notice that only rarely do we use sugar in our recipes. And here in this section we do find some things, otherwise good and wholesome, that just don't turn out as well without it. Also we wish to offer some area of choice to our readers who may not object to moderate use of sugar.

Note one important point: in all of our recipes you can interchange sugar and honey. One c. sugar equals ¾ c. honey. When using honey, reduce the liquid by ¼ c. If there is no liquid to reduce, add 4 T. of flour for each ¾ c. honey used, especially when making cookies. Other substitutes for sugar are maple syrup, molasses, malt syrup, date sugar, fruit juices, and sorghum.

Baking Powder

Many health food stores and markets now carry a healthful low-sodium baking powder containing no aluminum compounds or lime; or, you can prepare a mixture of 2 c. arrowroot flour (high in protein), 2 c. cream of tartar, and 1 c. potassium bicarbonate; or, you can substitute other leavening agents such as yeast, sourdough starter, corncob ash (see Corn section).

Cornstarch

Cornstarch is harmful because it is usually treated with sulphur dioxide. You can substitute arrowroot measure-for-measure with cornstarch. It is a natural thickening agent and a good source of protein. Keep in mind that arrowroot, if undercooked, will produce a gritty texture, an unpleasant taste, and possibly a stomachache!

Baking Soda

Baking soda can cause inflammation of the stomach.

Chocolate

Even though we love chocolate it is not good for you and you will want to be aware of that even if you choose to use it in some of our recipes. It is a stimulant and an irritant; and, of course, is usually combined with sugar.

Carob is a substitute for chocolate: ¾ T. carob = 1 square chocolate. Carob is available in pods or in powdered form.

Yield: enough to fill a 3-layer cake.

Cake Fillings and Icings

Custard Filling

½ c. honey
4 eggs, beaten
1½ c. milk, scalded

¼ c. unflavored gelatin
1 T. unbleached white flour
dash sea salt

First, scald milk. In the top of a double boiler (don't let water touch top) cream together honey, eggs, gelatin, and flour. Slowly stir in scalded milk. Stir constantly until mixture comes to a boil. (It is important that this filling sets up thick because it is to go between cake layers.) Remove from heat and add 1 t. vanilla.

If this filling is for the Poppy Seed Cake add 1 t. lemon rind, ½ t. nutmeg.

Yield: enough to fill a 3-layer cake.

Raspberry-Ricotta Filling

1 c. ricotta
¾ c. sugar
1 T. gelatin dissolved in 2 T.
   water

1 c. sour cream
2 c. fresh raspberries*
   (or fruit of your choice)
1 t. vanilla

In a small pan dissolve gelatin in water over low heat and cook for 3 minutes. Cool. Mix together ricotta, 1 c. of raspberries, sugar, vanilla, and gelatin. Add remaining cup of raspberries and the sour cream. Cover and refrigerate for 2 hours or until it is set.

* If canned raspberries are used, drain well and use the juice instead of water to dissolve gelatin.

Carob- or Cocoa-Ricotta Filling

1 c. ricotta
3 T. cocoa (unsweetened) or
   carob powder
8 T. brown sugar

½ t. vanilla
⅔ c. walnuts or almonds
   (or half and half), chopped

Combine ingredients. Refrigerate until ready to use. *Yield: enough to fill a 3-layer cake.*
Also try adding shavings from chocolate or carob bars.

Almond Filling

1 c. almonds, finely ground
½ c. butter
8 T. sugar or 6 T. honey

½ t. almond extract
1 T. milk powder (optional)

Cream butter and sugar, add almonds and extract. If using honey, and mixture isn't quite thick enough, add 1 T. milk powder. *Yield: enough to fill a 3-layer cake.*

For other cake filling ideas see some of the pie fillings such as Apricot Whip or Persimmon Cream Cheese.

Basic Cream Cheese Icing

8 oz. cream cheese   ¼ c. honey

Cream the two together. *Yield: enough to frost a 2-layer cake.*

Variations:

Fruit-Cream Cheese Icing: use ¾ c. jam in place of honey. If the icing gets too thin add 1 or 2 T. milk powder.

Lemon or Orange Icing: add 3 to 4 T. lemon or orange rind grated.

Pineapple-Whipped Cream Frosting

1 pt. whipping cream   ½ c. sugar
1¼ oz. or 1 T. unflavored   1 c. pineapple, diced
   gelatin   2 T. warm water

In a small saucepan dissolve gelatin in water over low heat. Put cream and sugar in a bowl, add gelatin and whip until it forms stiff peaks. Add pineapple and refrigerate for 4 hours.

This is enough to frost the top of one 2-layer cake. If desired for filling also, double the recipe.

Fudge Frosting

2½ c. natural sugar   2 c. half and half
5 squares baker's unsweetened   1 c. butter
   chocolate   2 t. vanilla

In a heavy saucepan, combine sugar and half and half. Bring to a boil, stirring constantly. Reduce heat and simmer for 6 minutes without stirring. Remove from heat and add chocolate, stir to blend, add butter and vanilla. Beat until thick and creamy. Cover and refrigerate until cooled. *Yield: enough to frost a 3-layer cake.*

Basic Butter Frosting

¾ stick or 6 T. butter   ½ c. milk powder
⅓-½ c. honey   dash sea salt

Soften butter at room temperature. Cream with honey and salt. Mix in milk powder a little at a time until the desired consistency is reached. If milk powder is lumpy it is best to sift it into the creamed mixture. *Yield: enough to frost a 2-layer cake.*

Variations:

Lemon Butter Icing: add 3 T. lemon juice or 3 T. grated lemon rind.

Carob Butter Icing: add ¼ c. carob and use only ¼ c. milk powder.

Peanut Butter Icing: substitute peanut butter for butter, or try a peanut butter and carob combination.

Fruit Icing: use fruit jams or sauces instead of honey. Adjust milk powder accordingly.

Cakes

Basic Sugar Cake

¾ c. butter   3 t. baking powder
1½ c. sugar   ½ t. sea salt
1 t. vanilla   1⅓ c. milk
2½ c. unbleached white flour   6 eggs, separated

Cream butter, sugar, vanilla, and egg yolks. Combine dry ingredients and add alternately with milk. Beat egg whites until stiff peaks form and fold into mixture. Pour into 2 oiled 8-inch, round cake pans and bake at 375° for about 25 minutes.

Yield: 2 layers.

Basic Honey Cake

⅔ c. butter
1 c. honey
4 eggs, separated
2½ c. whole wheat pastry
flour
1 T. baking powder

½ t. sea salt
2 t. vanilla
1¼ c. milk
¼ c. orange peel, grated
(optional)

Follow directions for Basic Sugar Cake. These basic cakes are fun because there is an endless variety of things you can do with them. Try various fillings and frostings. Add various spices. Substitute various extracts for vanilla.

Carrot Cake

1½ c. oil
1 c. honey
3 eggs
1½ c. grated carrots
3 c. flour
1 T. baking powder

¾ t. sea salt
1 T. cinnamon
¾ t. nutmeg
1 T. vanilla
1 c. pineapple
½ c. milk

Cream together oil, honey, and eggs. In another bowl, sift together flour, baking powder, salt, cinnamon, and nutmeg. Add to creamed mixture, then add milk, vanilla, carrots, and pineapple. Bake in a 9-inch x 13-inch rectangular pan at 375° for about 25 minutes.

Variations:

Add 1 c. raisins or 1 c. coconut.
Ice with Cream Cheese-Pineapple Icing or Pineapple-Whipped Cream Icing.

Honey-Date Cake
(Rich and moist.)

1½ c. dates	1½ t. vanilla
1½ t. baking soda	2 c. flour
1½ c. boiling water	1 t. sea salt
1 c. butter	1 t. nutmeg
1 c. honey	1½ t. cinnamon
3 eggs, well-beaten	1 c. walnuts, chopped

Put dates in bowl with baking soda and boiling water. Let cool. In another bowl, cream butter with honey. Add well-beaten eggs. Add date mixture. Mix well. Add vanilla, flour, salt, nutmeg, and cinnamon. Fold in chopped walnuts. Bake in an oiled, floured bundt pan at 350° for 45 minutes. Use Honey Butter Icing.

Susan's Poppy Seed Cake

1⅛ c. poppy seeds	4½ t. baking powder
3 c. milk	¾ t. sea salt
¾ c. butter	1½ t. vanilla
2 c. natural sugar	4 egg whites
3 c. unbleached white flour	

This makes 3 layers. Scald 1¼ c. milk. Blenderize poppy seeds, add to scalded milk. Let cool. Cream butter and natural sugar. (When using a natural sugar like this the crystals are sometimes large so I like to run it through a blender.)

In a separate bowl, sift flour, baking powder, salt.

Add vanilla to poppy seed mixture. Add dry ingredients, one-third at a time. Then add 1¾ c. milk. Fold in stiffly beaten egg whites.* Pour into 3 oiled, floured cake pans. Bake at 350° for 25 minutes.

* Use the egg yolks in custard fillings. Prepare Custard Filling recipe and spread thick between cake layers. Ice with Cream Cheese Fruit Icing.

Applesauce Spice Cake

1 c. butter
1½ c. honey
3 eggs, separated
3½ c. pastry flour
1 t. sea salt
2 t. baking powder
2 t. cinnamon

1 t. nutmeg
½ t. cloves
½ t. allspice
1¼ c. currants or raisins
1 c. walnuts, chopped
2 c. buttermilk
¾ c. applesauce

This makes 3 layers. Cream butter with honey, add beaten egg yolks. In a separate bowl, mix flour, salt, baking powder, cinnamon, nutmeg, cloves, allspice. Slowly add dry ingredients to wet. Then add currants or raisins and walnuts. Then add buttermilk and applesauce. Fold in 3 well-beaten, fluffy eggs.

Pour into 3 oiled, floured cake pans and cook at 350° for ½ hour. Use cream cheese or butter icing.

Susie Spunky's Chocolate Fudge Cake

10 oz. baker's unsweetened
   chocolate
¾ c. sour cream
4¼ c. natural sugar
¾ c. butter
5 eggs, separated

3 c. unbleached white flour
1½ t. baking powder
¾ t. sea salt
¾ c. milk
2 t. vanilla
4½ T. water

Make a chocolate "custard" by melting and mixing in a double boiler the chocolate, sour cream, 2 egg yolks, and 2¾ c. of the sugar.

Next, cream butter with remaining 1½ c. of the sugar. Add 3 egg yolks. Sift together flour, baking powder, salt. Slowly add mixture to butter mixture, alternating with milk, vanilla, and water.

Now stir in the chocolate custard. Fold in 5 stiffy beaten egg whites. Bake at 350° in 3 oiled, floured cake pans for 30-35 minutes.

Frost with Fudge Frosting—lots and lots!
Yield: 3-layer cake.

Froggy's Famous Cheesecake
Filling:

5 eggs plus 2 yolks	3 T. unbleached flour
2½ lbs. cream cheese	¼ c. whipping cream
1¾ c. turbinado sugar	1 t. vanilla

Soften cream cheese. Add sugar, vanilla, flour. Beat until well-blended. Add eggs and 2 yolks, one at a time, beating each one in well. Add whipping cream and beat about 3 minutes.

Crust:

6 oz. zwieback, crushed	½ t. cinnamon
6 T. natural sugar	½ t. nutmeg
¾ stick butter	

Melt butter and mix into dry ingredients. Press into the bottom of a spring form baking pan (10-inch diameter).

Preheat oven to 475°. Pour filling into spring form. Bake for 8-12 minutes. (This is to brown the top.)

Reduce heat to 250° for 1½ hours. Turn off the oven and let the cheesecake remain inside for 1 hour. Remove and let cool completely, but not in a draft. Refrigerate.

Yield: 16 servings.

Raw Cheese Cake
(Made with your own homemade cream cheese.)

Mix soft homemade cream cheese (which has been hanging in cheesecloth for a few days) with honey, vanilla—and crushed fruit if you like. Add some lemon juice.

Make a crust of ground nuts (walnuts, almonds, sunflower seeds) and honey (see Pie Crusts). Line a cake pan with crust. Put filling in pan. It may be topped with sliced fruit and/or nuts. Serve raw. *Yield: 6-10 servings.*

Cheesecake

1½ lb. cream cheese, softened	1½ t. vanilla
¾ c. honey	1 t. fresh lemon rind
½ t. sea salt	4 eggs, well-beaten
2 T. flour	

Combine and mix well. Slowly add eggs. Pour into graham crust shell. Bake at 350° for 45-60 minutes.

Top with slices of fresh fruit, such as strawberries, peaches, cherries. Also good with fruit and whipped cream.

Yield: 6-10 servings.

Sunray Cheesecake

8 oz. cream cheese	½ c. nonfat milk powder
8 oz. ricotta cheese	2 T. flour
8 oz. sour cream	¼ t. baking powder
¾ c. honey	1 T. vanilla
4 eggs, beaten	1 c. mild cheddar, grated

Cream, until smooth, the cream cheese, ricotta, and sour cream. Slowly add honey, then eggs (one at a time).

Mix together milk powder, flour, and baking powder, and beat into the creamed mixture. Stir in grated cheese and vanilla.

Line a 9-inch deepdish baking pan with a graham cracker crust (see Pie Crusts) and fill with cheese mixture. Bake at 350° for 35 minutes or until firm. You could also do this in custard cups, baking 20-25 minutes; or in muffin tins, 15 minutes.

Yield: 6-10 servings.

Persimmon Cake

2 c. raisins
2 c. nuts
2 c. natural sugar or
1¾ c. honey
4 c. flour
2 t. cinnamon
3 t. baking soda

2 t. ground cloves
2 t. allspice
1 t. sea salt
4 eggs
½ c. oil
2 c. persimmons (cut up skins,
mash pulp)

Combine raisins, nuts, sugar (if you are using honey, don't add it at this time). Then mix in flour and spices. In a separate bowl, beat eggs.

Add oil, persimmons, soda, and mix well. If you are using honey instead of sugar, mix it in at this time. Then combine with the dry ingredients and mix well.

Pour into an oiled and floured tubular pan or bundt pan. Bake at 350°-375° for about 1½-2 hours. Don't overbake or you'll dry it out. Cake should be moist like a fruit cake. Test it by sticking in a knife; if it comes out clean, the cake is done.

You can also bake this as muffins!

Peach Custard Cake

1½ c. unbleached white or
whole wheat pastry flour
½ t. sea salt
½ c. soft butter
2½ c. fresh peaches (or canned
or sliced)

⅓ c. honey
½ t. cinnamon
1 T. unbleached flour
1 egg
1 c. evaporated milk
¼ t. nutmeg

Mix flour and salt with butter until it is coarse like meal. Press mixture half way up the side of an 8-inch square pan. Slice peaches, or drain syrup from canned peaches, reserving ½ c. syrup. Arrange well-drained slices on top of the crust.

Sprinkle over peaches a mixture of honey, cinnamon, and unbleached flour. Bake at 375° for 20 minutes.

Mix egg, slightly beaten; evaporated milk; nutmeg; and peach juice or syrup (if you are using fresh peaches, squeeze out juice or use water and honey to make up the difference). Pour over peaches.

Bake for 30 minutes more, until custard is firm except in the center. (That will become firm on standing.) Serve warm or cold—best when cold!

Orange Cake

1 lg. orange (pulp and rind)	1 t. sea salt
1 c. raisins	⅔ c. honey
⅓ c. walnuts	½ c. shortening
2 c. whole wheat pastry flour	1 c. milk
1 t. soda	2 eggs, beaten

Grind orange, raisins, and walnuts. Set aside. Mix honey, shortening, and ¾ c. milk. Add to flour, soda, salt. Beat again for about 1½ minutes.

Fold in orange-raisin mixture and pour into a greased and floured pan. Bake at 350° for 40-50 minutes. This cake is very moist. Ice with Honey Butter or Orange Rind Icing.

Banana-Walnut Cake

1¾ c. whole wheat pastry flour	1 c. honey
3 T. milk powder	1 t. lemon rind
2 T. protein powder	3 eggs
2 T. baking powder	1¼ c. mashed banana
1 t. sea salt	¼ c. raisins
⅓ c. oil	¼ c. walnuts

Combine dry ingredients in a large bowl. In separate bowl mix oil, honey, lemon, eggs, and banana until well-blended. Then add to dry mixture. Blend well and add raisins and walnuts. Bake in an oiled and floured loaf pan or a bundt pan at 350° for 45 minutes. Ice with your choice of icing.

Apple Crumb Cake

6 apples, cored and sliced	1 t. cinnamon
1½ c. grated tangy cheese	¾ c. sugar
3 c. coarse bread crumbs	¼ c. cold water

Combine crumbs and cheese. Mix cinnamon and sugar. Arrange layers of apples, sugar mixture, and crumb mixture in greased casserole—3 layers of each. Drizzle water over last sugar mixture and top with last crumb mixture. Bake 45 minutes at 375°. Serve plain or with cream.

Oatmeal Cake

1 c. quick oats　　　　　　　1 stick margarine
1½ c. hot water

Pour water over oats and margarine. Let stand for 20 minutes. Add the following ingredients and mix well.

1 c. sugar　　　　　　　　　1 t. baking soda
2 c. brown sugar　　　　　　1 t. cinnamon
2 eggs　　　　　　　　　　½ t. nutmeg
1⅓ c. sifted flour

Bake for 30 minutes at 350° in an oiled and floured 10″ x 13″ pan.

Topping:

1 stick margarine　　　　　1 c. coconut
¼ c. brown sugar　　　　　1 c. nuts
1 t. vanilla

Combine margarine, sugar, and vanilla and boil into a syrup. Sprinkle coconut and nuts over cake when it is hot. Pour syrup mixture over and put under broiler until browned.

Walnut Coffee Cake (Without the Coffee)
(From our bakery.)

2½ c. whole wheat pastry　　1⅓ c. honey
　flour　　　　　　　　　　3 eggs, beaten
1 T. baking powder　　　　1 t. vanilla
1 t. sea salt　　　　　　　¾ c. milk
⅓ c. butter

Mix together flour, baking powder, salt. Cream butter and honey, then add eggs, vanilla, and milk. Pour into a greased and floured baking pan.

Topping:

¼ c. melted butter　　　　2 T. flour
¾ c. honey　　　　　　　2 t. cinnamon
1 c. chopped walnuts

Mix well, making sure flour doesn't lump, and pour on top of batter.

Bake at 350° for 1 hour.

You can add 1 c. sliced apples or 1 c. sliced pineapple to topping for variation.

Jam Cake

1 c. butter
1⅔ c. honey
2 c. jam of your choice
3¼ c. whole wheat pastry
    flour
1 t. baking soda

1 c. buttermilk
1 t. cloves
1 t. nutmeg
1 t. cinnamon
3 eggs

Cream butter and sugar. Add eggs and jam. Beat thoroughly. Sift the flour, measure and resift with soda, salt, and spices. Add alternately with milk to the first mixture. Beat well, pour into well-greased, tube-type cake pan. Bake at 350° for 55 minutes.

Yield: 2 layers.

Chrissie's Traditional Fruit Cake

2 c. whole wheat flour
1 c. butter
½–¾ c. honey
2 eggs, separated
1 c. raisins
1 c. walnuts, broken

1 t. sea salt
2 t. vanilla
½ c. citron
¼ c. cherry juice
1½ c. mixed fruit (dried,
    candied)

Cream the butter and honey. Add egg yolks. In a separate bowl, put mixed fruit, citron, and 1 c. of flour. Mix until the fruit is well-distributed. To the batter mixture, add cherry juice, salt, vanilla. Add remaining 1 c. flour, the candied fruit and flour mixture, raisins and broken walnuts. Fold in egg whites, stiffly beaten.

Bake in an oiled, floured loaf pan (10" x 13") for 1 hour and 15 minutes.

Walnut-Pero Quick Cake

2 c. unbleached white flour
¾ c. butter
¾ c. natural sugar
1 T. milk

2 t. instant pero* (dissolved in
    a little water)
½ c. walnuts, chopped

Cream butter and sugar. Add eggs, milk, and pero; and, while beating slowly, add flour. Add the walnuts and put into an oiled and floured bundt pan and bake at 350° for 1 hour. Lightly ice when cool with Honey Butter Icing.

* Pero is a coffee substitute.

Blueberry Cake
(From our bakery.)

¾ c. oil
3 eggs
1 c. honey
2¾ c. pastry flour
1 T. baking powder
2 t. cinnamon

1 t. nutmeg or allspice
½ c. walnuts
½ c. fresh blueberries
  (drained, if canned)
½ c. blueberry juice or milk

Cream together oil, honey, and eggs. Combine flour, baking powder, cinnamon, and nutmeg and add to creamed mixture, alternating with juice or milk. Add blueberries and walnuts. Pour into oiled and floured cake pans and bake at 350° for 25-30 minutes. Ice with Cream Cheese Fruit Icing. *Yield: 2 layers.*

Cookies

Date or Fig Bars
(From our bakery.)

Crust:

Combine ¼ c. oil and ½ c. honey. Mix in the following:

¾ c. pastry flour
1 c. oats
2 T. soy flour

½ t. baking powder
½ t. sea salt
2 t. orange rind

Filling:

To 1 c. hot water, add:

2 c. chopped dates or figs
1 T. fresh lemon juice

1 t. lemon rind
1 t. orange rind

Press half of crust mixture into a baking pan. Spread on the filling. Cover with the rest of the crust. Bake at 375° for ½ hour. Cool and cut into squares.

Honey Macaroons
(From our bakery.)

2 c. rolled oats (or rye or whole
    wheat flour)
½ c. wheat germ
½ t. sea salt
1 t. cinnamon
½ t. nutmeg

½ c. oil
½ c. honey
½ t. vanilla
½ t. almond extract
½ t. allspice
½ c. chopped nuts

Combine dry ingredients. Mix liquid ingredients and combine with dry ingredients. Add nuts. Drop by tablespoonfuls on well-oiled baking sheet. Bake 10-15 minutes or until browned. Makes about 36 macaroons.

Date and Nut Squares

2 eggs
½ c. sugar
½ t. vanilla
½ c. flour

½ t. baking powder
½ t. sea salt
1 c. walnuts, chopped
2 c. dates, finely chopped

Beat eggs until foamy. Beat in sugar, vanilla. Mix in remaining ingredients. Put into 8-inch square pan and bake at 375° until top has dull crust—approximately 25-30 minutes. Cut into square and cool. Remove from pan. Makes 12 squares.

Verenicky (Russian)

Pot cheese (1 carton or ¾ lb.)
1 or 2 eggs

2 T. unbleached white or
    whole wheat flour

Mix ingredients, reserving 1 egg. The consistency should be thick. If needed, add the other egg. Form mixture into 1½- to 2-inch balls. Roll in flour.

Put balls in cold, salted water and bring to a boil, covered. The Verenicky will float to top when ready (about 3-4 minutes). Remove with a slotted spoon. Cool slightly and roll in sour cream, honey, or jam.

Butter Cookies

Cream together 1½ c. butter and 1 c. sugar.

Add 3 beaten eggs, 2 t. vanilla, and ½ t. almond extract or lemon rind.

Slowly mix in 3 c. unbleached flour. Chill mixture for 2 hours or more. Roll out ½-inch thick, and cut into desired shapes.

Mix 2 eggs and 2 t. water. Spread egg mixture over each cookie. Optional: sprinkle with cinnamon or finely chopped nuts.

Bake until slightly brown at 375°. Makes 40 cookies.

Almond Gems

Cream together 1 c. butter and ¾ c. honey.

Add 1¾ c. whole wheat flour; 1¾ c. ground, toasted almonds; 2 t. almond extract; 2 t. lemon rind, and ½ t. sea salt.

Drop by tablespoonfuls on an oiled cookie sheet and press to ½-inch thickness.

Dip an almond in honey and press it into the center of each cookie.

Bake at 400° for 10 to 15 minutes. Makes about 25 cookies.

Pumpkin Cloud Cookies
(Very light—not for the "crunchy cookie craving"!)

½ c. butter or margarine	1 T. baking soda
1 c. honey	1 t. sea salt
2 beaten eggs	2 t. cinnamon
1 c. steamed, mashed pumpkin	1 t. mace
2 c. whole wheat flour	2 c. walnut halves, chopped coarsely

Cream butter; add honey. Add eggs and pumpkin. Mix dry ingredients together and add to the rest, including the nuts. Drop on greased cookie sheet. Bake in 350° oven for 15 minutes. Makes 30 cookies.

Peanut Butter Cookies

Cream together ½ c. butter and 1 c. sugar or ¾ c. honey (if using honey, add 4 T. flour).

Mix with 2 eggs, 1½ c. peanut butter, 1 t. vanilla.

Combine 1½ c. whole wheat pastry flour, ½ t. sea salt, 1 t. baking powder. Add to wet ingredients. Use small scoop and press out on an oiled cookie sheet. Bake at 375° for 12 minutes. Makes about 24 cookies.

Thumb Prints

1 c. butter	1 t. vanilla
2 egg yolks	½ t. sea salt
2 c. sifted flour	1 c. walnuts
½ c. brown sugar	

Roll into balls the size of walnuts. Dip in slightly beaten egg whites. Roll in finely chopped nuts.

Bake at 375° for 5 minutes, then press in the center to make a dent. Bake 8 minutes or a little longer. Cool and fill with jelly (currant jelly is great). Makes about 24 cookies.

Carob Brownies
(From our bakery.)

Melt 1 c. butter and mix in 3 c. carob powder.

Beat 1½ c. eggs and add 2 c. honey and 1 T. vanilla. Combine with butter mixture and whip really well.

Barely mix in 2¼ c. whole wheat pastry flour, 1 T. sea salt. Add 2 c. chopped walnuts.

Bake in an oiled pan at 350° for 45 minutes.

Country Granola Cookies

½ c. butter
⅓ c. molasses
½ c. honey
1 t. lemon juice
1½ c. whole wheat pastry
flour

2 eggs, beaten
1 t. sea salt
2½ c. granola
1 c. nuts, chopped
1 c. raisins

Cream butter, honey, and molasses. Add lemon juice and eggs and mix well. Add flour and salt, then mix in granola, nuts, and raisins.

Drop by teaspoonfuls onto a lightly oiled cookie sheet and bake at 400° for 8-10 minutes.

Granola cookies can vary greatly depending on the type of I've found it's not hard to recruit testers! Makes about 36 cookies.

Maple Refrigerator Cookies

½ c. butter
1 T. maple extract
1 t. vanilla
⅔ c. raw sugar

1½ c. flour
¼ t. cream of tartar
¼ t. sea salt

Cream butter with extracts, sugar, and honey. Sift together flour, tartar, and salt. Add with milk to creamed mixture. Shape into a roll and set in the refrigerator until chilled.

Cut into ¼-inch thick slices and place on an oiled cookie sheet. Bake at 400° for 8 minutes. Makes 24 cookies.

Large Oreo Cookies

1½ c. raw sugar
1 c. butter
1 egg, beaten
¾ c. cocoa

2½ c. unbleached white flour
¼ t. baking powder
½ t. sea salt
1 t. vanilla

Cream butter with sugar, add eggs. Add flour, cocoa, baking powder, salt and vanilla. Mix well. Roll out and cut into either rounds or squares. Bake at 400° for about 15 minutes, until crisp. Cool.

On one cookie, put a spot of filling made of cream cheese, honey, and vanilla. Top with another cookie. Makes 12-15 large cookies.

Chocolate Chip Cookies

1 c. butter	1½ c. unbleached white or
2 c. brown sugar	2 c. whole wheat pastry flour
3 eggs, beaten	½ c. wheat germ
1 t. vanilla	1½ c. chocolate chips
1 t. sea salt	1 c. walnuts, chopped

Cream butter and sugar. Add eggs, vanilla, and salt. Blend in flour and wheat germ. Mix in chocolate chips and walnuts. Spoon by tablespoonfuls onto oiled cookie sheet. Press down and bake at 350° for 15 minutes or until brown around the edges. Makes 24 cookies.

Sesame Cookies

2 eggs	1½ c. whole wheat pastry
½ c. date sugar	flour
¾ c. honey	½ lemon rind, grated
¼ c. vegetable oil	¼ t. sea salt
½ t. vanilla	½ c. sesame seeds
½ c. soy flour	

Beat eggs; add sugar, honey, oil, and vanilla. Mix well. Add flour and salt, lemon rind, sesame seeds. Drop by tablespoonfuls onto well-greased cookie sheet. Bake at 375° for 15-20 minutes. Makes 30 cookies.

If a crunchier cookie is desired and you don't mind the sugar, try adding ¾ c. sugar and ½ T. baking powder.

Oatmeal-Molasses Cookies

¾ c. butter	2 t. baking powder
⅔ c. molasses	3 c. oats
2 eggs	1 c. walnuts
2 t. vanilla	1 c. raisins
½ t. sea salt	1 c. sunflower seeds
1 c. flour	

Cream butter, molasses, eggs, and vanilla. Add remaining ingredients, mixing well. Drop by tablespoonfuls onto greased cookie sheet. Bake at 375° for 10-15 minutes or until crisp. Makes 30 cookies.

Oatmeal Cookies
(From our bakery.)

½ lb. butter
1¼ c. sugar
½ t. sea salt
1⅛ t. baking powder
1 egg, beaten

¼ c. milk
1¾ c. rolled oats
1 c. walnuts, chopped
1 c. raisins

Cream together butter and sugar. Mix in flour to a smooth paste. Add salt, baking powder. Add egg and milk, then mix in oats. Add walnuts and raisins. Drop by large soupspoonfuls (or larger if desired) onto oiled cookie sheet and press down. Bake at 350° for 10 to 15 minutes or until golden brown. Makes 30 cookies.

Honey-Lemon-Walnut Cookies
(From our bakery.)

1¼ c. whole wheat pastry
   flour
¼ lb. (½ c.) butter
½ c. honey
1 egg

¾ t. lemon extract
1¼ c. walnuts, chopped
½ t. baking powder
⅛ t. sea salt

Cream together butter and honey. Mix in flour. Add salt, baking powder, and egg. Add lemon and walnuts. Drop by large . spoonfuls onto oiled cookie sheet. It is not necessary to press this cookie because when the honey melts, the cookie will spread out. Brush each cookie with egg white and bake at 375° for about 15 minutes or until golden brown.

Coconut Cashew Bars

Cream together 1½ c. honey and ¾ c. butter.

Add ¼ c. lemon juice, ⅓ c. water, and 1 t. vanilla.

Mix together 3 c. oats, ½ c. soy or whole wheat flour, 1½ c. ground cashews, 1½ c. coconut, 1 t. sea salt, 2 t. baking powder. Combine with wet ingredients.

Press into baking pan, and bake at 350° for ½ hour. Makes 18 bars.

Nut Pastries

1 c. soft butter	4 egg yolks
3 c. sifted flour	1 c. dairy sour cream
1 pkg. active yeast	1 t. vanilla
4 T. warm water	½ c. honey
1 T. honey	nut filling (below)

Cut butter into flour. Dissolve yeast in warm water and 1 T. honey. Add to flour mixture with remaining ingredients (except filling and honey). Mix thoroughly and chill a few hours.

Roll dough to ⅛-inch thickness on a floured board. Cut in 3-inch squares. Put 1 T. filling in the center of each square. Moisten the edges of the pastry with water and pinch corners up and together.

Bake on ungreased cookie sheets at 375° for 15 minutes. Cool, swirl on honey and sprinkle with nutmeg.

Filling:

Force 3 c. walnuts through a food chopper or blender. Add ¾ c. honey, 3 t. vanilla, and ½ c. milk or cream. Mix well.

Optional: mix in 1 beaten egg. For variation, mix in ¾ c. ricotta cheese.

Candies

Carob Crunchies

½ c. peanut butter
½ c. granola
2 to 4 T. honey

1 c. carob powder
¼ c. honey
milk

Mix peanut butter and granola and honey. Shape into domes or balls. For topping, blend carob powder and honey and add enough warm milk to make a thick liquid. Dip the balls in carob.

Carob Fudge

1 lb. butter
3 c. honey
2½-3 c. milk powder

2 t. vanilla
1 to 2 c. carob

Melt butter, add honey, milk powder until smooth, thick texture. Add some vanilla. Add 1-2 c. carob—as you like (sift into mixture and stir it well.)

Add lots of nuts (walnuts preferrably). Then taste it to make sure it's good.

Wheat Germ Balls

1 c. coconut
3½ c. wheat germ
2 c. milk powder

½ c. raisins
¾ c. peanut butter
2 c. honey

Toast coconut and wheat germ. Mix milk powder, raisins, and peanut butter with wheat germ and coconut. Add honey, and roll into balls. If too thick, add a tiny bit of milk. If too runny, add powdered milk. Balls are best when they have set for a day or two.

Sesame Halvah

3 c. hulled sesame seeds   honey

Grind sesame seeds. Add enough honey to the seeds to make them hold together. Halvah can be plain; or, add other nuts, seeds, dried fruit.

Dried Fruit and Nut Balls

You can use any dried fruits or nuts of your choice. You just run them through a grinder and roll into balls. The fruit makes a sticky paste which holds the balls together. You can roll them in toasted wheat germ, coconut, or carob powder. Here is one example:

¾ c. dates   ¼ c. toasted wheat germ
¼ c. raisins   ⅛ c. carob powder or milk
¼ c. almonds   powder
¼ c. sunflower seeds   coconut
⅛ c. sesame seeds

Grind nuts and seeds. You can either grind fruit or chop fine and combine. If your mixture isn't sticky enough, add honey. Form balls and roll in coconut.

Variations:

Try using bee pollen in some.
Try mint leaves; chia seeds.

Peanut Butter-Carob or Chocolate Bars
Filling:

¼ lb. peanut butter   ½ c. milk powder
¼ c. sugar

Top Layer:

1½ c. carob or chocolate chips   ½ c. butter

Prepare a graham cracker crust (see Pie Crust). Press into bottom of a 9″ x 13″ baking pan. Next, mix filling and spread on. In a double boiler, melt butter and add carob or chocolate chips. Cook just until melted and no longer. Pour over top. Refrigerate. When carob just begins to set up, make cut lines for bars. After it has hardened, it becomes brittle and hard to cut. *Makes 16 bars.*

Sesame Candy

1 c. roasted sesame seeds
½ c. molasses (unsulphured)
3 t. milk powder

1 t. oil
dash sea salt

Roast seeds. In a bowl, add molasses, slowly mix in milk powder to a smooth consistency. Add oil, salt, and sesame seeds. Shape into 16 little balls and roll them in toasted wheat germ or coconut.

For variation, try adding ¼ c. tahini.

Seeds, Nuts, and Dried Fruit

These are high energy foods, good for breakfast or a pick-me-up anytime during the day. They are also excellent back-packing foods—small in bulk and weight, yet packed with energy.

Grind singly or any combination of the following: sesame and sunflower seeds, cashews, almonds, walnuts.

Add honey and molasses and you've got a treat.

Add carob powder and/or milk powder to make a complete protein.

Add ground cloves as you grind the seeds and nuts.

Add currants or raisins.

Add shredded coconut.

Some Sunburst Combinations

Raisins, walnuts, and carob chips.
Sunflower seeds, cashews, almonds, raisins, pumpkin seeds.
Almonds, dates, shredded coconut.
Carob chips and roasted salted peanuts.

Pies and Puddings

Is there still a desire for something sweet even after thumbing through all those pages of Cakes, Cookies, and Candies? Well, try this chapter; you just may find something pleasing—like Blueberry-Ricotta Pie.

Feeling more extravagant? How about some Walnut Pie? Still not the one? Well, maybe some Deep Dish Apple Pie smothered in fresh cream? Or something a little simpler, like pudding. The only way you'll know is if you try some, because it is still true that "the proof is in the pudding"!

Flaky Pie Crust
(Mom's best.)

2 c. unbleached flour	¼ t. sea salt
¾ c. shortening	4 T. ice water

This recipe will make top and bottom crusts for 1 9-inch pie.

Add salt to flour. Add ⅔ of the shortening. Mix with a dough cutter until mixture is in pea-size chunks. Add remainder of shortening and 4 T. ice water.

Mix with a fork until mixture leaves the sides of the bowl clean. Divide the dough in half. Form into 2 balls. Roll each out on a floured table top to fit to your pie pan.

If you are prebaking the shell without filling, be sure to first prick the bottom and sides with a fork, and on the top crust make a design or indentation to allow steam to escape.

Whole Wheat Pie Crust

3 c. whole wheat flour   1 c. oil
1½ t. sea salt   ⅔ c. water

This recipe makes top and bottom crusts for 1 9-inch pie.
Mix flour and salt. Slowly add oil and water, mixing.

Form into a ball. Divide in half and roll each out as thin as
possible on wax paper to fit pie pans. Flute edges and add filling,
or bake 20-30 minutes at 350°. (See note under Flaky Pie Crust
for prebaking.)

Graham Cracker or Zwieback Pie Crust

1⅓ c. crushed graham   1 t. cinnamon
    crackers or zwieback   2 T. natural sugar, if desired
⅓ c. butter, melted

This recipe will make bottom crust for 1 9-inch pie.

Melt the butter. Add to the dry ingredients and mix well.
Press into bottom of a pie pan or casserole dish.

You may vary this recipe by adding ⅓-½ c. chopped walnuts
or almonds.

Raw or Roasted Nut Pie Crust

½ c. walnuts   ¼ c. honey
½ c. almonds   1 t. cinnamon
¼ c. currants   ½ t. sea salt
¼ c. Sesame Tahini

This recipe makes bottom crust for 1 9-inch pie. Grind nuts.
Mix all ingredients together and press into pan. Put in freezer
until chilled. You may also roast nuts first, then grind.

Honey-Coconut Pie Crust

1 c. raw wheat germ   ¼ c. oil
⅓ c. unsweetened coconut   2 T. honey
¼ t. sea salt

This recipe makes bottom crust for 1 9-inch pie.

Mix all ingredients together and press into pan. Either chill
raw, or bake at 350° for 10 minutes.

Granola Pie Crust
(This is a good way to use up old granola.)

2 c. granola, ground*
¼ c. butter
2 T. honey

½ t. cinnamon
¼ t. nutmeg

This recipe makes bottom crust for 1 9-inch pie, plus enough to cover top.

Melt butter, add honey, spices. Mix with granola. Press into a baking pan and add filling; or, first bake and then add raw filling. Sprinkle remaining crust on top.

* Your blender will work well.

Oatmeal-Wheat Germ Pie Cust

1 c. oatmeal
½ c. wheat germ
4 T. whole wheat flour
2 t. sea salt

5 T. melted butter
⅓ c. honey
½ c. oil
1 t. vanilla

This recipe makes bottom crust for 1 9-inch pie.

Mix oatmeal, flour, salt. Mix separately the honey, oil, and vanilla.

Stir honey and oil mixture into oatmeal mixture. Press into pie pans, ready for baking. This crust may be also used as a crisp or may be sprinkled on top of filling.

Raw Coconut-Banana Pie

1-1½ c. bananas, sliced in
  rounds
½ c. coconut, grated and
  toasted

1½ c. yoghurt
¼ c. honey
1 t. cinnamon

Mix together the yoghurt, honey, cinnamon, and bananas. Pour half of mixture into Raw Nut Pie Crust or Honey-Coconut Pie Crust. Layer sliced bananas and coconut. Pour remaining mixture on top. Cover with coconut and more sliced bananas. If you wish, you can top it off with whipped cream.

Raw Apple Pie

Crust:

Make 1 recipe Raw Nut Pie Crust (using all walnuts). Save 1 c. for top of pie. Or make Oatmeal-Wheat Germ Pie Crust.

Filling:

1½ c. walnuts, chopped	¾ c. raisins
3 c. apples, grated	2 t. cinnamon
½-¾ c. honey (depends on	½ t. nutmeg
your sweet tooth)	juice of ½ lemon

Mix ingredients. Press crust into pan, reserving 1 c. for top of pie. Spoon in filling. Sprinkle remaining crust on top and serve.

Persimmon-Cream Cheese Pie

2 c. cream cheese	4 c. persimmons
½ c. honey	

Prepare 1 recipe for Granola Pie Crust and press into pie pan.

Cream the cheese and honey. Mash persimmons and add to mixture. Fill pie crust and refrigerate. Great with whipped cream.

You may substitute 3 c. mashed bananas for the persimmons. Try adding 1 t. cinnamon and ¼ t. nutmeg or mace.

Apricot Whip Pie

1½ c. kefir cheese	½ c. maple syrup
1½ c. apricots (very ripe)	

Prepare 1 recipe of Raw Nut Pie Crust and line a pie pan. Set in freezer so crust may firm up.

Mix kefir cheese with half of the apricots and all of the maple syrup. Remove crust from freezer and line bottom with apricot slices, then filling. Return to freezer until filling sets up.

Now put on a topping of whipped cream, flavored with vanilla and maple syrup. Serve, or return pie to freezer for keeping.

You may substitute sour cream or yoghurt for the whipped cream.

Avocado-Lime Pie

2 large avocados, well-mashed
½ c. fresh lime juice
1 can condensed milk

2 t. grated lime rind
⅔ c. honey
pinch sea salt

Prepare 1 recipe of Graham Cracker Pie Crust; line the bottom of 9-inch pie pan. Mix together the filling ingredients. Pour into shell and top with remaining crust and refrigerate.

For variation, slice bananas and lay on bottom pie crust.

Lemon No-Bake Filling

1 c. powdered milk
½-¾ c. water
3 T. honey

½ c. lemon juice
1 t. lemon peel
2 egg yolks

Prepare crust of your choice; line a 9-inch pie pan.

Blend powdered milk and honey with water. Add juice and peel. Stir in yolks. Stir until thickened. Pour into pie shell and refrigerate.

Blueberry-Ricotta Pie

1½ c. ricotta cheese
½ c. honey or maple syrup
1½ c. fresh blueberries

½ t. sea salt
3 T. agar-agar

Prepare 1 recipe of Raw or Roasted Nut Pie Crust; in this case, roasting nuts before grinding.

Combine the filling ingredients (mash half of the blueberries, leave the rest whole). Pour filling into crust. Add a topping of sour cream flavored with dissolved honey or maple syrup. Refrigerate.

For variation, you may substitute cherries or peaches for the blueberries.

Mom's Apple Pie

5 to 6 c. apples*
½ c. honey
⅛ t. sea salt
1 T. flour

½ t. cinnamon
¼ t. nutmeg
2 T. butter

Prepare 1 recipe for Flaky Pie Crust; line the bottom of a pie tin.

Core and thinly slice apples and lay on the pie crust. Next, drizzle the honey over, then spices and flour. Dot with butter. Top with a pricked pie crust.

Bake at 450° for 10 minutes. Reduce heat to 350° and bake 45 minutes to 1 hour.

* Select a good cooking apple such as McIntosh, pippin, Rome or Gravenstein. If apples lack flavor you may want to sprinkle with a little lemon juice and/or vanilla.

If apples are not very juicy, add 2 T. water, apple juice, or cream. If they are really juicy you may need to add another ½ T. flour.

Lemon-Honey Pie with Meringue

1 c. honey	3 egg yolks, beaten
6 T. arrowroot	3 T. butter
dash sea salt	1/3 c. lemon juice
1 c. cream	peel of 1 lemon, grated
1 c. milk	

This recipe fills 2 9-inch pie shells. Choose a crust recipe that needs no cooking or precook the shell.

In the top of a double boiler mix arrowroot, honey, and salt until it is a smooth paste.

Boil water in bottom of double boiler. Reduce to medium heat. Make sure water doesn't touch the top pan.

Slowly add milk and cream, stirring constantly, and continue cooking 8-10 minutes. Cover and let cook 10 more minutes, stirring occasionally to keep from sticking.

In a small bowl beat egg yolks, mixing in a few tablespoons of the hot mixture. Cook for 2 more minutes.

Remove from heat. Add butter, lemon, and grated peel. Stir very gently, to remove steam, and pour into cold pie shell.

Meringue:

4 egg whites	3 t. sugar (or date sugar)
1/2 t. cream tartar	1 t. vanilla

Beat egg whites until frothy. Add rest of ingredients and beat.

Cover filling with lots of meringue. Put pie in oven for 10 minutes or until peaks are light brown.

Simple Cheese Pie

1 1/2 lb. cream cheese	3/4 c. honey
4 eggs	2 T. lemon or vanilla

Prepare 2 9-inch Graham Cracker Pie Crusts.

Whip filling ingredients together and pour into crust. Sprinkle a little of the crust on the top. Bake for 12-15 minutes, until just solid.

You may layer fresh fruit slices on bottom or put them in the filling and on top.

Toyon-Apple Pie

4 c. apples, sliced
4 c. toyon berries, leached*
1½ T. butter
½ c. honey

¼ t. cinnamon
⅛ t. nutmeg
⅛ t. sea salt
1 T. arrowroot or flour

Prepare 1 recipe for Flaky Pie Crust; line a pie tin with a bottom crust.

Lay in apple slices and toyon berries. Drizzle honey over apples and berries. Sprinkle seasonings and arrowroot; dot with butter. Cover the pie with a pricked upper crust. Bake at 450° for the first 10 minutes. Reduce heat to 350° and bake pie 45 minutes to 1 hour.

* To leach toyon berries put in a bowl, pour boiling water over them and let sit for 10 minutes. Strain. Leave in strainer and pour boiling water over them two or more times. This should remove the bitter taste.

Banana Cream Pie

Graham Cracker Crust
Vanilla Custard Pudding
4 c. bananas, sliced

¼ c. toasted coconut
whipped cream

Press crust into pan. Lay 2 c. bananas on bottom then pour on pudding and put remaining 2 c. bananas on top. Add whipped cream and top with coconut.

Peanut Butter Pie

½ c. honey
2 T. gelatin
pinch of salt
1 Graham Cracker Crust recipe
¾ c. peanut butter

1 t. vanilla
1¾ c. milk
2 egg yolks (beaten)
2 T. butter

Mix in a saucepan honey, gelatin, and salt. Add milk, egg yolks, and butter. Line bottom of a 9-inch pie pan with crust.

Heat and stir filling until it is slightly thickened. Add some of this mixture to peanut butter, then add peanut butter mixure and 1 t. vanilla to the custard. Chill a bit, stirrring occasionally (don't allow it to harden).

Pour into shell and let set. Serve with whipped cream and/or honey topping.

Deep Dish Pie

Filling:

4½ c. fresh fruit, sliced
⅓-½ c. honey (depending on
   sweetness of fruit)
1 T. plus 1 t. lemon juice

1 T. 1 t. lemon juice
1 t. vanilla
thickening (flour, arrowroot, or
   quick-cook tapioca)

Combine ingredients in a saucepan and heat. Spice specific fruits according to J. M. B.'s Fruit Crisp recipe below.

Dough:

1 c. unbleached flour
1½ t. baking powder
½ t. sea salt

2 t. honey
4 T. butter or shortening
⅓ c. milk or cream

Use a fork to mix lightly. On floured board, knead for a minute or two. Roll out to cover 8-inch square greased pan.

When fruit filling is hot, pour into greased pan. Dot with 3 T. butter. Cover the fruit with dough. Sprinkle top with cinnamon and bake at 450° for 20-30 minutes. Serve with fresh cream.

J. M. B.'s Fruit Crisp

Crust:

1½ c. oatmeal
½ c. flour
⅔ c. butter

¾ c. honey
½ t. sea salt

Melt the butter and mix the crust ingredients.

Filling:

2½ c. fruit, sliced
¼ c. butter

¼ c. flour
¼ t. sea salt

Mix the filling. If using apples, add 1 t. cinnamon; peaches or apricots; ½ t. nutmeg, mace, or allspice; prunes or plums, ½ t. cloves.

Layer the two—first crust, then filling; then crust, filling—and sprinkle the top with crust mixture. Press down firmly. Bake at 375° for 30-45 minutes.

Green Tomato Crisp

4 c. granola, ground
½ c. butter
½ c. honey
1 t. cinnamon
½ t. nutmeg
4 c. green tomato slices

¼ t. sea salt
1 c. date sugar
3 T. butter (for top)
¼ t. cinnamon
1 T. lemon juice

Melt ½ c. butter, add honey and spices. Mix with ground granola. Pat half of mixture into an 8-inch square oiled pan. Lay down tomato slices and top with sugar, 3 T. butter, and spices. Top with rest of granola and bake at 375° for 35-40 minutes.

Pumpkin or Squash Pie

2 c. steamed squash
1 c. milk
4 eggs
½ c. honey
¼ c. molasses
½ c. milk (or soy milk powder)

½ t. sea salt
½ t. ginger
½ t. cinnamon
¼ t. nutmeg
1 t. vanilla

This recipe makes 2 9-inch pies.

Prepare 1 recipe Flaky Pie Crust; line 2 9-inch pie pans and prebake at 425° for 10 minutes.

Combine squash, milk, and eggs. Mix until smooth and pour into crusts. Bake at 375° for 45 minutes, until firm in center.

Walnut or Pecan Pie

Partially bake an empty pie shell for 5 minutes at 350°. Let cool.

Cream ⅓ c. butter, ¾ c. honey. Beat in 3 eggs, one at a time.

Add 2 T. molasses, 1½ c. broken walnuts, 1 t. vanilla, ½ t. sea salt.

Fill shell and bake for 30 minutes at 375°. Serve with whipped cream, if you like.

Molasses Pie
(Very simple and inexpensive.)

1 egg
1½ c. soft bread crumbs
1 c. molassses

1 t. cinnamon
dash sea salt

Choose a crust that can be baked and line a 9-inch pie pan. Mix filling ingredients, pour into pie shell, and bake at 400° for 20 minutes.

Try using 2 eggs and 1 t. cinnamon.
Add nuts or sliced apples.
Add ½ c. cream, yoghurt, or sour cream to filling.

Puddings as Fillings

You can use any of the crust recipes, choose a pudding, decorate if you like; and, voilà!—a quick treat.

Quick Vanilla Pudding
(A basic pudding that's quick and easy and tastes great!)

½ c. honey	4 well-beaten eggs
¼ c. flour or 2-4 T. arrowroot	1 t. vanilla
1½ c. milk	⅛ t. sea salt

Scald 1½ c. milk; set aside. In top of a double boiler, cream together honey, flour, eggs, and gelatin. Add milk. Stir constantly until mixture comes to a boil. Remove from heat and add vanilla and salt. Let cool and serve. Cover and refrigerate.

For variation add 1 t. lemon rind and ½ t. nutmeg.

Chocolate Pudding

Follow recipe for Quick Vanilla Pudding. When scalding milk, add 2 squares unsweetened chocolate. When chocolate has melted, mix with other pudding ingredients and continue as in recipe.

Carob Pudding

Follow Quick Vanilla Pudding recipe, substituting ½ c. carob powder for ¼ c. flour.

Carob-Mint Pudding

Make Carob Pudding. Add some spearmint leaves when scalding milk, or use mint extract.

Basic Vanilla Pudding
(Made with milk powder.)

1⅓ c. powdered milk
½ t. sea salt
3 c. milk

½ c. honey
5 eggs, beaten
1 t. vanilla

Slowly, with a whisk, mix powdered milk into the milk. Stir to a smooth paste; make sure there are no lumps. Scald 2 c. of the milk and set aside. In the top of double boiler, cream honey, eggs, salt. Add milk mixture and continue cooking. Slowly stir in scalded milk and cook until mixture reaches boiling point. Remove from heat; add vanilla. Chill. *Yield: 6-8 servings.*

Orange Pudding

Follow recipe for Basic Vanilla Pudding, adding 2 T. orange rind.

Indian Pudding

2 c. cornmeal
4 c. milk
¾ c. molasses or honey
1 t. sea salt
3 well-beaten eggs

4 T. butter (or ½ stick, or
　¼ c. oil)
1 t. cinnamon
½ t. ginger

Soak cornmeal in milk for a few hours (or cook for 25 minutes). Add other ingredients. Bake at 325° for 1 hour.
Yield: 6-8 servings.

Baked Custard

½ c. powdered milk
¼ t. sea salt
⅓ c. honey

3 whole eggs or 6 egg yolks
½ c. fresh milk
1 t. vanilla

Mix until smooth, then add 1½ c. liquid milk and mix thoroughly. Pour into shallow baking dish; sprinkle with nutmeg. Place in pan of water (important!). Bake at 300° for 40 minutes.
Yield: 4 servings.

Banana Pudding

10 ripe bananas
⅔ c. honey
3 T. butter
2½ c. water

1 t. nutmeg
½ t. allspice
1½ t. vanilla
½ c. sliced almonds

Melt butter in a frying pan. Cut bananas into ½-inch pieces. Fry in butter for 5 minutes. Mash. Add ½ c. of the water and heat with bananas. Gently stir for 3-4 minutes. Mix honey with remaining water. Pour over bananas and stir. Boil for 15 minutes, stirring often so mixture doesn't stick. Remove from heat. Add vanilla and spices. Pour into a dish and top with sliced almonds.
Yield: 6-8 servings.

Carrot Pudding

3 lbs. carrots
2½ cups fresh fruit juice (such as apple)
3 T. butter
3 T. arrowroot

¾ c. ground nuts (walnuts or almonds)
1 t. cinnamon
½ t. sea salt

Slice carrots into ½-inch rounds. Fry in butter for 10 minutes. Add 1½ c. of fresh juice. Cover and simmer for 20 minutes.

Drain the juice; save. Remove the carrots and mash. Return the juice to a frying pan. Stir in 3 T. arrowroot until dissolved.

Add remaining cup of fresh juice, the mashed carrots, ground nuts, cinnamon, and salt. Pour into a bowl and it is ready.
Yield: 6-8 servings.

Squash or Pumpkin Pudding

2 c. squash or pumpkin
¾ c. honey
4 eggs
¼ c. molasses
2 c. milk (evaporated milk, half and half, cream)
¼ c. milk powder
1 c. cornmeal

2 c. apples, sliced
1¼ c. raisins
2 t. vanilla
1 t. cinnamon
¾ t. nutmeg
⅓ t. cloves
¼ t. ginger

Steam or bake squash until soft and easy to mash. Let it cool down, then mash. In another bowl, beat eggs with honey and molasses. Mix with squash. Add 1 c. milk. Mix cornmeal and milk powder in remaining cup of milk until smooth. Stir in spices, apples, and raisins. Combine mixtures and pour into a baking pan. Bake at 450° for 10 minutes.

Reduce heat to 350° and continue baking until custard is firm. Test doneness by sticking a table knife in the middle; it should come out clean. Cool a little and serve warm with cream or milk, or serve cold with whipped cream. Watch out—it's filling!

Yield: 6-8 servings.

Rice Pudding

2 c. cooked brown rice
1 c. cream or condensed milk
2 well-beaten eggs
½ c .chopped walnuts
⅓ c. currants

1 t. cinnamon
½ t. nutmeg
¼ t. cloves
1 t. vanilla

Combine ingredients. Put into a pan. Top with bread crumbs or ground seeds. Bake 25 minutes at 375°. *Yield: 4-6 servings.*

Acorn Pudding

In a double boiler, heat:

4 c. milk
⅔ c. cornmeal

⅔ c. acorn meal, leached*
½ c. molasses

Cook mixture until it thickens, stirring occasionally. Remove from heat and add:

¼ c. butter or oil
½ t. sea salt
1 t. ginger

½ t. cinnamon
2 beaten eggs
½ c. raisins

Pour into oiled baking pan. Bake at 325° for 1½-2 hours. *Yield: 4-6 servings.*

*For instructions of leached acorns, see Acorn Bread in Bread section.

Maple Pudding

1 T. oil
3 T. date sugar
¼ c. nonfat milk powder
1 c. unbleached white, or
    whole wheat pastry flour,
    sifted

½ c. cold water
2 t. baking powder
¼ t. sea salt
2 egg whites
1 c. maple syrup

Mix thoroughly the oil, date sugar, and milk powder. Gradually add the cold water and stir until smooth.

Add and stir in thoroughly the flour, baking powder, and salt. Fold in stiffly beaten egg whites.

Meanwhile, heat the maple syrup to boiling and add to mix. Pour into a baking dish. Pour hot syrup over the pudding and bake at 400° for 25 minutes. *Yield: 4-6 servings.*

Parfait in a Tall Glass

Papaya-Mango

Line bottom of glass with fresh papaya. Spoon in a mixture of kefir cheese, mashed mango, and maple syrup. Alternate layers. Sprinkle nutmeg on top.

Apricot

Alternate layers of apricots with tapioca.

Banana-Pear

Alternate layers of bananas and pears with chocolate pudding. Sprinkle with toasted coconut.

Pineapple-Orange

Alternate pineapple and orange fruit mixture with pineapple or orange gelatin. Mold the gelatin with half water and half fruit juice or all fruit juice.

Beverages

Tea

Tea is an important part of our daily diet. For a tasty refreshment, as a preventive or tonic; or, most important, as medicine.

We gather most of our teas from the local hillsides. Some we use fresh; the rest we dry for storage. Most markets and health food stores carry good herbal teas.

In preparing tea, there are two basic things to remember: a. never boil stems or leaves; b. always boil roots, barks, and berries.

Bring a pot of water to a boil. Add enough tea to lightly cover the top of the water. Remove from heat, and cover to steep (15-20 minutes.)

Ice Tea

Prepare as for hot tea but let it steep longer, so that it becomes strong, before pouring over ice.

For extra pizazz, add a little lemon and honey while steeping.

To keep tea on hand, make a concentrate by adding a lot of tea to a small amount of water. Steep 20-30 minutes. Store in icebox. Dilute when ready to serve.

I like to keep cinnamon sticks and orange peel on hand to add to teas. You can dry orange peels on a tray in the sun, or in the oven on very low heat. Make sure you're not using an orange peel that will be too bitter.

Sun Tea

This is a great way to prepare tea you want to keep on hand. All you have to do is put tea in a jar (¼-inch in a quart jar), and fill with water. Cover and set in the sun until it reaches desired strength. This usually takes about 4 hours. The sun brings out the sweetness of the herbs. This is one of my favorite summertime refreshments.

Sun Punch

Fill a 1-gallon jar full of fresh-picked mint. Add slices of limes, lemons, oranges. Fill jar with water. Cover with a lid and set in the sun for a few hours.

When using packaged mint, you will have to use only half the amount. You may like this tea with honey added.

Tea Blends

Spearmint, eucalyptus.
Orange peel, anise, licorice.
Cinnamon sticks.
Raspberry, orange peel with a little milk, cinnamon and nutmeg.
Toyon and manzanita berries.
Lemon grass.
Chamomile and peppermint.

Indian Tea

(This tea has a very spicy flavor.)

2 c. water
4 peppercorns, ground
6-8 cardamom seeds, whole
1 T. gresh ginger, grated

1 cinnamon stick
¼ t. nutmeg. ground
6 cloves

Heat water to boiling; add other ingredients. Let simmer for 10 minutes. Add milk and honey to taste.

Rice Tea

½ c. rice

4 c. water

Pan-toast rice over high heat, stirring constantly until browned. Add water, bring to a boil, and simmer approximately 15 minutes. Strain and serve hot or cold.

Hot Spiced Milk

1 qt. milk
1 T. cinnamon

½ t. nutmeg
½ t. cloves

Combine and heat to scalding. Remove from heat and add 4 T. honey (and 1 T. vanilla if desired).

Carob Milk

1 qt. milk
5 T. roasted carob powder

2 T. honey

Serve hot or cold. For a richer milk, add 2 beaten eggs to cold milk.

Mocha Milk

To the above recipe, add 3 T. pero (a coffee substitute).

Fig Milk

To 1 qt. milk, add 2 c. figs sliced in halves. Let stand overnight. Pour off milk. Use soaked fruit in cereal, breads, or just to eat.

Try the same recipe with raisins or dates.

Yoghurt Protein Drink

2 c. milk
1 c. yoghurt
4 T. protein powder

1 c. fresh fruit
1 T. honey

Blend all ingredients. You may also try adding 3 T. carob powder, or use 1 T. molasses instead of honey, or replace milk with soy or nut milk.

Lemonade or Limeade

1½ c. lemon or lime juice
2 c. melted honey

1 gal. ice water

Mix together. You may also use orange juice alone, or with lemon; or lemon and lime.

Fruit Smoothies

This is a great way to cool off and quench your thirst in the summer heat. Also, it helps you to utilize any fruit that may spoil by using it right away or freezing it.

I like my smoothies best when made with frozen bananas. They are best when made in a blender but then can be made by hand.

Blender Method

Put in a blender 2 ripe bananas, ½ c. fresh fruit, ½ c. juice. Add a couple of ice cubes and blend.

Try using peeled and frozen bananas; you can eliminate the ice. Or, add honey and/or cinnamon, and vanilla.

Hand Method

Mash bananas and fruit with a fork. Add juice and mix well. Try putting in a jar and shaking.

Fruit Shakes

There are many variations possible here. The difference between fruit shakes and smoothies is that in shakes you use dairy products and eliminate ice.

Follow the recipe for smoothies but in place of juice, use milk. You may add a scoop or two of ice cream if you wish; or, use half and half or nut milk.

Fruit Combinations for Shakes

Cantaloupe and banana, with cinnamon.
Strawberry, peach.
Papaya, mango.
Pineapple, coconut.
Half a medium avocado, ½ c. apple, 2 bananas.
Juice of 2 fresh oranges, 2 bananas, 2 t. honey, dash ginger, dash lemon.
Carrot juice and carob ice cream.
Carob, pero, ice cream.
Orange juice, ice cream, protein powder, raw egg.

Nut Milks

Almond or Cashew

½ c. almonds or cashews   1½ c. water

First blanch almonds by pouring boiling water over nuts. After one minute, slip off skins. Blend ingredients in blender until smooth. Add water a little at a time. Strain through a cheesecloth. For better flavor, add 1-2 T. raw honey, a little at a time. Try mixing almond and cashew.

Sesame or Sunflower

½ c. sesame or sunflower   1½ c. water
    seeds

Follow directions in above recipe.

Egg Nog I

1 qt. milk   1 t. vanilla
4 T. honey   1 t. lemon rind
4 egg yolks   ½ t. nutmeg

Blenderize or beat well.

Egg Nog II
(Richer.)

1 pt. half and half or cream   1 t. vanilla
1 pt. milk   1 t. cinnamon
4 T. honey   ½ t. nutmeg
4 egg yolks

Blenderize or beat well.

Buttermilk Egg Nog

2 egg yolks
¾ c. buttermilk

½ c. low fat milk
1 T. molasses

Blenderize or shake in a jar.

Eye Opener

1 c. tomato juice
1 lemon or lime
1 t. sea salt

1 t. Worcestershire sauce
1 t. brewer's (nutritional)
   yeast

Mix by hand or in a blender.

Soy Milk

(See Soybeans.)

Ginger Ale

½ c. ginger root, chopped
2 lemon rinds

3-4 T. honey
1 qt. plain soda water

Slice lemon rinds thin; chop ginger. Boil just enough water to cover them. Pour boiling water over rinds and ginger and steep for 5 minutes. Strain. Stir in honey and chill. When chilled and ready to serve, add to the soda water. You'll be surprised how good it is! Try adding a cinnamon stick to the ginger and lemon.

Cream Soda

1 qt. plain soda water
¼ c. honey

3 t. vanilla extract

Follow recipe for Ginger Ale.

Variations:

Use peppermint extract in place of vanilla.
Use almond extract in place of vanilla.
Use lemon juice—about ¼ c.
Try adding cinnamon sticks.

Fruit

Our Mother Earth in all her delight
Raises her blossoms to the light
Seeking the blessing our Father bestows—
Life in abundance.

The blossoms to grow into
A profusion of fruit varieties,
Rainbow-hued, the gifts of her work
Simple and true.

Fruit Salads

There is no limit to the beauty you can create in arranging a bowl of fresh fruit. You can cut and scoop and shape—be a real artist.

The fruit doesn't even have to go into a bowl—how about using those cantaloupe shells you just scooped your melon balls from? Or, if you can cut a coconut in half with a saw, you have an instant bowl. Or arrange a beautiful platter.

You need no recipe for a mixed fruit salad, just go ahead and do it! Some nice dressings are suggested in this chapter.

Pear and Cheese Salad

pears
lemons or limes

cheddar or muenster cheese
ground almonds

Slice or halve pears and arrange them on a platter, alternately with cheese slices. Sprinkle juice on pears to prevent discoloration. Top with Mint Sauce, ground almonds—or try another dressing.

Papaya-Mango Salad

2 papayas
2 mangos
kefir cheese

pineapple juice
cinnamon
vanilla

Cut papaya in half and scoop out meat, being careful not to penetrate the skin. Set skins aside. Cut mango on each side of the pit, and scoop out. Cut meat from the pit also. In a bowl, mix kefir cheese with pineapple juice and spices, then add fruit. Put into the freezer for about 1 hour.

Scoop filling into the papaya shells. Top with a fresh mint leaf and a sprinkle of nutmeg. Serve immediately.

Pineapple-Apple Salad

2 c. apples, chopped
2 c. pineapple, cubed

½ c. walnuts
juice of 1 lemon

Prepare fruit. Make a sauce by mixing 1 c. plums (mashed or blenderized), ½ c. buttermilk, ¼ t. mace, and 2 dashes sea salt. Pour over fruit. Chill and serve.

Apricot-Peach-Strawberry Salad

peaches
apricots

strawberries
walnuts

Slice fruit and add walnuts. Top with sour cream and pineapple juice.

Orange-Grapefruit Salad

oranges   pink grapefruit
recipe for Lemon-Honey   lemon
   Dressing (or your choice)   coconut

Divide oranges and grapefruit into sections. Put into a bowl with coconut. Pour dressing over and chill. Serve with yoghurt.

Avocado-Banana-Orange Salad

Slice avocado and banana in rings. Section oranges. Arrange attractively and top with Lemon-Honey Dressing, or other dressing of your choice.

Gelatin-Apple Salad

1 pkg. unflavored gelatin
1 c. hot water
1 c. apple juice

1 c. grated apple
½ c. seedless grapes

Dissolve gelatin in hot water; add apple juice. Put in refrigerator until gelatin begins setting. Add grated apple and grapes. Return to refrigerator until gelatin has molded.

Baked Apples

6 apples
¼ c. raisins
¼ c. walnuts
¼ c. honey

2 T. butter
2 t. cinnamon
1 t. nutmeg
½ t. coriander

Core apples and place in a baking dish. In a small pan, melt butter, honey, and cinnamon. Fill each apple with raisins and walnuts. Pour sauce over. Bake at 350° for 40 minutes or until done. (Remove and baste a couple times while baking.)

Fruit Salad Dessings

Yoghurt

1 c. yoghurt
¼ c. orange juice
2 T. honey

1 t. vanilla
¼ t. cinnamon

Experiment with different herbs such as crushed anise seed or mace. Add ¼ c. milk powder if you like a thicker mixture.

Lemon-Honey

½ c. honey
½ c. lemon juice
¼ c. milk powder (optional)

2 t. mace
¼ t. lemon verbena (optional)

Blend ingredients and pour over fruit.

Sour Cream or Yoghurt

You can blend sour cream or yoghurt with fruit salad or first mix it with a fruit sauce of your choice.

Papaya-Orange Sauce

(See Sauces and Gravies.)

Mint Sauce

(See Sauces and Gravies.)

Some Suggestions for Serving Fruit

Apples

Cooked or raw. Whole, chunks, slices, or grated. Of the many varieties, golden and red delicious are best eaten raw. McIntosh, pippin, Johnathan, Rome are good both ways. Good stewed in sauces, butter, jam, pies, tarts, puddings, cakes, bread, muffins, pancakes; as juice, dried, in salads, baked.

Apricots

Can be used the same as apples.

Avocados

Sliced, in chunks, or mashed. Great by themselves or in sandwiches, guacamole, salad dressings, salads, soups, pie fillings.

Bananas

Whole, sliced, mashed, sliced with cream, salads, smoothies, breads, fried, pancakes, cakes, cookies, muffins, pies, puddings, or dipped in sweet sauce.

Berries

Blackberries, blueberries, boysenberries, cranberries, elderberries, raspberries. As berries and cream, in salads, stewed, in sauces, preserves, pies, cakes, breads, icings, smoothies.

Cantaloupe

Halve, clean out seeds, and put in a scoop of yoghurt or ice cream with honey or sauce. Chunks, slices, salads, smoothies.

Cherimoyas

A custard-like fruit that tastes like pineapple and banana. Great as it is or in salads, jams, smoothies.

Cherries

Many varieties. Use as you would berries.

Dates

Dried, in salads, breads, cakes, pancakes, puddings, candies, smoothies.

Coconut

Good milk. The flesh is usually dried by the time we get it. Great in salads, pancakes, for baking, in smoothies, juice.

Custard Apple

Soft, creamy, custard flavor. Eat as it is or use as cherimoyas.

Figs

Dried, fresh, stewed. Good alone or in salads, preserves, cookies, or soaked in milk overnight.

Grapefruit

Eat raw in sections, chunks, halved. Try drizzling with honey and heating under broiler, or in salads.

Grapes

Raw, in salads, in juice, or dried as raisins.

Lemons

Juice, or with tea or other beverages. Salads, bread, pies, salad dressings, and marinades.

Limes

Same as lemons.

Mango

One of the best tropical fruits. Cut lengthwise on either side of the pit, then cut diagonally into cubes, fold back peeling, and it's ready to eat. Also eat what remains on the pit. Good in salads, jams and chutney, raw pies, smoothies.

Nectarines

Use same as apples.

Oranges

As is or in salads, juice, marmalade, sauces, cakes.

Papayas

Just a bit of papaya aids digestion because it contains a digestive enzyme. Cut in half and remove seeds. Great alone or in salads. Use as mango.

Peaches

Use same as apples.

Pears

Use as apples, glaze and bake, try them with sauce.

Persimmons

Great as they are. Must be ripe or they will make you pucker! Great in salads, raw pies, cakes, breads, juice.

Pineapple

Sliced, chunked, crushed, dried. Good in salads, jams, pies, puddings, gelatins, cakes.

Plums

Sauces, jams, icings, sauces, puddings, fillings.

Pomegranates

Fresh or in juice.

Prunes

Fresh, dried, or stewed. Use as figs.

Raisins

Dried, use as grapes. Good as they are or in breads, cakes, cookies, pancakes, puddings, syrups, cereals.

Rhubarb

Good cooked in pies, sauces.

Tangerines

Use as oranges.

Watermelons

Good as they are or in salads or juice.

Pancakes and Crepes

Pancakes are a great American tradition that should be used as more than a breakfast standby—serve them any time of the day.

Plain or fancy, the base is the same. Ground grains, water or milk, eggs, oil, and a leavening agent to make them light. For variety and change you can make additions to your batter such as fruits, nuts, or even seafood.

If you feel like being even fancier, try crepes. You can fill them with fruits, cheese, vegetables, seafoods.

To cook pancakes, prepare your griddle or fry pan by first rubbing it with oil, then preheat to about 400°. To test it, sprinkle on a few drops of water, the water should bounce and move.

Carefully pour on the batter. Cook the first side 2-3 minutes or until bubbles appear on the surface, but before they break. Turn the cakes over and cook the second side 1½-2½ minutes.

It is best to serve them right away. If you have many to prepare keep them in a covered dish set inside a warm oven.

Yeast-Rising Pancakes

1 pkg. yeast	¼ c. honey
¼ c. warm water	¼ c. oil
1 t. honey	2 eggs
¼ c. dry milk powder	½ t. sea salt
2 c. warm water or milk	2 c. whole wheat flour

Dissolve yeast in warm water and add honey. Combine milk powder, milk, honey and oil, and add to yeast mixture. Add beaten eggs and salt. Mix in flour. Cover and let rise, covered, for 20-30 minutes. Drop on hot, oiled griddle or large skillet. Cook over medium heat and turn when bubbles appear. *Yield: 18 cakes.*

Basic Pancakes

2 c. flour	2 t. oil
1 t. sea salt	2 eggs
2 t. baking powder	½ c. honey, optional
2¼ c. milk	

Let the ingredients sit until they are at room temperature, then add liquid to dry ingredients. Cook on a griddle or pan with evenly distributed heat until bubbles appear, then flip over. *Yield: 18-20 cakes.*

Banana-Walnut Pancakes

Prepare Basic Pancake recipe. Add to it:

2 mashed bananas (or sliced)	½ c. chopped walnuts
1 t. vanilla	

For variation, try grated apples and grated lemon rind, or chopped fresh fruit of your choice or serve these goodies on top of pancakes. *Yield: 20-24 cakes.*

Soy Flour Cakes

Use Basic Pancake recipe but substitute ¾ c. soy flour for ¾ c. whole wheat flour.

Quick Buckwheat Cakes

1 c. buckwheat flour
¾ c. whole wheat pastry flour
2½ t. baking powder
1 t. sea salt

1 T. molasses
2 eggs, separated
⅓ c. butter, melted
1½ c. milk

Combine flour, baking powder, and salt in a large bowl. Mix molasses, egg yolks, butter, and milk in another. Combine the two mixtures. Beat egg whites until stiff and fold in. Cook on a griddle or pan with evenly distributed heat until bubbles appear, then flip over. *Yield: 16-20 cakes.*

Sourdough Pancakes

Starter Batch:

1 c. sourdough starter
(see Bread section)
1 c. warm water

1½ c. unbleached white, whole
wheat, or buckwheat flour

Mix warm water with starter and add flour slowly, stirring continuously until all lumps are removed. Cover and let sit in warm place for 12 hours. Check once in a while; if crust or liquid forms on top, stir.

The Pancakes:

1 egg
1 T. sugar
1 T. melted butter

¾ t. sea salt
2 T. milk

Let ingredients sit until they are at room temperature. Beat egg with rest of ingredients, mixing well, then add to starter batch.

Drop by tablespoonfuls on a hot griddle or skillet. When bubbles appear, flip over. Serve with honey or syrup; or sour cream. *Yield: 16-20 cakes.*

Corncakes

(See Corn section.)

Apfelschmarren

(German apple pancakes.)

4 pippin apples
2 eggs
¾ c. milk
½ t. vanilla
¾ c. flour

⅛ t. sea salt
2 T. butter
cinnamon and sugar
　　(or cinnamon and honey)

Beat eggs, then add vanilla and milk. Sift in flour and salt. Add thinly sliced apples. Melt butter in skillet with oven-proof handle.

Pour batter in skillet and bake at 350° for 10-15 minutes, until batter is set. Sprinkle the cinnamon mixture thinly on top. Cut into slices and serve.

Creamy Waffles

1½ c. flour
3 t. baking powder
½ t. sea salt
1 t. sugar

3 eggs, separated
1 c. cream or condensed milk
¼ c. melted butter

Mix the sugar, egg yolks, milk, and butter in one bowl. Sift the flour, baking powder, and salt together, then add to the liquid ingredients. Fold in stiffly beaten egg whites and pour into waffle iron.

French Toast

4-6 eggs, well-beaten
¼ c. milk, evaporated milk,
    or cream
honey or sugar to taste

bread slices (best to use
    2-day-old bread)
cinnamon, nutmeg, salt

Dip bread in milk mixture. Allow to really soak up mixture, then put slices on a medium-hot skillet with a little melted butter. Brown and turn. Add more butter if needed. Serve with butter and honey, syrup, or jam.

Fruit French Toast

French Toast recipe
fresh fruits of your choice
    (colorful)

yoghurt or sour cream
cinnamon, syrup

Cut toast in half, diagonally. Arrange nicely on a plate (slices overlapping each other). Top with yoghurt or sour cream, then lay fruit in a nice arrangement on top. Pour syrup over and sprinkle with cinnamon.

Scotch Oat Cakes

3 c. cooked oats (or leftover
    oatmeal)
1½ c. water

½ t. sea salt
2 T. oil

Combine ingredients. Drop by large spoonfuls on griddle or in a heated skillet. Fry until brown on both sides. Serve with sryup or honey. *Yield: 3-6 servings.*

This same kind of cake can also be made with other leftover cereals.

Fried Bananas

4 bananas, mashed
12 T. flour
2 eggs, well-beaten

3 T. honey
1 t. cinnamon
¼ t. nutmeg or mace

Combine ingredients and mix well. Spoon a heaping tablespoon for each cake onto a greased griddle or skillet. Cook until browned or crisp on each side. *Yield: 3-5 servings.*

Fried Pineapple

6 to 8 pineapple slices, ½-inch
thick
2 T. flour

1 egg
lemon juice

Combine flour and egg. Sprinkle a little lemon juice on pineapple. Dip in batter and fry until crisp on both sides. *Yield: 3-5 servings.*

Fritters

2 eggs
⅔ c. milk or fruit juice
1 T. butter
fruit of your choice

1 c. flour
½ t. sea salt
1 T. honey

Beat eggs, add milk or juice, and butter. Combine flour, salt, and honey. Let sit for 2 hours in a cool place.

To cook: have oil hot, but not smoking, in a frying pan (no more than ⅓ full of oil).

Slice or chop fruit, no more than ¾-inch thick. Pat dry so that fritter batter will adhere to it, and drop into oil. Cook 3-5 minutes. Drain on paper towels.

You can use apple slices, banana rounds or lengths, pineapple wedges, orange or tangerine sections, apricot halves, peach slices—or something exotic like elderberry or yucca blossoms!

When done, swirl on honey, and dust with cinnamon.

Syrups

Basic Syrup

½ c. butter   ¼ c. honey or molasses

Melt butter. Stir in honey or molasses and serve. *Yield:* ¾ *c.*

Variations:

Orange Syrup. To above mixture, add ½ c. fresh squeezed orange juice and grate a little rind into it.

Fruit Syrup. Put fruit of your choice in a blender with vanilla, and add to Basic Syrup. You may also add half and half. If syrup is too thin, thicken with milk powder or cook a little more with some arrowroot.

Spice Syrup. Add 1 t. cinnamon, ¼ t. nutmeg, and 1 t. vanilla (optional).

Also see Dressings for some fruit sauce recipes.

Papaya Syrup

1 papaya   1 t. cinnamon
2 T. honey   ¼ t. nutmeg
4 T. butter   dash sea salt
half and half

Blenderize ingredients and serve. You may heat the mixture if you wish.

Crepes

(Use with fillings below.)

3 eggs   ½ c. milk
½ c. water   1 T. oil
2 T. unbleached flour   ½-1 t. sea salt

Beat eggs, add water, beat more. Add unbleached flour, beat more. Add milk, oil, and salt to taste. Let sit for half an hour or more to develop gluten in flour.

Heat skillet with 1 T. oil in it. When medium-hot, pour in 1½ ounces batter, and tilt pan around so that the batter covers the entire bottom. Cook 1-2 minutes. Loosen around the edges with a spatula, and flip, cooking on other side until slightly brown.

Don't be discouraged if your first crepe doesn't turn out right. It takes practice to develop a 'feel" for them. Your skillet must be hot enough to prevent the crepe from coming out too thin; but not so hot that the batter bubbles up immediately, making the crepe too thick. *Yield: 8 crepes.*

Persevere—crepes are really fun when you get the hang of making them!

Spinach Crepes

1½ c. ricotta cheese
½ c. spinach, cooked and
   drained
⅓ c. sautéed mushrooms
⅓ c. green onions, chopped

⅓-½ c. sliced almonds
¼ c. Parmesan cheese
½ t. garlic powder
½ t. nutmeg
¼ t. sea salt

This is enough filling for 8 crepes. Put 3 T. of the mixture along each crepe and roll up. Place the crepes in a casserole pan, bake in oven at 375° until hot. Serve with cream sauce.

Sour Cream and Fruit Crepes

1 c. sour cream
3 T. honey

½ t. cinnamon
¼ t. nutmeg

Combine ingredients. Put 1 T. or so of this mixture along each crepe. Cover with sliced fresh fruit such as peaches, bananas, strawberries, apricots, whole blueberries. Roll up, place in casserole, and heat at 375° until it is warmed through. Serve with whipped cream.

Seafood Crepes

1 c. fish
1 c. shrimp
¼ c. green onions

¼ c. celery
1 t. sweet basil
sea salt to taste

Mix just enough cream sauce with filling to moisten. Fill each crepe and serve with hot cream sauce on top.

Canning and Drying

When winter comes and the fresh fruit and vegetable selection begins to dwindle, it's time for a look into your pantry. There you may have a wide choice from the selection of colorful fruits and vegetables you have canned.

Your family's pleasure in being able to enjoy these things is your reward. Now aren't you glad you set aside the time to prepare these foods for the winter months?

Part of "living on the land" is being in tune with the cycles of the seasons. There is a time to sow and a time to reap. Much planning is done, much work is performed to grow enough food to feed the family and to store something for the winter.

Because of the mild climate where we live we are able to plant in both the spring and the fall. Fall crops are much more limited, of course—to the very hardy plants. What we plant in the spring will be harvested in both the summer and the fall. Much of what we harvest is prepared for storage by either drying or canning.

There is so much information on drying and canning (enough, in fact, to fill a book), that I decided to give only a basic outline here, along with some helpful things we have learned. We are fortunate to have in our family some devoted and experienced canners.

There are some very good books on canning and drying that can give you more information.

The Basic Canning Process

Canning is simple, but it takes time and patience and care. Here is a basic outline of the canning process:

Check jars for nicks and cracks—discard defective jars (lids won't make a perfect seal if the surface is nicked); always use new lids (used lids will not seal), or good rubber seals.

Wash jars, covers, and seals in hot, soapy water. Rinse well.

Select firm, fresh fruit. Do not use fruit that is too overripe. Be sure to cut off all bad parts of the fruit.

Prepare the food according to recipe.

Sterilize the jars, rims, and lids in boiling water.

Pack jars. Be sure to leave enough head room. Add extra sterile liquid if necessary.

Release air bubbles by stirring with a knife.

Wipe the top of the jar and the threads so that no food clings (a dirty rim may cause an imperfect seal).

Place lid on jar, screw on rim snuggly, but do not tighten down completely.

Process in a boiling water bath, or a pressure cooker, according to recipe.

Remove jars from processing bath and tighten down rims.

Let cool 12 hours, remove rims (if using metal lids), test seals.

Label jars with contents and date; store in pantry or cellar.

Test seals. One sign of a perfect seal is the indentation of the lid; another is a high, clear ring when the lid is tapped. (If the jar is too full, the sound will be lower and duller, so be sure to leave ¼-inch space when filling jar.)

Tips for Successful Canning

Once you understand the basic canning process there are always a few things to be learned through experience that can make it all a little easier. Here are some tips to help your canning go smoothly.

Be careful; take the time to do it right.

Keep everything as clean and sanitary as possible. All utensils, containers and food should be *sterile*. (Food or packing liquid should be boiling.)

Always use fully ripe food, making sure to remove all spoiled, discolored, or wormy parts.

Try to get as much air out of the jar as possible to ensure a perfect seal.

Oven canning is not recommended. It is dangerous and less than foolproof.

To lift empty jars out of sterile water, use the handle of a wooden spoon; much easier than using tongs.

Put a cookie sheet under the jars you are packing to catch the spills.

Be organized; have everything you need within your reach and a place for everything.

If you are canning at higher altitudes, add 2 minutes to the processing time for every 1,000 feet elevation. (For example, if you are at 7,000 feet, add 14 minutes.)

Avoid exposing hot jars to a cold draft to prevent cracking.

If you're going to be doing a lot of canning or canning large quantities, it is really nice to build an outdoor canning kitchen. All you need is a screened-in area to keep out flies, work tables, water, and heat for cooking. You may include a whole stove or just a grate with a fire under it. It is really a lot nicer to have lots of air circulating about and no one to bump into, than being in a steamy, crowded kitchen.

It is possible for low-acid foods to develop *Clostridium botulinum*, a bacterium that produces botulin, a fatal toxin that is very hard to detect. So when you are ready to serve a low-acid food that is home-canned, it is essential to boil it uncovered for 15-20 minutes. Pickled vegetables and most fruits will not develop *botulinum* because of high acid or sugar content. If you are uncertain about a jar of food, don't even taste it. Throw it away or bury it where even an animal won't find it.

Fruit sauces and fruit butters have a tendency to become discolored. The best way to avoid this is to use a double boiler, and to pack jars while the fruit is piping hot.

The way in which we decide to process food we are canning is determined by the relative acidity of the food. Yeasts, molds, and bacteria won't live as readily in high-acid environments as in low-

acid ones. Generally speaking, vegetables are low-acid and most fruits are high acid. To make sure we have food free from bacteria, molds, and yeasts we can add various natural preservatives to the food:

Lemon and apple-cider vinegar provide acid.

Tamari is also high in acid.

Salt is a natural preservative.

Honey is a natural preservative.

Vegetables may be canned in a tamari-water solution (make it as strong as you like but remember that it will become stronger sitting in a jar for a couple of months). Add vinegar and/or spices for pickles or extra tanginess. Fruits may be canned in a honey-water syrup. Add spices if you wish. Make the syrup thick or thin. Vary the sweetness to your taste (2 c. honey to 4 c. warm water).

Low-acid foods *must* be processed in a pressure cooker. High-acid foods may be processed in a boiling water bath. The packed jars are immersed in water (be sure water completely covers the jars). Use a wire rack to lift jars in and out of the water. Processing time varies according to each recipe. I have found it best to set hot jars on a towel to drain and cool.

A *boiling water bath* means the packed jars are processed in a kettle of boiling water.

Pressure canning means the packed jars are processed in a pressure cooker to reach high enough temperatures to kill all harmful organisms.

Recipes may be hot-pack or cold-pack. *Hot-pack* means the food is packed in the jars hot; *cold-pack* means the food is packed in the jars raw.

Headroom. Be sure to leave the appropriate amount of headroom at the top of the jar before closing (headroom is the space between the food and the top of the jar). For most foods it is about ½-inch. For jams and jellies—usually not more than ¼-inch.

Canning Equipment

Equipment You'll Need
1. Jars and appropriate sealing lids (see below).
2. Good sharp knives (1 large, 1 small).
3. Big pots for cooking or steaming food and for processing of jars (with a wire rack that fits inside).
4. A pressure canner if you're doing vegetables.
5. A couple of wooden spoons with really long handles.
6. A ladle.
7. A strainer, blender, or ginder may be needed for some recipes.
8. A canning funnel is nice but not essential.

Types of Glass-Jar Seals
1. Red rubber sealing ring and porcelain-lined screw cap.
2. Red rubber sealing ring and metal screw cap.
3. Reusable metal screw band (rim) and metal cap (cap not reusable).
4. Glass lid and red rubber ring with a wire bail (old-fashioned European type).
5. Metal lid or screw band, hard plastic insert, and soft rubber gasket (Aunt B's).

A note on the scarcity of canning jars, rims and lids:

Canning supplies are becoming more in demand and a lot harder to find when you need them. Plan ahead—buy your jars in January when no one else could be bothered. Don't wait until the height of canning season (summer to fall) or you may be disappointed.

Try thrift stores; they often have beautiful old jars, but be sure to check for cracks and nicks.

Try ordering from local merchants. Order long before the canning season to be sure you'll have the supplies you need.

Resources

The Ball Blue Book
Ball Corporation
Muncie, IN 47302

The Kerr Home Canning Book
Kerr Glass Manufacturing Corporation
Sand Springs, OK 74063

Canning Vegetables

Green Beans

Snap into ½-inch pieces. Pack into jars raw. Fill jars with boiling tamari water, leaving ½-inch headroom. Seal and process for 75 minutes in pressure canner.

Beets

Steam and peel beets. Dice or leave whole. Pack hot. Fill jars with boiling solution of vinegar, salt, water, and pickling spices. ½-inch headroom and process in pressure canner for 65 minutes.

Pickles

Slice cucumbers, zucchini, or melon rind. Pack raw. Fill jars with boiling solution of vinegar, salt, water, and pickling spices. Leave ½-inch headroom. Seal and process in boiling water bath for 30 minutes.

Peaches or Berries

Wash well. Pack into jars raw. Fill jars with boiling water or boiling honey syrup. Seal with ½-inch head room. Process in boiling water bath for 30 minutes. For extra flavor add a peach pit to the peaches jar.

Tomato Sauce

Quarter and cook down to a thick, chunky sauce for several hours (for a smooth sauce, put through a food mill or blender). Pack hot with ½-inch headroom. Seal. Process in boiling water bath for 20 minutes. May be seasoned with Italian spices, chilies for Mexican style, or just salt or tamari.

Applesauce

Quarter and cook down apples. Mash well. Add lemon and honey. For variations, add raspberries, or spices, nuts, and raisins. Leave ½-inch headroom and process in boiling water bath for 20 minutes.

Preserves and Conserves; Jellies and Fruit Butters

Conserves are combinations of mixed fruits and nuts. Try plum-peach-walnut or apple-berry conserves. Anything you can imagine!

Sweet butters can be made from almost anything. Simply puree, add spices and honey, and cook until really thick. Pack hot. Seal with ¼-inch headroom.

Some of my favorites are apple butter and pumpkin butter. Other possibilities are peach butter, plum butter, apricot butter, and strawberry butter. Make them thick but don't overcook as all jam-type foods get thicker as they cool.

Jellies are made from the juice of the fruit (no pulp at all), honey, a little acid (lemon), and a thickener such as pectin or agar-agar. Be sure to cook well or you'll have soup instead of jelly. Old favorites are apple-mint; and, of course, grape. Jellies may be sealed by pouring melted paraffin on top instead of using a metal lid.

Peach or Pear Butter

6 c. peaches	½ t. cinnamon
1½ c. honey	¼ t. nutmeg
¼-½ c. lemon or orange juice	¼ t. ginger (optional)

Cut peaches into eighths and cook until very soft. Run through a food mill, sieve, or blender until smooth. Return to pan, add remaining ingredients, and cook until thick, about 90 minutes. Stir frequently to prevent sticking. Store in refrigerator or can. No processing is necessary. Fill to ½-inch of rim.

Apple Butter

Cover 5 lbs. apples, sliced and cored, with cider and bring to a boil. Simmer until mushy; about 20 minutes. Remove from heat and push through a sieve. Add the following:

2 lbs. brown sugar or	1 t. nutmeg
3 c. honey	1 t. cloves
1 t. cinnamon	

Stir in and return to heat and boil. Turn heat to low and simmer 2½ hours, stirring often, until very thick—until it sheets from a spoon.

Spoon into hot, sterile jars and seal—no processing necessary.

May be scalded with paraffin. The juice of one lemon may be added for tartness. Half a cup of chopped nuts may also be added.

Strawberry Jam

1 qt. strawberrries	1 stick agar-agar or pectin
1½ c. honey	½ lemon, juiced

Wash and stem strawberries. Cook slowly in a heavy pot until warm and juicy throughout. Then stir in honey and mix well.

Prepare the agar-agar by flaking, and soaking for 15 minutes. Add it to jam after honey has been well-mixed. If using pectin, you need only half the amount that jelly would take. The addition of agar-agar or pectin quickens the process—the end result is a spoon-dropable product.

You can do it without agar-agar or pectin but you must allow more time for the jam to thicken while simmering and there is no quarantee that it will become spoon-dropable. While the jam is cooling, sprinkle lemon juice over the top to brighten the color and add more flavor.

For variation, use blackberries, boysenberries, or loganberries.

Aunt Bea's Spiced Apples

4 qts. boiling water
2-4 c. sugar or honey
2-3 t. cinnamon
1 t. ginger

1 t. allspice
1 t. cloves, ground
4 qts. apples, quartered and
    diced or cut into rings

Heat water to boiling. Add 2 c. honey or sugar. Add more to taste. Stir until it is dissolved. Add cinnamon, allspice, and ginger. Then add the apples. Heat until the apples begin to turn clear.

Pack into hot, sterile jars, ½-inch headroom, and process in boiling water bath 20 minutes.

Spiced apples can be used in cobbler, pie, apple crisp, or served plain.

Applesauce 'n Raisins

5 lbs. pippin apples
½ to 1 c. honey
1 T. cinnamon
1 t. nutmeg

2 T. vanilla
½ c. lemon juice
½ lb. raisins

Core and cut apples. Cook down until very soft. Add raisins until sauce is a darker color and pulpy. Add remaining ingredients. Cook about 10 more minutes. Store in refrigerator or can it. Fill to ½-inch of rim. Processing time is 10 minutes in boiling water bath.

Rosehip Jam

4½ lbs. rosehips
4 c. water
5½ c. sugar (substitute can be
    date sugar)

gelatin (or substitute 1 c.
    apple juice for 1 c. water
    —try agar- agar)

Remove blossom end, split and remove balls of seeds. Crush fruit, add water, bring to a boil, and simmer covered for 10 minutes. Pour into cloth bag and allow all juice to drain from bag. Yield: 4 c. juice.

Mix gelatin or agar-agar with juice in saucepan. Bring to hard boil over high heat. Add sugar and bring to rolling boil for 1 minute, stirring constantly. Remove, skim, and pour into sterile jars and seal. No processing necessary. Leave ½-inch headroom.

For variation, add slices of 1 small orange and 1 T. of ginger.

Raspberry-Rhubarb Jam

1 qt. raspberries
2 c. rhubarb, diced

3 c. honey
1 T. lemon

Steam rhubarb until soft. Follow directions for Strawberry Jam. Pack into hot, sterile jars; no processing necessary.

Pineapple-Guava Jam

6 c. guavas (65)
¼ c. water
3 lemons (juice)

¼ stick agar-agar
½ c. honey

Scoop out guavas into a pan. Add water and lemon and cook down about 1 hour. Add agar-agar. Run through a mill or sieve or blender until smooth. Add honey to taste. Pack into hot, sterile jars. May be sealed with paraffin. No processing necessary.

Tomato Ketchup

8 qts. tomatoes (about 10 lbs.)
½-2 cloves garlic, minced
3 large onions, diced
2-3 dashes sea salt
¼ t. kelp
1 t. ginger, ground

2 t. mustard
2 t. mace
1 T. tamari
½ c. honey or sugar
2 c. vinegar

In a cloth bag, tie:

1 T. whole cloves
1 T. peppercorns

1 stick cinnamon
1 T. pickling spice (optional)

Quarter tomatoes, add rest of ingredients, bring to a boil. Simmer for several hours, stirring often, until thick. Pack into hot, sterile jars with ½-inch headroom. (Remove cloth bag.) Process in boiling water bath for 20 minutes.

Bread-and-Butter Pickles

12 cucumbers, sliced
   crosswise
6 large onions, sliced
4 cloves garlic, chopped
1 T. sea salt
2 t. cinnamon
1 T. mustard

1 T. pickling spice
2 c. vinegar
1 t. cloves
1 t. allspice
1 t. celery seed
½ t. tamari
1¼-1½ c. honey

Soak cucumbers and onions overnight, with vinegar and salt,

in a glass or stone jar. Put a plate with a weight on top to keep them submerged.

It is important to cook them after soaking overnight; they lose their crispness within a day. Cook cucumbers in their soaking juices, with spices added, until they are soft. Be careful not to cook them too long or they will fall apart.

Pack into hot, sterile jars with ½-inch headroom. Process in boiling water bath for 30 minutes.

Chili Sauce

6 qts. tomato puree*
4 cloves garlic, minced
3 large onions, diced
2 c. celery, diced
2 bell peppers (red or
   green, diced)
1 T. black pepper
1 c. vinegar

½ t. cayenne pepper
1 t. sea salt
1 t. chili powder
1 t. cinnamon
1 t. allspice
2 t. dry mustard
⅓-½ c. honey
½ c. molasses

Simmer all of the ingredients until thickened and the flavors are well-blended; 30-35 minutes. While still hot, ladle into canning jars, leaving ½-inch headroom. Process in boiling water bath: 10 minutes for quarts and pints; 20 minutes for half-gallons.

*If you are preparing this from scratch, strain 9-10 qts. of cooked tomatoes down to 6 qts. puree.

Green Tomato Relish

6 qts. green tomatoes,
  uncooked
2 large onions, sliced
1 clove garlic, chopped
2 bell peppers (red or green),
  chopped
1 c. vinegar
½ c. honey
1 T. sea salt

2 T. dry mustard
1 t. pepper
¼ t. cayenne
1 t. cinnamon
1 t. allspice
1 t. ginger
1 t. cloves
1 t. celery seeds
1 t. lemon rind (optional)

Cook all ingredients together in a large pot for about 45 minutes. Pack into hot, sterile jars, leaving ½-inch headroom. Process in boiling water bath for 25 minutes.

Drying

We are finding ourselves turning to drying many of our foods, due to the rising cost of canning jars, and not having a freezer. Also, it allows us a quick method of using fruits and vegetables which are soon to spoil.

Our best drying method is sun-drying with screens. When using this method, select screens which are in wooden or fiberglass frames; metal can give the fruit an undesirable taste. The screen should be raised slightly so that the air can circulate freely.

The screens may be set on top of the roof or propped up (with bricks, etc.), and put in your yard, or tied to a branch or pole. If on the ground, and ants are a problem, place legs in tubs of water.

If the top screen is larger than the bottom, you can keep out insects. Also, mosquito netting may be used.

Selecting Fruit

Of course, fruit in perfect condition is our first choice. However, many times we find ourselves with fruit that is on its way to spoilage, and we must do something fast. So you can cut and remove the bad spots and dry the rest. Slice thin and even.

Apples
Good when done in slices. Keep checking and removing them when each slice is done. This will prevent them from burning in the sun.

Apricots
Halved. Save pits and sun dry; good for crushing—use like vanilla, or oil can be extracted too.

Bananas
Best whole, but will dry faster when split in thirds lengthwise. Slice in circles; dry and roast for chips.

Nectarines and Peaches
Best halved.

Pears
Best halved, but will dry faster when sliced thin.

Grapes and Cherries
Dried whole. Check through for bad ones.

Papayas
Half-moon slices.

Figs
Whole.

Pineapple
Sliced in rounds about ¼" thick.

Drying time depends on climate. If moist and damp, bring fruit in at night.

Try honey-dipping fruit first.

It is good to check fruit daily and move it around. When dry, remove. Make sure it's dry or it will mold in containers.

To store: cool from the sun's heat. Pack in airtight jars or containers. (Bakeries will sell you used cans with lids, or plastic tubs which work nicely.) You can also use well-sealed plastic bags. Store in a cool, dry place.

To prevent insect breeding, you can pasteurize fruit by placing it in a hot (175°) oven for 15 minutes.

Wash screens to ensure sanitary conditions and be ready for the next load.

Vegetables

What a wonderful discovery drying vegetables has been. It has always been exciting to find them in the cupboard during the winter to use in your favorite recipe or in soups—or as bouillon.

Dry as fruit or string and hang in the sun, or shade with cheesecloth over them.

Chilies and Garlic

Hang up as a decoration while drying.

Bell Peppers

Cut up in rings.

Cherry Tomatoes

Halves.

Eggplant

Slice thin for crispies; a little thicker for a "moister" vegetable when it is soaked.

Okra

String and hang in shade.

Potatoes

Slice thin.

Leafy Vegetables

Can be placed on racks and dried like herbs.

Squash, Pumpkins or Mushrooms

Whole or slices.

Garlic

Braid and hang as a decoration.

Herbs

A large percentage of herbs are collected for their leaves. They are at their highest strength just before they bloom.

Drying: On burlap stretched between racks, or tied up and hung upside down in bunches so oils go down into the leaves and keep their full strength.

When they are collected for their flowers, they are dried the same way, never in direct sunlight. Need good ventilation.

Store in airtight containers or they lose their strength.

Braid garlic and hang for decoration.

Eight Paths
of Right Cooking

1. Begin with a short moment of meditation to reach that point of calm.

2. Have a clean, orderly kitchen.

3. Plan your menu. Have the picture clear in your mind. Make sure it is a well-balanced meal.

4. Make sure that you have all of the ingredients.

5. Decide which dish requires longest preparation and/or cooking time so you can prepare it first. You may possibly want to prepare sauces the evening or morning before.

6. Assemble all the necessary utensils and ingredients.

7. You can chop up all your vegetables, nuts, or whatever ahead of time—so your preparation will go smoothly.

8. Smile—for it's a joy to cook for your family! The rewards are seen in their healthy bodies.

Some Helpful Ideas

1. Measuring honey. If you first measure your oil—or rub a little oil inside the cup the honey will slide out and not stick to the cup.

2. When combining flour, arrowroot, milk powder, etc. with liquid, put a little of the liquid in a jar and add the dry ingredients. Cover and shake well and the mixture will be smooth when it is all combined.

3. To freshen stale granola put in the oven until crunchy.

4. When frying foods you can drain them on paper bags or egg cartons.

5. Put a cracker in your salt to keep out moisture.

6. Don't store dried fruits, nuts, or cereals in paper bags. The moisture is quickly removed. Store in air tight containers or plastic bags.

7. When cooking corn-on-the-cob in boiling water remove it from the water as soon as it is done or it will become tough.

8. Always cover food in your refrigerator.

9. Store onions in a separate container from fruits. Onions will flavor them.

10. When making guacamole save the avocado pits. Put them in any leftover guacamole to keep it from turning brown.

11. To clean your blender put in a little soapy water and turn it on. Rinse well.

12. To help in cleaning burned pots, put water and baking soda in and bring to a boil. Then simmer 45 minutes. This method helps to loosen burned particles.

Equivalents

dash = 2-3 drops

1 T. = 3 t.

2 T. = 1 liquid oz.

¼ c. = 4 T.

⅓ c. = 5⅓ T.

½ c. = 8 T. or 4 oz.

1 c. = 16 T. or 8 oz.

1 pint = 2 c. or 16 oz.

1 qt. = 4 c.

1 gal. = 4 qts.

1 peck = 8 qts.

1 bushel = 4 pecks

1 lb. = 16 oz.

1 T. active dry yeast = 1 compressed cake or
1 pkg. active dry

1 c. sugar = ¾ c. honey

1 T. white flour = ½ t. arrowroot

1 c. unbleached white flour = ¾ c. whole wheat flour or
⅞ c. whole wheat pastry flour

Glossary

Agar-Agar

Gelatin that comes from sea weed. It is a good source of minerals. Comes in flakes, granulated, or in bar form. Can use instead of gelatin or pectin. With 1¾ c. liquid, use 1 T. flakes, or 1½ t. granulated, or 7-inches from a bar.

Arrowroot

A natural thickening agent. It is also a good source of protein. Substitute for cornstarch.

Baking Powder

Choose one which has no lime or aluminum compounds and is low in sodium. See the Cake section for a recipe to make your own.

Baking Soda

Can cause stomach inflammation; avoid using whenever possible.

Bran

Residue after whole wheat flour is ground and sifted. Provides roughage which aids in keeping you regular.

Brewer's Yeast

Also known as nutritional yeast. Nonleavening agent. Comes in powder or flakes. High in B vitamins. Also a good source of protein, minerals, and viatamins. There are many different brands so try them until you find the taste you like.

Carob

Also known as "St. John's Bread." You can eat the pods or grind them into flour. It is the best substitute for chocolate. High in iron, minerals, calcium, vitamins; low in fats and starch. Try different brands until you find the one you like. I like the roasted powder best.

Date Sugar

Made from dried, ground dates.

Flax Seed

High in minerals; aids in constipation. Use in baking; grind or whole. You can soak overnight. It has a natural gelling agent—see Cakes. Use when baking; or grind, then soak an hour or two, simmer over low heat 20-30 minutes. Set in refrigerator when it cools; beat as you would egg whites.

Flours

There are so many kinds of flour; don't limit yourself to whole wheat or unbleached white. It is important to remember that you will still need a glutenous flour when baking, or use part gluten flour. (See Gluten.) Try grinding some of these: brown rice, garbanzos, granola, millet, oats, potato, rye, soy, tapioca, whole wheat, corn, and acorns.

Gluten

Gives adhesiveness to dough, coagulates when heated, gives shape; high in protein, low in starch.

Kelp

Comes from seaweed. Good source of protein, iodine, calcium. Comes in powder or granulated form. It is often used as a salt substitute.

Lecithin

Comes from the soybean. It breaks up fats and is a cell builder. Widely used as a preservative. It can be used in baking or raw in smoothies and protein drinks. If it won't overpower the other flavors, try it in salad dressing. It comes in liquid or granular form.

Malt

Usually made from barley. Very nutritious. Can be used as a sugar substitute when in syrup form. Use in smoothies and protein drinks.

Miso

Comes from the soybean. Its other ingredients are barley and salt. High in protein.

Protein Powder

Source of protein. Can be used in baking or in drinks such as smoothies.

Sorghum

A syrup made from a grain which is grown in a way similar to corn.

Tamari

Naturally fermented soy sauce made from wheat, soybeans, water, and salt. It is aged in wood for 2 years. It provides protein, natural sugars, vitamins and minerals. Good seasoning with grains, vegetables, in salad dressings, sauces.

Tapioca

A root product. It comes from a plant called cassava. It makes great pudding and when ground into flour it is a good thickening agent.

Seaweeds

Vegetables from the sea! There are several kinds: kelp, dulse, nari, hiyuki, kombu, agar-agar. High in minerals.

Tofu

Made from soybeans—the curd. High in protein and minerals.

Vanilla

A bean or seed pod used in making vanilla flavoring. You can make your own by soaking the beans in the liquid you are going to use in your recipe until they are soft. Slit beans vertically and scrape out inside. Soak both the shell and the inside for several hours; or, you can cover and simmer half an hour or longer for more flavor.

Index
and List of Recipes

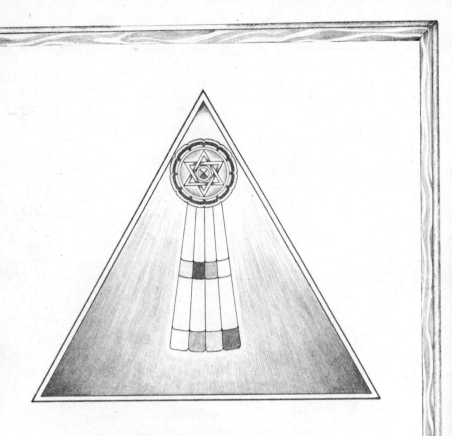

This ancient symbol represents the truth by which we guide our lives. To live by this truth is to embark upon a journey that leads to the essence of your own existence.

The central circle is a picture of the Sun, and the symbol of the Creator in whose image we were made.

The twelve divisions, formed by the interlacing triangles symbolize the union of Heaven and Earth, the masculine and feminine principle in the universe. These twelve divisions formed, are the gates of virtue that surround the heavenly abode where the true Light dwells.

The twelve scallops on the outside of the outer circle symbolize the twelve great earthly temptations that must be overcome in order for man's soul to reach these heavenly gates.

The eight lower divisions symbolize the eight paths of Truth that we must walk; they tell what a man's actions and thoughts must be in order to overcome the temptations and pass through the gates of virtue into the Kingdom of peace and happiness that dwells within you.

The surrounding triangle represents the great pyramid, "Cheops," the all-seeing eye that gives strength and power to all those who choose to live in the light of virtue.